KADYA MOLODOWSKY

KADYA MOLODOWSKY
THE LIFE OF A YIDDISH WOMAN WRITER

ZELDA NEWMAN

ACADEMICA PRESS

LONDON-WASHINGTON

Library of Congress Cataloguing-in-Publication Data

Names: Newman, Zelda Kahan.
Title: Kadya Molodowsky : the life of a Yiddish woman writer / Zelda Kahan Newman.
Other titles: Yiddish woman writer
Description: London ; Washington : Academica Press, [2018] | Includes bibliographical references and index.
Identifiers: LCCN 2018020530 | ISBN 9781680530568
Subjects: LCSH: Molodowsky, Kadia, 1894-1975. | Women authors, Yiddish--Biography. | Women poets--20th century--Biography.
Classification: LCC PJ5129.M7 Z76 2018 | DDC 839/.113 [B] --dc23
LC record available at https://lccn.loc.gov/2018020530

Copyright 2018 by Zelda Kahan Newman

All rights reserved. Printed in the United States of America. No part of this book may be used or reproduced in any manner whatsoever without written permission except in the case of brief quotations embodied in critical articles and reviews.

Academica Press
1727 Massachusetts Avenue, NW, Suite 507
Washington, DC 20036
editorial@academicapress.com

For orders call

(978) 829-2577

Table-of-Contents

No.		Pages
Introduction		vii
Acknowledgements		xi
Chapter 1	Early life	1-30
Chapter 2	Kiev, two men enter, one man leaves	31-66
Chapter 3	Warsaw, Kadya becomes famous	67-108
Chapter 4	The US - (1935-1950)	109-186
Chapter 5	Paradise lost: Three years in Israel	187-244
Chapter 6	Return to the US: The first decade (1953-1962)	245-292
Chapter 7	The US (1963-1975)	293-322
Bibliography	Bibliography of Kadya Molodowsky's works	323-320
Index	Index of people	32-323
	Index of places	324-326
	Index of work discussed	327-328

INTRODUCTION

Learning about a writer from her autobiography is like watching her enter a ballroom all dressed up and bejeweled; learning about a writer from her correspondence with her loved ones, on the other hand, is like watching her stumble out of bed and amble into the bathroom, all disheveled and in her pajamas. This biography is based not just on what Molodowsky tells us about herself, but also, and primarily, on what her documents and those of her friends and family tell us about her.

Is there a married woman who does not remember some details of her wedding vividly? Some remember the dresses worn; some remember the songs sung; some remember the food, some the guests. But when Kadya Molodowsky wrote about her wedding in her memoir, she mentioned none of these. All she said was that she bought new shoes for the occasion and that it snowed that day. None of the material that the author published explains this strange silence. But a careful reading of the archival material reveals the reality that the author attempted to skirt in her later years.

Kadya Molodowsky was a writer, not a politician. Yet for most of her young adulthood in Europe, she flirted with Socialism, and for a while, even with Communism. Nowhere in her published writings does she ever discuss the change of heart she underwent over the years. But from her letters to her loved ones and her dear friends this change of heart is quite apparent.

Molodowsky wrote an autobiographical memoir late in her life. There she embeds the story of her naming within a wider account of life in Europe in the years of her childhood. When she begins this story, she tells of her visit to Pruzhene, her grandmother's *shtetl*:

"This grandmother of mine was not my real grandmother. She was my mother's stepmother. She was not my grandfather's first wife, but his third wife. In Pruzhene she was already married to her second husband, the man she married after my grandfather left her a widow."[1]

We see here not the usual, sanitized tale of a perfect society, with each nuclear European family consisting of one Matriarch and one Patriarch, but the genuine reality as Molodowsky knew it: men who married serially, usually because their former wives died from overwork or childbirth, and women who remarried to sustain themselves and their children.

Molodowsky continues her story about this grandmother, noting that the older woman waited till her present husband was out of the house before telling tales about her former husband:

"She was a smart woman. When her husband was not at home, she'd tell me about my grandfather, her first husband, a man I never knew. I am named after him. His name was "Kadish", and that's where the name "Kadya" comes from. She spoke lovingly about my grandfather and about her stepchildren.[2]"

If all we knew about Molodowsky were this autobiography, we would know only this: that at her birth her parents named her "Kadya" in memory of this beloved grandfather. But there are other sources for knowledge of the author's life. In particular, there are documents that she left behind in archives: one in the YIVO archive New York and one in the Makhon Lavon archive in Israel. As it turns out, in the latter archive we find out that the story as we know it from Molodowsky's autobiography does not at all square with the facts.

Among the documents in the Makhon Lavon archive are Molodowsky's Polish passport, issued in 1935, her passbook from the Pennsylvania [bank] Company and a postcard from the US Immigration and Naturalization Service, both issued in 1937, and a health certificate (in Hebrew), issued in 1950, and sent on to the Israeli immigration authorities. In all of these documents the author's given name is "Kiejla Lew". The author's husband's name was Simche Lev (spelled "Lew"); that explains the last name on every one of these documents. But what about this unexpected first name: "Kiejla"?

Before we attempt to square the autobiographical account with the facts that turn up in the archive, we should consider another document that can serve as evidence of the author's given name: a letter Kadya wrote to her husband Simche in November of 1937. At the time, she was in the US, but he was still in Warsaw.

Frightened as both were of his prospects in Poland, they tried desperately to get permission for Simche to immigrate to the US and join Kadya there. They could

Introduction

not say what they truly believed: that life in Europe meant likely death for Simche; that was true for all the Jews of Poland. Instead they based their request on their desire for family reunification. To prove that they were indeed married, Simche needed the documentation provided by a marriage certificate. In the letter that Kadya wrote to Simche, she reminded him that in the official Polish records her name will be the same name that appears on her *ksube* (her Jewish marriage certificate): "Kiejla". The archival documents are historical bits of incontrovertible evidence. Apparently, the author really was named "Kiejla" in some official capacity. This is the objective truth.

Still, Kadya would certainly not have needed to remind her husband of her official name if it were the one they ordinarily used. Kadya, who clearly knew about this official name, made sure her husband used it when searching for proof of their marriage. Why then, did she tell an entirely different tale when she wrote her autobiography?

Apparently when she wrote her autobiography she was telling her readers her own subjective truth. And subjective truths can be, and often are, very different from objective facts. It seems as though the author disliked the name "Kiejla" and never used it. Moreover, by the time she wrote her autobiography in her late sixties, she had been called "Kadya" ever since she could remember.

As we learn from the author's autobiography, "Kadya", the name the author preferred, was attached to a personally unknown, but much-admired grandfather. The grandmother she knew, loved and obviously wanted to emulate, had loved this man and still loved her mother. Surrounding this man there was a wealth of good feeling. What could be better than taking on his name?

This re-fashioning of the facts so that they fit a psychologically genuine "truth" cannot be avoided. For the re-fashioners, this narrative becomes their personal "truth". For researchers, however, the issue is more complex. We need to balance this personal, subjective "truth" with the historical truth of objective facts. Then we need to compose a picture that presents both truths and does justice to them both. Only then can we begin to approximate "the whole truth". That is why this biography relies not only on the printed material found in books, but also on material found in the Molodowsky archives in New York and Israel, and on the Rokhl Korn and Ida Maze archives in the Montreal Jewish Public Library.

I have chosen to highlight those of Molodowsky's literary works that I consider worthy of note. Neither the children's poems nor the poems for adults are quoted in their entirety; I hope interested readers will seek out the fuller versions. If that will happen, I will have done what I set out to do.

After the Holocaust, Kadya Molodowsky was unable to resurrect the cultural milieu of Jewish Warsaw, despite her concerted efforts. In this book I have tried to give the reader a sense of what was lost, what Molodowsky did to replace the lost world, and why she ultimately failed. If to remember is to live again, then we are all keeping that world alive by remembering it.

---

[1] *Svive*, no. 23, p. 22.
[2] Op. Cit., p. 23.

ACKNOWLEDGEMENTS

This book could not have been written had I not had a sabbatical year off from my teaching duties in the Languages and Literatures Department of Lehman College/CUNY. I had no idea what awaited me in the Makhon Lavon archive; all I knew was that there were tens of folders each with letters and documents that no one had looked at since they were deposited there in 1952. As it turned out, many of the important and surprising "finds" were in that archive.

I would like to thank Shannon Hodge and Daniela Ansovin of the Montreal Jewish Public Library, Gunnar Berg and Yeshaya Metal (now retired) of the YIVO archive and Yishai Ben-Arieh and Alexandra Tumarinson (now retired) of the Makhon Lavon archive for their kind help. In addition, I would like to thank my readers, my proofreading friend and the friend who helped format this book for publication. None want to be mentioned by name. Their suggestions, questions and corrections were invaluable. I am deeply indebted to them.

CHAPTER ONE: EARLY LIFE

What we remember from childhood we remember forever — permanent ghosts, stamped, inked, imprinted, eternally seen.

Cynthia Ozick

The Uniqueness of Kadya Molodowsky

Kadya Molodowsky, the most prolific woman writer of Yiddish, wrote poetry, short stories, novels, essays, plays and a novella. She was the only woman writer of Yiddish who edited a literary journal, and single-handedly decided what and who could be published. Virtually every well-known writer of prose and poetry appeared in her journal. Her unique status among her contemporaries led one of her male colleagues to quip: she was "…the very first [woman] in Yiddish literature to wear editorial pants."[1]

She was not only a connoisseur of good writing, she was a fine writer herself. Her children's poems and stories are rhythmic and lilting even in translation, and her short stories open a window into a bygone era. When she wrote for children, she let her imagination gallop untethered; when she wrote for grown-ups, she was sometimes an astute observer, sometimes a mystic.

She lived through all the major upheavals known to twentieth century Jewry: the chaos of WWI, an inter-war pogrom, and the destruction of European Jewry in the Holocaust. She was a participant in the pre-WWI revival of Hebrew in Europe, the flowering of Yiddish literature in pre-WWII Warsaw, and the attempt to reconstruct Yiddish culture in the early years of the State of Israel and in the US. The story of her life, then, reflects the story of twentieth century Jewry. Molodowsky was also a Jewish feminist before Jewish feminism was a movement. To follow the twists and turns of her feminism is to follow the challenges that Jewish women faced as they confronted modernity.

Kadya Molodowsky left behind multiple sources of information about herself. There are letters she wrote to her father, and letters he wrote to her; letters she wrote to her husband, and letters he wrote to her; letters she wrote to her sister, and letters her sister wrote to her. There are tens of letters she wrote to colleagues and friends, and tens of letters they wrote to her. Neither of her sisters, Lina and Dora, left accounts of Kadya's childhood.

Kadya did write an autobiographical memoir that covers these years, but this memoir, written many years later, leaves many missing pieces in the narrative. In addition, recollections resurrecting the past need to be treated with a bit of skepticism.

The problem, as Jean-Baptiste Alphonse Karr noted, is that a person has three characters: "that which he exhibits, that which he really has, and that which he believes he has."[2] Put differently, not only do we not see ourselves as others see us, not only are there parts of ourselves that we hide even from ourselves, but we also see our own actions differently over time.

Since Kadya Molodowsky's account of her early life was begun when she was in the seventh decade of her life, and since this autobiography omits many crucial details of her life, we need to confront her own account with facts known to us from other sources. As we review the facts we have, we will constantly ask ourselves: what did Kadya not tell us? And why did she omit these details? Here, then, is what is known about Kadya's early life, tempered by what is not known.

The Shtetl, Education and a Wandering Life

Kadya Molodowsky, was born in an ordinary small town (Yiddish, *shtetl*) in (what the Jews called) Lithuania. But the Jewish name for the town and the region differed from the names used by gentiles.

When Kadya Molodowsky was born in 1894, the Jews called her hometown "*Berze*". The ruling government, however, then Czarist Russia, called the town "*Kartuskaya Beryoze*". The Jews of this town called their Yiddish dialect

"*Litvish* Yiddish", or Lithuanian Yiddish, even though the town had ceased to belong to Lithuania in the 14th century.

Both Jews and non-Jews lived together in this town on the western edge of the Russian Pale of Settlement[3], but they did not live side by side. The non-Jews lived in one section of the town, while the Jews lived in a different section of the town.[4]

Although the Chinese and the Japanese were warring in 1894 when Kadya was born, and ten years later, that conflict re-emerged as the Russo-Japanese war, the period immediately preceding and following the dawn of the 20th century were relatively peaceful for the Jews of *Berze*. The conflicts of the larger world did not reach the Jews of this small village. The virulent anti-Semitic sentiment that surfaced in later years, when first the Poles, and then the Germans, actively persecuted Jews, may have lain dormant then. There is no knowing for certain whether it did. But when Kadya Molodowsky was growing up in *Berze*, Jews and non-Jews lived in a mutually wary state of co-existent insularity. This self-contained Jewish existence, unchallenged by the need to adjust to gentile mores, may explain the later self-contained Jewish world described by the mature Kadya Molodowsky, the Yiddish writer. It is not as though the outer world did not impinge on the Jewish world at all in these years; it most certainly did. But the Jewish self-containment of those early years remained with Kadya for the rest of her life. For the mature Kadya, the writer of poems and stories and novels and essays, the world that truly mattered was always the world of Jews, coping, adjusting, grieving, but firmly moored in the language and culture of a Jewish world.

Much is missing from Kadya's memoir account of herself as a young girl. Nowhere in that document does Kadya tell us what she looked like. But from what we know of her photographs as a young woman, we can project backwards and venture a guess. Kadya was most probably thin. Her dark hair was luxuriant, her eyes were bright and curious, and she was a bundle of energy. Since she viewed the autobiographical memoir as a kind of "portrait of the artist as a young woman", she concentrates in that work not on outer appearances, but on her inner life and on formative people and events.

In that memoir, there is no hint of any resentment Kadya felt toward her mother. But in a personal interview that she gave an Israeli newspaper reporter when she was 78 years old, her resentment slipped out.

The interviewer first put her at ease, and then calmly asked her to describe her early life. At this point, she blurted out her earliest experience of writing in her parents' house. She told the interviewer that when she began writing as a child, "My mother got angry at the mess I made. She said 'Look at the mound of paper that the child made', and she threw the papers into the fire [of the fire-place]."[5] It seems as though the young writer-to-be was devastated. But youngster that she was, she said nothing.

It is possible for adults to re-think their relationship with their parents from a mature perspective. Had Kadya done this, she might have realized that her mother, knowing only *shtetl* life, had never known, or heard of, a woman-writer. She had certainly never known a woman who earned a living from her writing. But Kadya didn't say this; it would seem she never thought this. The burning of her papers did not bring on an ordinary hurt. It was an offense that struck at the very core of her being. Her sense of affront, it would seem, stayed with her throughout her life.

Although Kadya and her mother were not on the same wave-length, Kadya and her father definitely were. Kadya and her father, Aizik, had much in common. Like him, she was a bookish person. Like him, she had an insatiable curiosity, and was a life-long student.

Even when she was an old woman, Kadya remembered with vividness the excitement she felt when she finally doped out the difference between two similar-looking Hebrew letters and found she had unlocked the door to the world of books. Once she got the hang of reading Yiddish and Hebrew, it was clear she could read Russian as well. She showed an interest in continuing her studies, and study she did.

It was Kadya's father who began her informal education at home and it was he who continued to encourage both her informal and her formal education. Kadya was one of three sisters. One, Lina, was older, and one, Dobbe/Dora, was younger. But from all that is known, of the three sisters, only Kadya was tutored by Russian-speaking students, and only Kadya sat for and passed the state high school matriculation equivalency exam. At no time in her memoir, does Kadya ever question this arrangement. Apparently, it seemed only natural to her when she was writing her autobiographical memoir in her late sixties, that of the three sisters, only she was entitled to an education outside the home.

From the archived letters that Dora wrote in Hebrew during the three years Kadya spent in Israel, we know that Dora learned to read and write Hebrew when she was middle aged. And she was quite proud of herself for that. Apparently, she had gotten the rudiments of Hebrew reading and writing back in Europe when she was a child, but she had never gone further than that.

Was it the family that designated Kadya as "the studious" one of the three sisters? That does often happen in families. Perhaps Kadya's unquenchable curiosity contrasted so much with the diffidence of her sisters, that educating only her seemed to all the most reasonable choice.

What we do know is that she acquired reading skills from her grand-mother, and writing skills from one "Berl, the writer", or as she later calls him "Leyzer-Ber", a man known for his penmanship. The poem entitled "Inheritance", written when she was past forty, speaks of her indebtedness to him:

"Nor di oysyes zaynen geyarshnt voylgibik
Fun dem altn melamed
Leyzer-Ber mitn tsibik."[6]

But the alphabet I inherited truly productively/From the elderly teacher/Leyzer-Ber with the pipe.

Once she could read and write, Kadya began studying the Hebrew Bible with her father. But because he was a man of broad horizons, Aizik Molodowsky knew that his daughter's education would be stunted if her education were to stop there.

After he had taught her the basic stories and lessons of the Bible, he hired Russian-language tutors for her. These were university students who gave private lessons in the summer time, when the university was not in session and students had vacation. In this way, Kadya learned arithmetic, and geography, history and the natural sciences.

The story of her arithmetic teacher is a telling story. When this young man finished giving Kadya a lesson, he told his friends that he was "going to accompany *the lady* [in Yiddish: *di dame*] home". The grown woman recalls that the young man's friends giggled. Hearing this, Kadya got insulted and decided she would never again study with this tutor. And she didn't.

What exactly happened here? Why was Kadya so insulted? It would seem that Kadya was a tween-ager at the time, no longer a child, but not really grown up either. Not knowing quite how to label her, this young man decided to accord her the more "grown-up" title. It may well be that he had no intention of hurting Kadya's feelings. But she was insulted anyway. Hypersensitive child that she was, she decided this was an insult, and nothing would change her feelings. This hypersensitivity stayed with her the rest of her life. Indeed, it is one of her trademark life-traits.

In her autobiographical memoir we get a sense of what *shtetl* life was like as well as what her tutors were like. Her vignette about the custom shoe-maker of the *shtetl*, Sholem Borukh, provides us with panoply of *shtetl* types and with a portrait of their differing heroes. But some background information is needed for us to get a sense of what is being reported.

First to appear in this story is the Russian-speaking tutor with the "cockade" on his hat. While many, if not most, of the Jewish men of the *shtetl* walked around hatted, no one else in the *shtetl* had a cockade on his hat. This was the identity badge of an assimilated Russophile, one who had, or wanted to have, some connection to the Czarist bureaucracy.

Each of the homes mentioned in this vignette have a portrait hanging on the wall, but only in the home of the Jewish Russophile, the tutor with the cockade on his hat, is this portrait one of the Czar and the Czarina. All of the other homes have a portrait of a Jewish man hanging on the wall. Four homes are mentioned here. Each has its own hero.

Chapter One: Early Life

Two of the four portraits are of rabbis: the Vilna Ga'on, and Reb Mordkhele of Slonim. The former, also known as Rabbi Elijah of Vilna, was a much-revered eighteenth century rationalist and a fierce opponent of Hassidism, while the latter, Mordechai Chaim of Slonim, was a twentieth century mystic, and a leader of a Hassidic dynasty. But for all that the Vilna Ga'on and Mordechai Chaim of Slonim held diametrically opposed world views, the two men shared a common interest. Both men, now seen as "proto-Zionists", viewed the settlement of what was then called "Palestine" and is now called "Israel", as crucial to the well-being of the Jewish people. The Vilna Ga'on sent a group of his own followers to settle in Palestine/Israel, while Reb Mordechai Chaim of Slonim, a grandchild of the first rebbe of Slonim, actually lived in Palestine/Israel in the city of Tiberias. Of the two non-rabbis whose portraits hung on walls, Moses Montefiore, a financier and philanthropist, is now best known for the establishment of the first Zionist Jewish settlement outside the walled city of Jerusalem, while Doctor Theodore Herzl was the theoretician behind the modern Zionist movement and the mastermind behind the world-wide organization of Jews dedicated to furthering the settlement of Jews in Palestine. All four men, then, two of them pillars of the religious Jewish world, one, Montefiore, an avowedly traditional Jew, and one, Herzl, an avowed secular Jew, were all part of the underground current that connected European Jews of every stream to the great well-spring of Jewish identity: the ancestral homeland, known then as "the land of Israel".

Here, then, is Kadya's vignette about Sholem Borukh, the custom shoe-maker of the *shtetl*:

"Sholem Borukh complained that not all Jews were like Moses Montefiore. And he brought support for this from a story about the teacher with the cockade [on his hat]. This teacher's wife ordered a pair of shoes from him. When he came to their house to measure her feet, he saw a portrait of the Czar and the Czarina hanging on the wall. So he immediately took off his hat. 'What choice did I have? How was I to know that the Czar and the Czarina would be hanging there? In your house [he says to Kadya's father, Aizik] there is a portrait of the Ga'on of Vilna; in my house there's a picture of Moses Montefiore; in Yosl the Miller's, there's a picture of Reb Mordkhele of Slonim; at Shimin the clockmaker's, there's a picture of Doctor Herzl. But did it ever occur to me that I'd go to measure someone's feet, and I'd have to remove my hat?! What do you think I did? When the shoes were ready, I sent them with my wife and she delivered them. No more hat removals. After all, my wife doesn't speak Russian and in that house, they all speak Russian, he and she and their children and her sister. Then they couldn't bargain with my wife and they paid her whatever she asked for. An end to that one.'"[7]

Kadya tells us more about this Russophile, the teacher with a cockade [on his hat]. The going price for a lesson with him was high: so high that her parents agreed to it only because lessons with him were crucial for someone who wanted to pass the matriculation equivalency exams. After a month of learning with him, the young Kadya brought his payment along with her to her lesson. As she was about to pay, the teacher said:

"Your father is also a teacher, so I'll take half the sum from you."[8]

The older Kadya reports that her younger self was very confused and said:

'My father learns *gemoro* with *kheyder* boys." The Russophile's retort was: "I know, I know". 'And the teacher smiled and said: 'Talmud'…I know…"[9]

Kadya returned home with half the money she was given, realizing that the Russophile had switched from the word "*gemoro*" to the word "Talmud", but unaware why the language change mattered. She repeated the story, and used the word "Talmud". Here is her version of what happened next:

"My father smoked a cigarette, as he always did when he had to think something over. He sighed, shook his head [and said]: '*Kol Yisroel khaverim*… A goyish Jew…What else can one expect? *Kol Yisroel khaverim'*…"[10]

These few lines use a short-hand known to Kadya, but one unlikely to be comprehensible to a 21st century reader. The lines speak volumes about the language sensitivity of the young Kadya, the value system of her father, Aizik, and the long-lasting effect the father had on his daughter. But to get the full impact of this story, we need to explicate some terms and provide some historical background.

"*Kol Yisroel Khaverim*" is the Hebrew name given to the "Alliance Israelite Universelle", the French-based world-wide organization that aimed to "civilize" or "enlighten" traditional Jews by giving them a secular education. Along with the acquisition of a non-Jewish language, in this case, French, and a marketable skill leading to economic self-sufficiency, this education brought with it a contempt for things uniquely Jewish. A typical Alliance student didn't want to look like a Jew, and didn't want to sound like a Jew.[11] When Aizik mentioned "*Kol Yisroel Khaverim*" in the same breath as the Russophile, he was clearly suggesting that the Russophile identified with their ideology.

In Aizik Molodowsky's Jewish world, one '**learned *gemoro***'; in the secularized world of the "Alliance," one '**studied Talmud**'. Unlike Talmud that is studied in an academic environment and eventually mastered, "*gemoro*" is something that Jews are supposed to engage in learning their whole lives long. Because it is felt to be the blue-print for Jewish thought and practice, one is supposed to "swim in its waters"[12] and *learn from* it.

In Aizik Molodowsky's Jewish world, young boys went to '***kheyder***'; in the Alliance world, young boys went to '**school**'. A traditional *kheyder* is an ungraded, class-less, one-room school-house; a secular school has classes and grades. The young Kadya was quite right: the small changes of language revealed a chasm of ideological difference.

Aizik's estimate of this teacher was by no means flattering. In his eyes, this Russophile was a "*goyisher yid*": a Jew ashamed of his Jewishness, a Jew whose identification with things Jewish was so reduced, that he was no better than/different from a *goy*/ non-Jew.

While Kadya almost certainly did not understand as a child why the substitution of "Talmud" for "*gemoro*" made this teacher into a "goyish Jew", she very definitely internalized Aizik's values once she was grown. When she left her native town on her own for the first time, it was to take those matriculation exams in the town of Libave.

In her memoirs, Kadya reports that as she was about to leave for Libave, her mother said simply:

"Well, as long as you're traveling, then be successful".

On the other hand, it was her father's parting words, she tells us, that saw her through the stress of test-taking. Her father said:

Don't take it too much to heart. If you manage, that's good; if not, so you won't. The world doesn't depend on this gymnasium [test]."[13]

That expedition was itself a learning experience. For one thing, Libave, unlike her home-town of Berze, was outside the Pale of Settlement[14]. While Kadya had traveled freely within the Pale of Settlement, in Libave she needed a permit to live in her lodgings, if only for the 2-3 weeks of test-taking. For another thing, like the proverbial farm-hand who has seen the city for the first time, Kadya's stay in Libave brought her an awareness of the larger world. As she put it her memoirs, she now realized that her *shtetl* had:

"no sea and no port, and no window displays of large shops, where one could buy lamps and fiddles, clothes and books, mirrors and even children's toys"[15].

Far more importantly, the Jews with whom she lodged in those weeks were German-speaking, assimilated Jews. Never before had she encountered a group of Jews so ashamed of traditional Judaism and of Yiddish.

She passed those exams and got her teaching certificate. Her first real job was teaching Hebrew at a privately-run girls' school in Sherps (Sierpc), in what was then Russian Poland. Here, too, she encountered assimilated Jews. The difference between them and the Jews of Libave was negligible, as far as she could see. In Libave the assimilated Jews spoke German, while in Sherps the assimilated Jews spoke Polish.

We know from Kadya's autobiography, that while still in Sherps working as a novice teacher, Kadya "used to relax a bit" when she went to the hairdresser. Although the style was then for young women to wear their hair in line with their ears, Kadya says,

"My own hair nevertheless wanted to grow. Before I turned around, my hair grew beyond my ears, and then I used to go to get it cut."[16]

Note that Kadya says her hair "**wanted** to grow". She speaks of her hair as though it has a will of its own. This is the only hint Kadya gives the reader of the

Chapter One: Early Life

importance she attaches to her hair. When Kadya suggests that her hair has a will of its own, it is not Kadya the girl or the poet speaking; it is Kadya the woman.

For Kadya, a woman's hair is not just one feature of her physical self, it is her most important, most alluring, feature. What's more, for her, hair grooming is bound up with physical pleasure. This is true of the fictional woman who appears in more than one work of hers, and it is true of her as well. At this point though, Kadya had not yet become a writer and had not yet found the person who would groom her hair and care about her.

It is no accident, then, that in Sherps, Kadya bonded with her Yiddish-speaking hair-dresser. But the two of them had more in common than their concern for her hair. This hairdresser called the assimilated Jews of Sherps: "Frenchies". She quotes him as saying of an assimilated Jew:

[Er] iz nisht keyn fish, un nisht keyn knish, un avade nisht keyn ish"[17]. [He] is not a fish, and not a knish and certainly not a man.

This hairdresser's rhymed folk-saying is far cleverer than it seems. Of the three rhyming words, "*fish*", "*knish*", and "*ish*", "fish" is one that Jews share with Germans, and "knish" is one that Jews share with Slavs; only "*ish*", a purely Hebrew word meaning "man", is a word known only to Jews. Because it belongs to the particularistic, national sphere of Yiddish, it is a stand-in for all that the assimilationists wanted to avoid and the Sherps hairdresser was so proud of: Jewish particularism. In the hairdresser's opinion, a Jew ashamed of his Jewishness is not worthy of being called "a man".

It is clear that Kadya was in complete agreement with the hairdresser. A proud Jew in the mold of her father Aizik, Kadya had little respect for Jews who willingly gave up on their Jewish identity. She found the assimilationist tendencies of the school in Sherps so distasteful, that she quit after only one year on the job.
It is ironic that the career of so fine a teacher should have had so inauspicious a beginning. This, of course, proved nothing about her abilities as a teacher. The family who ran the private school wanted her back, she tells us. But she would not stay one day beyond the agreed-upon first year.

To recover from the disappointment of her first-year debacle, Kadya went to visit her aunt in Bialystok. It was there that she joined the organization known as "lovers of the Hebrew language" ("*Khovevei Sefat Ever*" in Hebrew), and it was there that she decided to join the group of youngsters being trained in Warsaw by Yehiel Halperin. But before she left for the Warsaw training, she spent the summer in Bialystok.

In her autobiographical memoir, Kadya informs us that during her summer stay in Bialystok, she rented a very large room because she "very much wanted"[18] her sister to join her there. Compared to Berze, where Dobbe, (as Dora was then called), and the rest of the family lived, Bialystok was a taste of the larger world. The exposure not just to city life, but also to an exciting intellectual environment, was something that Kadya wanted to share with her sister. Kadya reports that her sister came to stay with her, and even wore stylish shoes that impressed Kadya's landlady. But Kadya's intellectual excitement was apparently not contagious. With what can only be said to be a note of regret, Kadya reports that "her Bialystok"[19] apparently didn't hold all that much attraction for her sister. After a mere two or three weeks, her sister left for Berze, while Kadya stayed in the summer cottage she had rented for them both.

It is no accident that one of the characters in Kadya's first play is "a dreamer". The intellectuals in Bialystok that Kadya so admired, were dreamers. Was there at the time a Jewish homeland where all the world's Jews could live and feel at home? Not at all. Palestine of the time (pre-World War I) was a backwater province of the Ottoman Empire; it certainly was not a habitable Jewish homeland. But that didn't stop the intellectuals in Bialystok from imagining such a homeland in Palestine. Like those intellectuals, Kadya dreamed it might come to pass, and loved imagining it could be so. Dobbe/Dora, on the other hand, was a practical person. If there was no such place, she saw no point in dreaming about it. What's more, these dreamers insisted on speaking a language that would get them nowhere any place in Europe (or in the New World) where Jews lived. Hebrew was the language of the Bible and the prayer book, but, unlike Yiddish, it was not an everyday language that an ordinary Jew could actually use. That made it uninteresting for Dora. And for just that reason, Kadya loved learning it. Just as she could imagine a time when there would be a homeland for the Jews, so she loved learning a language that might someday be used in this homeland.

The differing views of the two sisters reflect the long-standing chasm between materialists and idealists. For materialists, what can be understood by the five senses is what is important. For idealists, on the other hand, the very fact that something can be comprehended by the five senses alone, makes it liable to decay, and ultimately, to death. In the view of an idealist, only intangible ideas live on. In this dichotomy, Dora is a superb example of the materialist, while Kadya is a superb example of an idealist. When Kadya invited Dora to come to join her in Bialystok, she had not yet realized that she and her sister differed on this crucial point. By the time Dora left, however, it dawned on Kadya that the two of them were unalterably different.

It was around this time that Kadya had her first disappointment in love. There was a young man who paid her compliments and flirted with her. And, she tells us "I was certain he was in love with me".[20] But then people who knew them both told Kadya the man had a fiancée, a dentist. Here is how she reports her reaction:

"What does that mean? If that was the case, it was in no way decent behavior...I began to doubt whether all male compliments are sincere...That's when I understood that God drove Adam and Eve out of the Garden of Eden because the snake intervened, and the snake, in fact, slinks around in the world till this very day. And I decided that I must indeed watch out for him, that snake."[21]

The Warsaw teachers' training that Kadya anticipated was something entirely new. Zionist visionary that he was, Yehiel Halperin was convinced that only a thorough grounding in Hebrew would prepare teachers to teach Jewish children for life in the Jewish state that would some day become a reality. His seminar, therefore, was meant to train teachers of young children in a school system run entirely in Hebrew. Kadya herself did not have the training to be a teacher in such a system. But then, neither did anyone else; the teachers were training for a reality that did not yet exist.

Before she took off for Warsaw, Kadya told her father in a letter that she suddenly realized how little she knew and how much she still needed to learn. When she said this, she touched on the crucial trait that she and her father shared: an intellectual curiosity than entailed a life-long need to keep learning. Her father recognized this need, and he encouraged her. She reports that he responded with:

"If that's how you feel, you will spend the rest of your life learning. But that's all right. The most important things are in the Torah, and that I have already taught you."

Aizik Molodowsky was not suggesting that the Biblical stories he told his children at every opportunity were a substitute for mathematics or science, or for that matter, for history and general literature. His horizons were broad enough to convince him that this was not so. What he was saying is that the moral foundation needed to lead an ethical life is to be found in the traditional, if informal, Jewish education he provided for his children in his home.

Those Biblical stories he told were far more than dry historical anecdotes that happened to coincide with Jewish holidays. Aizik was so fine a story-teller, that for Kadya these Biblical stories came alive and captured her imagination. Here is her autobiographical account of the Holiday of *Shavuos* and its connection to the Biblical story of Ruth as Aizik told it:

"The first day of [the Jewish holiday called] *Shavuos*, our father would wake us up early and read the story of Ruth. Just getting up early was like preparing for a long journey. The [Biblical] story of Ruth starts with the [Hebrew] word "*Va-yehi*", and our father translated that for us: "and it happened, long, long, ago". And the word "*va-yehi*" together with the words "long, long, ago" began turning like wheels of fantasy across far-off time into far-off places, and even before we got to the story of Naomi and Ruth, we had already traveled somewhere far away, to the land of "*va-yehi*" and "long, long ago".[22]

Once she had Aizik's blessing and reassurance, Kadya was able to leave for Warsaw comforted. She was off to widen her horizons in the Polish city that provided the richest of possibilities for a curious Jewish youngster. She had been in Warsaw on her way to Sherps, and on her way home from Sherps, and she was impressed. The stream of people, the electric tram system and the commotion of the big city, impressed her immensely. As she put it:

"Once I'd seen Warsaw, I didn't want to return to *Berze*."[23]

While we know from her autobiography that she returned occasionally to visit her family in the small town of *Berze*, she always sought out city living. She needed to be in a place where she could interact with and learn from others, and only city living provided this for her. And city living was her choice throughout her life. When she arrived later in the US, she ended up living in New York, and during her 3-year stay in Israel, she lived in its largest urban metropolis: Tel Aviv.

It would seem that Kadya's stay in Halperin's Hebrew teachers' seminar had far-reaching consequences. From all the evidence, her experiences affected her father's career choices, as well as her own.

In the *shtetl*, most Jewish families eked out a living by selling goods and services. Typical methods of earning a living were shoemaking, tailoring, buying and selling lumber and woodworking, the making, buying or selling of food-stuffs and providing whatever the Russian army stationed nearby might need. Aizik Molodowsky did none of these. According to Kadya, he was a teacher of *gemoro* in a *kheyder*, the classical one-room school-house of Jewish education in the *shtetl*. This, at any rate, is what the mature Molodowsky tells her readers in her autobiography.

What is remarkable is that in this autobiography, written during the last decade of her life, she portrays her father **only** as a *gemoro* teacher, and a poorly paid one at that. However, we have other accounts of what Aizik did in his home town, and they differ greatly from Kadya's memory. From accounts of Holocaust survivors from their home town, an entirely different picture emerges.

In these accounts, Aizik Molodowsky is remembered as a Hebrew teacher and an active Zionist. In an online memoir written for the site called "Jewishgen", the former resident of Berze, Yakov Gorali says that Aizik Molodowsky was one of the two major Hebraists and "Zionist activists" in his home town. Aizik Molodowsky, he says, "raised a whole generation of Hebrew speakers."[24]

Was Aizik simply a Hebraist? The picture is more complicated than that.

The early part of the twentieth century was a time of great ideological ferment among East European Jews. There were Yiddishists and Hebraists, those who are what might now be called *Haredim* (usually translated as "Ultra-Orthodox"), as well as secularists. In a book made up of a collection of short pieces written by those who lived in Bereze and eventually settled in Israel, Aizik Molodowsky, Kadya's father and Leibl Molodowsky, Kadya's brother, are both mentioned. Leibl is listed as one of the first graduates of the Yiddish school[25], while Aizik himself is said to be a "teacher of [Hebrew] grammar and Jewish history".[26] The facts that emerge from this book, then, are that Aizik, like Kadya after him, supported the study of both Yiddish and Hebrew. The picture of him that is probably the most accurate description of his "both-and" approach is this one:

"He was a modern teacher, very well informed on general Jewish culture,…with a slight tendency to Yiddishism".[27]

Finally, those who remembered him well, pointed out that Molodowsky Sr. was a teacher for the rich folks, and he worked, not in the one-room school-house typical of a *kheyder* (as Kadya claimed in her memoir), but in a modern educational system that had graded levels of classes.[28]

The differing accounts of Aizik Molodowsky's putative wealth are the easiest to understand. Kadya remembered the years of her youth, when all the Molodowsky children needed to be cared for, and Aizik was hard-pressed to provide for them all. The Holocaust survivors from her home town, more than twenty years younger than Kadya, knew Aizik Molodowsky when the children had grown, and two of his daughters, married and living in the United States, were able to send money "back home". Then, too, what appeared as wealth to the youngsters growing up in the *shtetl*, may well have looked entirely different to Kadya, living years later in New York.

The not-so-easily resolved discrepancies between Kadya's autobiographical account and the account of the Berze inhabitants who survived WWII, center on what Aizik taught and where he taught. While Kadya claimed Aizik taught *gemoro* in a *kheyder*, the later residents of Berze claimed that Aizik taught Hebrew and worked in a "modern" educational system that had graded levels of classes. We have no reason to believe that the younger Holocaust survivors of Berze imagined a reality that never existed. How, then, to validate both accounts? In the manner typical of Talmudic efforts to resolve a discrepancy between two conflicting positions, we will decide that both positions are correct: Aizik began his working life as a *gemoro* teacher and continued to work as a *gemoro* teacher as long as Kadya was a young woman, just as Kadya reported in her autobiography. And then, after Kadya left home, Aizik became a teacher of Hebrew in a "modern", graded school system, just as the Holocaust survivors of Berze remembered.

Such a "modern" graded system was pioneered in Europe early in the twentieth century by Yehiel Halperin, the man who energized the group of young men and women that Kadya joined in Bialystok. We know that Kadya shared her enthusiasm for reviving Hebrew as a spoken language with her father; she tells us so in her autobiography. Here, then, lies the only possible explanation for Aizik's career switch: Kadya's enthusiasm for reviving Hebrew and teaching the language to young children in a modern, graded, school system, "infected" her father. Although Kadya never tells the readers of her autobiography that this is in fact what happened, there is no other plausible explanation for the known facts. Upon reflection, this is not surprising. Aizik and Kadya learned not only with, but also from, each other. This is a natural development for soul-mates, and Aizik and Kadya were definitely soul-mates.

Kadya's father was not the only non-conformist in her family. Although Kadya never knew her great-grandfather personally, the man made his way into the title of her autobiography. Entitled "My Great-grandfather's Legacy", the autobiography begins with the story of the trip Kadya's mother made to retrieve her share of this legacy left to her by this great-grandfather. As it turned out, that legacy was not especially large. Still, it was not entirely negligible. For Kadya, this escapade brought her imagination into a wider world, one that extended all the way to Paris, where her great-grandfather had lived and died. It also gave her a sense of the family inclination to independence of mind and non-conformism. That great-grandfather, who lived in Paris, she was told, was hounded out of his home town because he dared to delve into the philosophical works of Maimonides. He had not abandoned traditional Jewish observance; her mother assured her of that. But he was not prepared to have his reading material chosen or approved by the self-appointed thought-police of the small-town Jewish community. And for that, he suffered. Because he did not want to buckle under social pressure and conform to the small-town norms, he moved to Paris, where he could be the sort of Jew he wanted to be. It is of no consequence whether this story is fully true or only partially true. What is important is that for four generations, as part of a shared family legend, this patriarch was respected for his principled independence of thought.

One generation closer to Kadya was her maternal grandmother. This woman was proficient enough in Hebrew to be a teacher of elementary Hebrew, and, as we have seen, it was she who taught Kadya the basics of elementary Hebrew. This grandmother lived alone and was financially independent. Twice a day, in the morning and in the evening, young girls would come to her house to be taught the fundamentals of Hebrew reading, and each paid a small fee. This woman must have made literacy seem of supreme importance, for when Kadya finally learned to distinguish one Hebrew letter from another, she felt, she said "as though a miracle" had happened. Unlike the elderly women of her time, this grandmother never slept at her children's house. She regularly visited Kadya's parents once a year, on the Holiday of Purim, but she always went home to sleep. What's more, every Purim, she recited the story of the Holiday in rhymed Yiddish verse, and sang it with a spirited tune. Years later, Kadya remembered lines of this verse and repeated them in her autobiography. There is no question that this woman's example of financial independence and intellectual acuity made a very strong impression on the young Kadya.

Kadya's two sisters, Lina and Dobbe/Dora, apparently took their mother as a role model. While naturally intelligent, shrewd and skeptical, Kadya's mother was not bookish. From all we can tell, she seems to have taken no active role in Kadya's education or spiritual development.

We know very little about Lina, Kadya's elder sister. Even in later years, when Kadya was living in New York while her sisters Dora and Lina were living in Philadelphia, it was Dora who wrote and sent regards from Lina. Lina herself wrote rarely, and even then, generally as an afterthought in a letter that originated with Dora. We do know that unlike Dora, Lina never worked and apparently never needed to do so. But as we will see later, when she and her husband's money were needed, Lina came to Kadya's aid.

While we are never told when Lina or Dora left *Berze* for the US, it does seem that by the time Kadya embarked on the course of study in Warsaw, Lina was gone. Kadya tells us that just as she was about to set off for Warsaw to begin her course of study in the Hebrew teachers' seminar run by Yehiel Halperin, she felt a chasm had opened up between her and her sister Dora and between her and brother. But there is no mention of Lina at that point. It is likely, then, that by the time Kadya set off for her independent course of study in Warsaw, Lina had already left home for the US.

For all that Kadya's intellectual model and inspiration was her father, there is no question that Kadya's mother was an industrious woman with a potential, if untutored, entrepreneurial bent. Proof of that is the few hundred-ruble legacy that she invested twice over.

First, she tried running a fabric store. With the family house as the store location, the table she used for her goods was the very same one that the Molodowsky children used to prepare their school lessons. She went as far as Brisk (Polish "Brest") to acquire the inventory for her business, and then piled the material high, till some bolts of cloth could be reached only while she stood on a ladder. The young Kadya, already then blessed with a vivid imagination, saw in these bolts of patterned cloth, "a full garden blooming with dots and speckles." The store was run on credit, however, and far more customers owed money than paid money. It was not long before the stock was depleted, and that first investment was written off as a failure.

The mother's second entrepreneurial venture was the production and sale of corn-kvass, a fizzy, slightly fermented drink, which (Kadya later described in her autobiography as something that) "did not exist in the entire region, and no one had ever tasted it or even seen [anything like it. Z.K.N.]". A little booklet provided by Kadya's uncle offered instructions on how to proceed, and all the children did their part to make the venture succeed. Inexperienced as they were, the first few tries were near-disasters, with the glass bottles exploding in the night from the excess pressure of built-up gas. The family then experimented with differing concentrations of the necessary ingredients, till they got the recipe that seemed right.

As a young girl, Kadya was sometimes called on to push or pull the cart that carried her mother's home-made drink through the streets of their *shtetl*. When she was approximately 40 years old, Kadya wrote about this venture and her place in it in a poem entitled "My Earth-biography". There she says:[29]

> The bottles are resounding bells
> And I – a wet choirmaster.

This must have been a deeply embedded melody, because so many years later she repeats the phrase about the "ringing bottles" three times:

> So those bottles keep ringing
> Green, young, clear
> In a carriage with water…
>
> So those bottles keep ringing
> All bundled together
> The bottles keep ringing
> My mother sent them off somewhere…

There was more to this incident that Kadya let herself speak about, even at the age of forty. It was not until she was in her late sixties, almost thirty years later, that she revisited this incident and finally admitted what it was about the ringing bottles that lodged so stubbornly in her memory.

The *shtetl* had no marketing or distribution system for innovative products of this sort. To get the product to potential customers, the glass bottles were loaded onto a wagon. This wagon was pulled by a string in front, and pushed by hand from behind. Kadya and a young gentile boy hired for the purpose did this in a turn-taking fashion: half the time he pulled and she pushed, and half the time she pulled and he pushed.

When she was older, Kadya called the humiliation brought on by her acknowledged poverty "*Malke*'s *nign*", *Malke*'s melody. An age-mate of Kadya's named "*Malke*", happened to be riding in her family's carriage when Kadya was pulling the cart with her mother's wares. This friend/age-mate took a stick and rolled it across the bottles as she passed by. In so doing, she created a "melody", and at the same time, deeply wounded Kadya. Kadya was certain that this child intended to mock her. Did *Malke* really intend to mock Kadya's poverty? Or was she, perhaps, just in the mood to see how the bottles would sound if they were scratched with a stick?

As was the case when Kadya's math tutor called her "a lady", the hypersensitive Kadya took offense easily. Even in her old age, Kadya did not see things differently. It never occurred to her that *Malke* may not have intended to mock her. No matter what this child intended, Kadya felt mocked. And that hurt stayed with her for years.

The corn-kvass venture, as it is related in Molodowsky's autobiography, reveals much about the Molodowsky family. First of all, it says much about her mother. The establishment of a small factory based on a trial-and-error scheme learned from a booklet is testament to her pluck and determination. Through her willingness to try what no one else had ever done, and to keep at it despite the setbacks, she gave her children a life-lesson. Though she may not have seen her mother's venture in this light at the time, Kadya goes out of her way to tell us in her autobiography that her father played no active role in her mother's business ventures, or as she puts it in the "legacy businesses". In part, this was due to his preference for book learning and his non-interest in business. But in part, we are led to understand, this was due to his feeling that his wife deserved autonomy in her own affairs. The money was hers, after all, and she had the right to invest it as she thought best. While this view is thoroughly consistent with Jewish thought and practice, it is nevertheless a fact that a man with a different disposition and less respect for his wife, might have mocked her failure, or intervened and taken over his wife's business affairs for "her own good". But Kadya's father was neither callous nor overbearing. It comes as no surprise, then, that when Kadya herself married, she found a husband who respected her autonomy and allowed her to do just as she pleased.

Before Kadya left for Warsaw, the family Molodowsky deliberated: if she was traveling to Warsaw to study, perhaps it would be better for Kadya to study dentistry? After all, a dentist earns more, and dentistry is a more socially respected profession. Kadya reports that during these discussions, her father stared out of the window and was silent. This is how she remembers the rest of that event:

"A bit later my father said to me: 'So you'll pull teeth: what will you get from it? But if you'll teach children, then you'll have accomplished something. The crucial thing is: you'll succeed in teaching them something.'"[30]

The heading for this chapter in Kadya's memoir is: 'The Crucial thing is..." Says My Father. In its Hebrew and Yiddish usage, the word for crucial, '*ikar/iker*' is always contrasted with its antonym, '*tafel/tofel*', insignificant. And Kadya makes sure the reader gets her meaning. She ends that paragraph by hammering out the fact that she learned a life lesson from her father, and his comment determined her career choice:

"In short, one needs to seek the crucial point. In everything there is, so to speak, an insignificant point, and a crucial point. I set off for Warsaw to take [those] Hebrew courses."[31]

Kadya spent one peaceful year, from 1913 to 1914, in Halperin's Warsaw-based seminar. She listened to lectures, all in Hebrew, she practiced teaching young children, again in Hebrew, and, when she was free, she attended lectures in and about Yiddish that were held on the same block. Because the funds she came with would not have supported her in Warsaw for long, Halperin found her a private tutoring job. With that income, she was able to rent a comfortable room which she shared with a room-mate. She says about herself that she was carefree then in a way then that she never was afterward.

She reports a practical joke that she played on her room-mate and then comments:

"Those were the days when I was mischievous and I enjoyed teasing folks."[32]

In her early poetry, she recalled this one year as a magical one. The way she put it, at that time:

"…the earth was soft everywhere for my feet

From Berze to Odessa".[33]

Yakov Fichman, one of the now-forgotten, but once well-known, writers of early Hebrew literature, knew Kadya during that peaceful year. This is the way he remembered her:

"Kadya was then a thin young woman, dark-skinned and charming, who loved to sing and tell children stories about the Jewish holidays and Jewish heroes. But she was not always happy. When she would pass the poor neighborhoods of the city, her heart would contract at the sight of the neglected, gaunt children, and she would begin to cry with pity. I believe it was about these sad children that Kadya wrote her first, secret, poems. ut then she didn't believe she was truly a poet. And after that years of hardship and war arrived."[34]

When WWI broke out in 1914, it changed everything. As Kadya put it in her memoir:

"Gone were the hopes of opening new kindergartens and new schools. No one knew what the next day would bring and where one might get thrown…Jews deserted their villages and towns, they wandered and suffered and one had to save them from neediness and homelessness.[35]

The war did not concern Jews directly; both the Allied and the Axis powers had Jewish populations. But Jews were unquestionably the victims, no matter which side advanced temporarily. Everywhere the troops advanced, no matter which side advanced and which retreated, Jews were beaten, and raped; their stores were looted and burned, and because law enforcement was absent, chaos reigned. The result was a tidal wave of refugees, as small towns emptied out and Jews sought refuge in the big cities.

To tend to the Jewish children, many of them witnesses to the horrors of pogroms and orphaned from one, or sometimes both, parents, Yehiel Halperin established a home for refugee children in Warsaw, and shortly after the war broke out, Kadya taught in this children's home. Some children were orphans; others had parents but no homes to live in. The composition of the "classes" was in constant flux as families came to pick up their children and place them in a safer environment.

When the children's home closed down at summer's end, and the front moved closer to Warsaw, Halperin moved his teachers' seminar to Odessa, and Kadya took the opportunity to go home to see her family. But she did not stay there long.

The Molodowsky family had an only son, Leibl. Ordinarily, Russian law exempted an only son from army service. But war-time was not ordinary time, and Leibl was due to be conscripted. However, music students were exempted from conscription. So Kadya's parents decided to enroll Leibl in a music school in Poltava. Not knowing any other way to ensure his registration in this school, they sent Kadya to Poltava. She had with her a small amount of money and instructions to send them a telegram when she arrived safely. The telegram would assure them that all was well with her, and they would then send on more money for her.

Kadya never tells us how her brother Leibl got out of the army, if indeed he was not conscripted. Apparently, in the chaos of World War I and its battles, Leibl's conscription was overlooked. We do know that for the rest of their lives, Kadya felt personally responsible for her younger brother. In fact, Leibl's safety was so important to her, that in an attempt to save his life when he was older, Kadya was prepared to turn to a man she personally loathed, a man who was publicly known as her adversary, if not her enemy.

As far as Kadya and her parents knew, the trip to Poltava was an effort to help her brother Leibl avoid the draft. In reality, that trip to Poltava did not work out as planned. Instead, it was the start of a nomadic life for the young Kadya.

Just getting to Poltava was by no means as easy as it should have been. The war had sent civilians fleeing, and the trains were overfilled beyond capacity. The tumult and the crowds were too much for Kadya. She saw no way to push herself through the crowds and get onto the transfer train that was to take her to her destination. But a total stranger, a young man who spoke to her in Russian, materialized out of nowhere, and made the crowds part for her. Here is her description:

"It seemed to me he was the Prophet Elijah (In Yiddish: *Eliyohu Ha-novi*). To this day I don't understand what happened, who that man was, or why he did what he did. It can only be attributed to the merit of my great-grand-father who learned Maimonides' Guide to the Perplexed and sent his grandchildren a trousseau without ever having met them."[36]

Like most Jewish children raised in a traditional home, Kadya knew the stories of Elijah the prophet who comes to all Jews on *Peysekh* (Passover) to drink from the cup that is prepared for him at the *seder*. She knew, too, that in Jewish folklore, he brings unexpected salvation to Jews in desperate straits, and he will announce the coming of the Messiah at the end of days. This image of Elijah stayed with her throughout her life. And, as she says in a poem written at the beginning of her career, like most traditional Jews, she keeps waiting for Elijah's ultimate arrival:

"I've just now smelled at winter-time

The *erev Peysekh* [Passover eve] pureness of nights

And the mild warmness of a thin satin rain,

And the shining rays of my children's dress.

Perhaps Elijah the Prophet is nearing

And in walking, lets fall somewhere a sweet word,

I waited for him in pure children nights

Year in, year out, near his cup

And I still hope to meet him.

And dark windows will light up and become pure

And mute hearts will move like a singing forest…"[37]

Kadya got to Poltava at night and found the hotel she sought out. For the first time in her life she was in a hotel in a strange city where she knew no one. In the morning, she sent her parents a telegram, as she had promised, and then went off to the music school. There she found out that the school was not accepting any more students; there were no available places. She made sure they knew how to contact the family in case a place should free up, but she realized her whole trip might have been in vain.

Returning to her hotel, she found out that there was a problem with the telegram to her parents. The front had moved, and the telegram had not been delivered. She felt, as she says in her memoir, "penniless and helpless." She paid her bill and asked for directions to a Jewish restaurant, hoping that there she would meet someone who would give her advice on what to do next.

Arriving at this restaurant, she heard Hebrew spoken at one of the tables. She spoke to the men at that table in Hebrew, and was immediately invited to join the group. As she put it: she felt as though once again that strange young man had approached her: once again Elijah the prophet saved her. When she told them of her plight, one of the men there said:

"Don't worry. You'll have where to stay. We were waiting here for you."[38]

This man brought her to his house, told his wife he'd brought home another daughter, and the whole family made her feel at home. But Kadya was not prepared to be idle or accept the kindness of this family on an unending basis. She put an ad in the paper offering to teach children in a school. She got more than one offer, but her hosts would only let her accept an offer that seemed promising. Finally, they agreed to let her go, but made her promise that if she were unhappy in her new post, she would return to them.

The Children's Home in the town of Romni, where Kadya next went, was run by a woman who clearly felt distanced from the orphaned children in the home. They were her wards, and she did what was necessary out of charity, but she did not empathize with the children. Kadya stayed there long enough to scrounge up the money for a new winter coat. But when a friend of hers wrote to tell her that they were opening up a Hebrew school in Saratov, she jumped at the chance to leave Romni. Saratov, on the Volga, was different from both Berze, her home-town, and from Warsaw, the big city she had begun to think of as her new home. She stayed and worked in Saratov for the rest of the school year, feeling as though she'd found a Jewish corner in the midst of an alien world.

All this time, she was financially independent, not only because the war had prevented her from going home and getting funds from her parents, but primarily because she had determined that she would not be a financial burden on her family once she went off on her own. Although teachers were never well-paid, and the war years were years of financial hardship and near-starvation for everyone, she always managed to make do with what she earned.

When the school-year was over, she re-joined Halperin's seminary, now stationed in Odessa. By now Halperin was asking from his students, not two years of preparation, but three. What's more, the young women were being trained not just to teach kindergarten, but also to teach children in upper classes. In Odessa, Kadya lived side-by-side with young men and women who later became the great scholars and leaders of the young state of Israel.[39] She thoroughly enjoyed this scholarly environment, and was delighted to renew friendships with some of these people in later years when she moved to Israel. As was the case when she was in Warsaw, she was a student in Odessa, and at the same time, she gave private lessons to maintain her financial independence.

When that school year was over, Kadya was still unable to get home to spend the vacation with her family; her home-town of *Berze* was occupied by the Germans. In need of a place to live, she joined one of her classmates in Nikolaev, located in the Volhin province of Russia. Once again, she was treated as an adopted daughter, and once again she learned to accept the kindness of strangers.

In her memoir, Kadya mentions the time of the Balfour Declaration, the 1917 declaration made by the then-Foreign Secretary of Great Britain, Arthur Balfour, that His Majesty's government views "with favour the establishment in Palestine of a national home for the Jewish people."[40] When that declaration was made, she was in Odessa. In her circles, the day of the declaration was a holiday: all rejoiced and congratulated each other. Kadya herself appended to her jacket a twig with a few leaves and a blossom. As she put it:

"In my youthful fantasy I saw this as a symbol of the twig that would bloom...It seemed as though Jews would take the Balfour Declaration and walk straight to Jerusalem."[41]

But the excitement died down fast. There was no instant redemption for world Jewry, and most Jews did not walk straight to Jerusalem. They continued to live where they had always lived. These were also the days of the Russian Revolution, and that, in itself, created new problems:

"After the revolution in Russia, Odessa became a different city. The speakers at the meetings spoke of freedom as if it were the coming of the Messiah. One morning I sat at the window and watched the passing of a military parade. The sweep of their song, a resounding and strong sound, and the echoes of their hooves, and the rhythm of their blows on the cobblestones, made me very fearful. It didn't look [to me] like the coming of the Messiah; it seemed like a storm had blown by."[42]

Nowhere in this description do we get a sense of how Kadya felt about the new Bolshevik regime. She tells us that the sound of the military parade made her fearful, but we have no way of knowing if the volume of the soldiers' song was a problem, or the message of their movement was a problem. It is instructive that here she recoils not from the message about the coming of the Bolshevik Messiah, but from its assault on her senses as a listener. It may be that this account, written many years after the event, is a recalibrated understanding of what happened years earlier. Or, alternatively, it may well be that the gut reaction she felt at the time, one which she ignored later in the heat of the political events in Jewish Warsaw, resurfaced later and took on a new significance after she found out just how badly the god of the Bolshevik Messiah had failed the Jewish people.

She continues:

"It was the time of the civil war. Power changed hands frequently, sometimes the city was taken by the Bolsheviks; sometimes it was taken by the "Whites". It was often hard to find food. Under these conditions, it didn't make sense to keep the courses in Odessa. It was a time of utter chaos."[43]

Naturally, Kadya wanted to get home. It had been years since she had left home for Poltava to take care of her brother's army exemption; she had no idea how her family was faring. She managed to travel as far as Kiev, but there she had to stop. There was simply no safe way for her to get from Kiev to her home-town.

Once again, Kadya was all alone in a strange city, and once again, she found someone to help her. She met an acquaintance who recommended her to a baker, and the baker's children needed tutoring in Hebrew and in Yiddish. That was an ideal situation: she taught the baker's children to read and write Hebrew and Yiddish, and in return, she got a solid mid-day meal and bread to take home.

It was in Kiev that Kadya got a taste of a pogrom. But it was also there that she met two men who greatly influenced her future: Dovid Bergelson, the man who recognized her talent and encouraged her as a poet, and Simche Lev (spelled "Lew"), the man she married and lived with till the day he died

---

NOTES

[1] Melekh. Ravitch. *Mayn Leksikon: Yidishe dikhter, dertseyler, dramaturgn in Poyln tsvishn di tsvey velt milkhomes.* Montreal, 1945. p. 124.
[2] See: Alphonse Karr, A Tour Round My Garden, Kessinger, 2008, p. 304.
[3] For a definition of the Pale of Settlement, see: http://www.yivoencyclopedia.org/article.aspx/Pale_of_Settlement
[4] See the PDF at: https://archive.org/details/nybc313701, p. 10.
[5] *Ma'ariv,* May 3, 1971, p. 25
[6] *In Land fun Mayn Gebeyn*, p. 82.
[7] *Svive*, no. 17, October, 1965, p.40.
[8] op. Cit., p. 41.
[9] Ibid.
[10] Ibid.
[11] It is unclear whether the Russophile in Berze was in fact connected directly to the Alliance movement. Of itself, that is of little importance.
[12] To be entirely fair, there were traditional books published called *Yam Ha-Talmud*, The Ocean of the Talmud, the first of these, published in 1755. Nevertheless, it was the secular world that used the term "Talmud", while the religious/traditional world stuck with the term *gemoro*.
[13] *Svive*, no. 21, December, 1966, p. 32
[14] See: https://en.wikipedia.org/wiki/Pale_of_Settlement
[15] *Svive*, no. 23, October, 1967, p. 22.
[16] Op. Cit., p. 28.
[17] Ibid.
[18] Svive, no. 25, p. 45.
[19] Op. Cit., p. 46.
[20] Op. Cit., p. 45.
[21] Ibid.
[22] *Svive*, no. 20, September, 1966, p.60.
[23] *Svive*, no. 24, February, 1968, p. 34.

[24] http://www.Jewishgen.org/Yizkor/bereza93/ber011.html
[25] *Kartuz-Bereza: Sefer zikaron ve-edut le-kehila she-hushmeda, H.Y.D.*, p. 56. Available in PDF form from yiddishcenteryizkorbooks See: https://archive.org/details/nybc313701
[26] Op.cit., p. 54.
[27] Op. cit., p.33.
[28] Op. cit., p. 54.
[29] This poem can be found in her book *In Land fun Mayn Gebeyn*, pp. 8-9.
[30] *Svive*, no. 25, June 1968, p. 48
[31] Ibid.
[32] *Svive*, no. 28, May 1969, p. 58.
[33] This poem can be found in *Kheshvendilke Nekht*, p. 22. The translation is my own.
[34] http://www.dafdaf.co.il/Details.asp?MenuID=2&SubMenuID=144&PageID=1257&Ot=ב&SubTextID=1258
[35] *Svive*, no. 30, January, 1970, 56.
[36] Op. Cit., p.60.
[37] This poem can be found in *Kheshvendike Nekht*, p. 31. The translation is my own.
[38] Op. Cit., p. 61.
[39] There she got to know Yehudit Simkhoni(t) and Sara Kafri, both women members of the Knesset, the Israeli parliament, in the early years of the State of Israel.
[40] See http://en.wikipedia.org/wiki/Balfour_Declaration
[41] *Svive*, no. 32, September, 1970, p. 56.
[42] Op. Cit., p. 57.
[43] Ibid.

CHAPTER TWO: KIEV, TWO MEN ENTER, ONE MAN LEAVES

Kadya's years in Kiev were crucial ones. Here she made the career-switch from teacher-to-be to writer; here she switched from moving among dreamers in Hebrew, to moving among social activists whose language was Yiddish. Here she swerved from the Zionist camp to the socialist and Communist camp. And here she replaced the dream of living in Israel among other Jews with the dream of living in the Diaspora and striving for the universal brotherhood of Jews and non-Jews.

Here, she began to acquire fame, but here, too, she had a revolver placed directly on her heart by an Anti-Semite. How she came out of that unscathed, she herself never knew.

In Kiev, Kadya met the two most important men in her life: Dovid Bergelson and Simche Lev. Dovid Bergelson launched her career, but Simche Lev kept her financially afloat while she was the most important woman writer and editor in the world of Yiddish letters.

Until her stay in Kiev, Kadya thought of herself as a teacher and only as a teacher. While she did write poems, she never showed them to any one or thought of writing as a profession for herself.

It was a pogrom that brought her to Bergelson's attention. In the post-revolution Russia of 1917, the Whites and the Reds fought for control of what had once been Czarist Russia. In the chaos that ensued, pogroms were quite common.

In her autobiographical memoir, Kadya tells us that when the political power-brokers in the city of Kiev, changed:

"…we prepared ourselves for a pogrom."[1]

The Jews of the city anticipated a pogrom. Even so, they could do nothing more than bolt the doors of their homes and hope for the best. At the time, the common belief was that riots would hit the poorer sections of town, but leave the up-scale neighborhoods intact. That is why Kadya's friend, a dentist, invited Kadya, along with other less well-off friends, to ride out the anticipated mob action in her supposedly safe home. But that home was not as safe as the young women supposed. Here is Kadya's description of what happened:

"One morning we heard a strong knock at the door. We understood [from the knock] that these were not invited guests. There was no alternative; the mistress of the house opened the door. Four fine young officers entered. They didn't greet us. They just ordered: 'Give us your money.' At the time we'd been sitting at the table eating breakfast. To hurry us up, they took out their revolvers from their holsters. One of the young men came over to me and pointed his revolver at my heart. I no longer felt frightened; apparently at the time I was already dead from fright. But it seems that the prophet Elijah came once more to my rescue. The officer pointed that revolver, but he didn't shoot. He had a fine, gentle face. To this day I cannot understand how such a man becomes so violent. Our group began removing their rings, their watches, and they took out whatever money they had. And the officers didn't forget to ask the dentist where she kept her spare gold teeth. In short, they elegantly stuffed everything into their pockets and they left. They were "gentle folk". They didn't beat anyone, they didn't curse anyone, but it has to be said that they left without saying "goodbye". They just closed the door and that was it. When they left, we, the robbed girls, praised them. They were truly fine people. They didn't send us off to the next world."[2]

From Kadya's description, it seems that although all the young men had revolvers, only one actually threatened them directly. And that one chose to threaten her. How is it that in a room full of young women, a gunman chose her? Naturally this is not a question she asks; she was far too traumatized at the moment to ask that question. But we can ask ourselves that question. It would seem that in a group, Kadya stood out, even when all were silent. She had the sort of charisma that made a total stranger focus on her, above all others. It was almost certainly that quality that made her "the person to know" in the Yiddish world in later years.

Had Kadya lived in the age of Facebook, she would have had thousands of followers. And there is little doubt that among those names would have been Bebe Idelson, nee Trachtenberg. Bebe and Kadya had much in common. Bebe was born one year after Kadya, in 1895, and she died one year later, in 1975. But the two

Chapter Two: Kiev, Two Men Enter, One Man Leaves

women shared a lot more than the coincidental overlap of life-span. Both women had fathers, who, though versed in traditional Jewish sources, respected general, secular studies, and both fathers encouraged their daughters to leave their native-born *shtetl* and acquire a secular education. Both women were independent, non-conformists, committed to financial independence for women, and both married in difficult times. Most importantly, WWI brought the plight of Europe's impoverished refugees to their attention. In the aftermath of WWI, there were pogroms in Kiev, as there were throughout all of the former Czarist Russia. Between 1919 and 1921, when both women were in Kiev, there were 1,236 murderous riots in 500 different cities and towns, during which an estimated 200,000 Jews were murdered.[3]

Kadya and her friends had a narrow escape during one such pogrom in Kiev, and Bebe was in Kiev during these pogroms. Did the two women meet then? Was Bebe, perhaps, present at the party that celebrated the escape of Kadya and her friends from the pogrom described above? It is likely, but there is no way of knowing for sure. Since the two women were fast friends when they met up in Israel in 1950, and Bebe left Europe in the inter-war years, it is more than likely that the two met sometime during the years that both of them spent in Kiev. We do know that the violence against Jews that both women witnessed then convinced them both of the need for some sort of Jewish self-defense organization, and ultimately, of the need for a Jewish state that would pledge itself to guarantee the physical well-being of Jews world-wide. Both women helped the WWI refugees in whatever way they could, and were sympathetic to Jewish Socialism, a solution, as they saw it, to the exploitation of Jewish workers who lived in poverty. If the two women did not actually meet, they must have communicated. More than thirty years later, in 1950, when the two women met up in Israel, it was Bebe, then head of the women's division of the Socialist Labor party, who provided funding and a home for Kadya's literary and social efforts. But unlike Bebe, Kadya did not leave Europe for Palestine in the inter-war years. Instead, she stayed in Europe.

When Kadya was still in Kiev, and the danger from further pogroms seemed to have been averted, Kadya's friend, the dentist, made a party to celebrate the deliverance of the group from the pogrom. In honor of this party, Kadya composed a humorous/satirical poem of 'thanks' to the pogrom perpetrators. In this poem, she described how, in heaven, these men were given a parade and celebrated as righteous men. Among the invitees to this party was the brother of the man known as '*Der Nister*'[4]. This man grabbed Kadya's notebook from her and put it in his pocket. He wanted to show the poem to his brother. The notebook contained other poems that Kadya had written. She had been writing poems since childhood, she tells us, but she had never taken the poems, or herself as a writer, seriously. She asked *Der Nister*'s brother to return her notebook, but he would hear none of it. A few weeks later this man told her that his brother had shown her work to other writers, and they wanted to meet her. He mentioned the names: *Der Nister*, Bergelson, Dobrushin, but she didn't go to meet them. This is how she puts it in her memoir:

"It did not occur to me that I could be in the writers' 'heavenly world'". I imagined that books came to this world from Mount Sinai."[5]

As it happened, Kadya worked in a Children's Home along with one of Bergelson's relatives. This woman approached her one day and told her Bergelson wanted to meet her. Kadya went to the co-worker's house, where Bergelson scolded her for not coming to meet him when she was invited to do so earlier. She was invited this time to come to his house. When she got there, she saw several well-known Yiddish writers, among them *Der Nister*,[6] Dobrushin and Leib Kvitko. These men had gathered at Bergelson's place to discuss the second edition of their literary journal, *Eygns* (Our Own). To her great surprise, they had chosen some of the poems that were in her notebook for publication in their journal.

It is a measure of Kadya's surprise at this turn of events that she asked Bergelson what would happen if she were no longer able to write poems:

"Everyone will laugh at me", she said. "They'll say: 'Big Deal, she was able to write a few poems, and that's it.'".[7]

Bergelson calmed her with his understanding, if humorous, response:

"No one begins at the end. Everyone begins at the beginning."[8]

When Dobrushin gave her a writers' handbook, one which she admits she never looked at, Bergelson said, once again, humorously:

"No writer learns [his craft] from books. Each writer goes to his own *kheyder* [school]"[9]

Despite the praise she got, as well as the warm and genuine welcome, the older Kadya reports that her younger self nevertheless left that meeting with the well-known writers still amazed that she had been chosen to be one of them. As she points out, each of the men there had an established reputation from before the War; she herself was then unknown; an entirely new addition to the world of Yiddish literature.

True to his belief that each writer needs to find his/her own way, Bergelson never told Kadya what she needed to do to improve a line of her poetry. But, taking out the Hebrew Bible, he did show her how to spot an effective, arresting line of text. From his example, she tells us, she understood that a "strong line of poetry" is always more than the sum total of its parts. It has multiple meanings, each of which the text points to, but does not necessarily make explicit. More than anything else, Bergelson encouraged Kadya. He knew how to build up her self-confidence, and he did so.

When the group celebrated publication of its journal, they insisted that Kadya recite her poems aloud. Shy as she was, she hesitated. But once again, Bergelson encouraged her. In the end, it was an uplifting experience for her. As she says in her memoir:

"I felt then that a poem belongs not only to its writer. It belongs to the public…In short, I realized that writing is a communal undertaking."[10]

In the poems she wrote after their meeting, she spoke openly of her emergence as a poet. For her, the full light of positive feedback was akin to discovering her potential power as a poet. In a poem dated 1920, she says:

"I've come out of darkness and hiding

And wide is the stride of a small foot

And strong is the beat

Of a thin fist

I've come out of darkness and hiding."[11]

Kadya tells us in her memoir that she visited the Bergelson home often when she was in Kiev. There she met the rising young stars of Russian Yiddish belles lettres: Peretz Markish, Dovid Hofshtein and Leib Kvitko. She reports listening to Bergelson read a piece he was in the middle of writing and becoming enchanted:

"As he read, I felt the heroes of his story come alive in front of me. And in his reading, there was such an intimacy, a kind of closeness to the people he was portraying. One felt that this was not a constructed plot, but one that was lived-through; this came from an inner depth."[12]

The mature Kadya tells us that these meetings with Bergelson stimulated her into thinking about the essence of the writerly experience. For the first time she realized that a writer's work draws on deep roots, communal as well as personal, and that each writer has his/her own peculiarities of language that mark him/her, and convey his/her understanding of the world.

Kadya devoted four pages of her autobiography to her stay in Kiev, her meeting with Dovid Bergelson and his influence on her writing. When she wrote this, she was past seventy years old; her meeting with Bergelson was then more than 45 years in the past. There is no question that their meeting was crucial for her artistic development; she is generous and honest in crediting him with encouraging her. But there is a lot that she doesn't say in her memoir.

Dovid Bergelson, already a famous Yiddish writer when Kadya met him, created in Kiev the *Kultur Lige*, the League for [Jewish] Culture, a group of young intellectual Jews who wanted to establish a national network of schools, publishing houses, theaters, libraries and clubs within the new Socialist/Communist political setting. Bergelson's journal, *Eygns* (Our Own), was part of this mission. As the title of Bergelson's journal suggests, for these intellectuals, Jewish identity was inherently and inexorably bound up with the Yiddish language.

This was a new view for Kadya. She had trained as a teacher of Hebrew; many of her fellow teachers at Halperin's seminar emigrated to what was then Palestine and took up positions of leadership. Kadya had taught Jewish children in

Chapter Two: Kiev, Two Men Enter, One Man Leaves

Yiddish till then, not out of any ideological conviction, but simply out of a practical motive. After all, Yiddish, not Hebrew, was the children's native language; for them Hebrew was a foreign language. Traumatized as her orphan students were, it seemed to her only humane to use their native language while teaching; this kept the upheavals in their lives to a minimum. From Bergelson and his circle, she heard a different message: that Yiddish, not Hebrew, was the genuine language of the Jewish people, and only it could be a vehicle for the modernization so necessary for Europe's Jews. Interestingly, despite Bergelson's personal charm and the sway he held over those who met him, he did not altogether convince Kadya on this point. After she and Bergelson left Kiev, Kadya continued to teach children in schools where the language of instruction was Yiddish, but she also taught children in schools where the language of instruction was Hebrew. Always the skeptic, and in the manner of her father, always the outsider looking in, she was moved by the message of Bergelson and his group, but she did not slavishly adopt all their positions.

The *Kultur Lige* was almost certainly Kadya's first serious confrontation with Communist sympathizers. Though the outlines of what was later to become Communist totalitarianism were not yet clear, the difficulties that lay in a total adoption/implementation of the Communist program were already evident, at least to some. And indeed, some of the original members of the *Kulture Lige* later split with Bergelson just because he was so keen a follower of Soviet Communism.

There were some topics which Kadya and her friends never wrote about. If they did write letters discussing these topics, they may have intentionally removed these letters from the material they deposited in their archives. Sometimes we know the facts from other archival material; sometimes we know them from material made public after Kadya was no longer alive. One such to pic is the fate of Dovid Bergelson under the Soviet Communist regime.

Kadya's friend, Rokhl Korn, the Yiddish poet and novelist, spoke publicly of how Bergelson suffered under the Communist regime. Of a visit she made in 1944 to Bergelson, then living in Moscow, she said:

"He took me by the arm and led me into his study. He stopped in front of his portrait which hung on the wall and asked: 'Do you see him?' I answered: 'Yes, who painted it?' being sure he wanted to comment on the painter. But as though he had not heard my question, he kept pointing his finger at his own portrait and like one possessed he shouted into my ear: 'Look at him; take a good look at him. I hate his guts, the filthy scoundrel!'

Only later did I begin to grasp the full tragedy of the scene. This was David Bergelson's way of turning to the free world and asking that he not be judged too harshly for having given in, and having served a false idolatry both in his work and in his personal life. He realized he was already a prisoner of Soviet reality, but I, who was still a Polish citizen, had a chance to leave this prison that housed 200 million."[13]

There is every reason to believe that Rokhl Korn told Kadya about this harrowing experience. But Kadya never mentioned it anywhere in her writing. Indeed, Bergelson's political orientation and his fate are singularly absent from her stories about him in her memoir. Nor did she leave an account of the extent to which she sympathized with the political positions she heard in Kiev. By the time she wrote her memoir in 1970, all knew that the Soviet regime had accused Bergelson in 1952 along with other Yiddish writers of "rootless cosmopolitanism" and had executed him by a firing squad. The fact that a later Soviet regime rehabilitated him along with other Yiddish writers and republished his works was cold comfort. For Kadya, as for many of her time.who were close to these writers, the bitter end of the victims brought on a shocked silence.

A complex knot of feelings came along with these murders. The Jewish writers were seen as martyrs: they died because they were Jews who wrote in Yiddish. There was no way to excuse the vicious anti-Semitism of the Stalinist Soviet regime. And yet, the writers were also blind, blind to the cruel realities of Stalinism, blind to their own prejudices against traditional Judaism, blind to the basic reality of Jewish nationalism and to the deeply-rooted bond between the Jewish people and the ancestral homeland they called "the Land of Israel". No one wanted to blame the martyred victims; they had paid dearly for their blindness.

Chapter Two: Kiev, Two Men Enter, One Man Leaves

What surfaced, then, was a sadness that could not find its voice. Even Kadya Molodowsky, a vocal woman and one of Bergelson's great admirers, could find nothing to say.

The only fair way to appraise Kadya's actions at this point is to examine them in their historical context. It is not hard to see why Kadya was attracted to the *Kultur Lige* in 1920-1921; its agenda was nothing less than grandiose. The political realities of Europe were changing. It looked like the Czar would be replaced by a new democratic order, and the Jews, formerly an oppressed minority people within the Russian Empire, would now be able to determine their own fate. Here were intellectuals who had thought seriously about the fate of their people and were determined to help their fellow Jews establish a new order.

Ten years older than Kadya, Bergelson achieved fame before the outbreak of World War I, when Kadya was still a teenager. At that point, she had just gotten her high school equivalency degree. In the 1920s, when the two of them met, Bergelson was said to be the "highest-paid" Yiddish writer of his time.[14]

Apparently Bergelson not only had talent; he also had charisma. Those who knew him personally later said that in any social circle, he was always the center of attention. He came from a wealthy family; he had had a broad education- both Jewish and secular-, and when he and Kadya met, it looked like his plan for state support of an autonomous secular Jewish/Yiddish culture might just materialize. Kadya joined his group partly out of curiosity, and partly out of admiration for their literary achievements. Indeed, as we have seen, she felt honored and amazed that they welcomed her into their circle. When Bergelson published Kadya's two poems, "*Dorsht*" (Thirst) and "*Shtot*" (City), in the second volume of *Eygns*, in 1920, he gave her just the critical boost that she needed; her self-confidence soared.

Despite the fact that Bergelson's public acclaim stemmed from the experimental nature of his novels, he did not find it demeaning to write for children. On the contrary; he viewed this writing as a critical and highly valuable tool in the repertoire of Yiddish culture. Practically speaking, if one captured the attention of young children with Yiddish stories, one had these children as a potential adult audience in years to come. More importantly, if a language aspires to cultural greatness, and Bergelson's group most certainly had such an aspiration, it cannot forego a well-written, enjoyable corpus of children's literature. That is why even before he met Kadya, Bergelson had published three of his own stories for children. As it turned out, the mature Kadya, perhaps even sub-consciously, took her cue from Bergelson's attitude and from the importance that he attached to literature for children. After she met him, she published Yiddish poems and plays and essays for adults, but also poems and stories for children. Indeed, her first award was for her children's book, entitled "*Mayselekh*", and it is on her poems for children that her fame now rests.

One of Bergelson's closest friends, a fellow author and sometime co-editor, Nachman Mayzel, said about Bergelson's desk that it always had on it "an ashtray overflowing with cigarette butts."[15] We know from a first-hand report, then, that Bergelson was a chain smoker. It is doubtful that the small-town Kadya smoked cigarettes when she was growing up in Berze. That was simply not something young women did. Nor is it likely that she picked up the cigarette habit in Halperin's seminary for Hebrew teachers. Those were war years, when everything was scarce. Even if one of the teachers-to-be in Halperin's seminary had had such a habit, in those years it would have been difficult to indulge. Early in her memoir, Kadya mentions her father smoking. In this, Bergelson was like her father. Here were two father-figures in her life, both of them men she admired, and both of them smokers. It is not surprising, then, that photographs of Kadya in her later years show her wrapped in a cloud of cigarette smoke. And in fact, in her last volume of adult poetry entitled *Likht fun Dornboym*, (Light of the Thorn-bush), there is a poem dedicated to her cigarette.[16]

There is one more item, circumstantial in nature, that can be marshaled for a personal connection between Kadya and Dovid Bergelson. The two of them met and worked together during the years 1919 through 1921. The young Kadya, entranced as she was by the older man, was not about to become his mistress. She was looking for an open connection, and that could have happened only if Bergelson would have divorced his wife. He obviously was not interested in doing so. Only after Bergelson left Kiev for Berlin in 1921, did Kadya look for, and agree

Chapter Two: Kiev, Two Men Enter, One Man Leaves   41

to, a serious connection with a man. It may not be an accident that she married her husband, Simche, in the winter of 1921, when it was clear to her that her connection with Bergelson would never develop into anything serious.

There is no question that a deep-seated emotional bond often forms between people who jointly engage in serious intellectual investigation or highly creative work. It would seem that such a bond existed between Bergelson and Kadya.

Kadya lived out most of her late adult life in New York City. After her death, her papers were deposited in an archive in YIVO, the center for Yiddish research in New York. Among the correspondence found there are 2 letters from Bergelson, written when he was in Berlin and she in Warsaw, and one slip of paper without an envelope.

In 1928, Bergelson told Kadya that he got her book of poems, and read them:

"with joy in [reading] each poem, each successful line, even though I remembered many of them from prior reading, when they were printed individually. For me this book is one of the best indications that our poetry has taken off and grown to a further level. I would like to be able to talk with you about your future path, but this is hard to do in a letter."

He then tells her he is planning to take a trip to the US, where he will stay for a few months. When he returns, he tells her, he plans to start a small, solely literary, journal which will print the best that Yiddish literature has to offer. He adds that he hopes she will help him with it.

In fact, he did travel to the US in 1929, and he did tour the country for 6 months. But he did not found a new journal and the two of them did not collaborate on the journal he dreamt of. The second letter, written in 1930, also came from Berlin. It was written before Bergelson returned to Warsaw that year:

"The day before yesterday I spoke of you, yesterday I spoke of you, today I spoke of you and decided to write you and tell you that: you and the poems that you read to me bring me back to my finest minutes in Warsaw. I took your book of poems out of my cabinet, and put it on my desk so I can read it more often.

Thank you, dearest [*libenke* in the original]. I'm writing to tell you what I thought today: as things stand now, it looks like you will be one of the greatest- if not the greatest Yiddish poet. This is not just my opinion. Remember this when you go on to other writings, because others as well as I will expect this [finest writing] from you. It's good that your book for children is about to be published. And may God save you from putting out a book with typos/mistakes. Write me from time to time and send me your new poems."

There is no doubt that this sort of praise from the most respected man of letters in Yiddish literature of the time was very flattering for Kadya. But we see in this letter not just a respect for talent but also a genuine personal concern, a human connection that goes beyond artistic appreciation.

The third bit of correspondence from Bergelson that is found in the YIVO archive is a note scribbled on a slip of paper. It has no envelope, and the handwriting on the bottom of that note, which appears to be Kadya's, has added: 29/V.[17] The official biography of Bergelson, claims that it was in 1930 that "Bergelson returned to Warsaw for the first time in twenty years."[18] If this is so, the two met in May of 1930.

Whatever the facts about the dates of Bergelson's appearance in Warsaw, it is worth repeating the contents of the note:

"Kadyele!
You've been invited through me to have dinner at the Vagman's. I'll be there too. If you'd be good, you'd take a few poems with you so we can read them. I'll be there and I'd like to see you.
A Kiss, D. Bergelson"

When Kadya first met Bergelson in 1919, she was 25 and he was 35. When the two of them parted ways, and Kadya married Simche in 1921, she was 27 and Bergelson was 37. By the time the two of them met up again in 1930 in Warsaw, Kadya was 35, and Bergelson was 45. At this point, the two of them were no longer so young, and Kadya was no longer Bergelson's unknown protégée, but a recognized writer with a name of her own.

It is quite likely that Kadya met Dovid Begelson one more time in 1933. Among the poems in *Dzshike Gas (Dzshike Street)* which was published late in 1933, is a poem entitled *"Nakht" (Night)*. Its heading says "Berlin 1933. [19] Nowhere in her memoir does Kadya mention a trip to Berlin that year. Nor is such a trip mentioned anywhere in her letters. While it is true that she may have gone to Berlin for any number of reasons, it is also true that Dovid Bergelson, the man she greatly admired, was living in Berlin at the time. Did the two of them meet then? That is certainly more than possible; it is probable. Since the heading of a poem mentions her presence in Berlin during that year, Kadya was obviously not out to keep her trip a secret. While the details of what took place cannot be verified, there is nothing to stop the reader from speculating.

Some time after that putative trip, Bergelson left Berlin for the Soviet Union. That sealed his doom. Once there, he was forced to "inform" on his former colleagues, the Yiddish writers he had so admired when he was in "the free world". In an undated letter that Kadya wrote to Opotashu, between 1933 and 1935, she expresses her shock that Bergelson, her former supporter and colleague, wrote in a Communist journal called "October," that she was a "traitor" to the [Socialist ZKN] cause, a bourgeois and "reactionary". She never saw the article that accused her of these things, she admitted, but she was told about it. She was hurt and shocked.

"I cannot understand what has happened. What's going on: Is it a psychosis…"

She ends this portion of her letter with "C'est la vie!"[20]

It is clear that at this point neither Kadya nor the rest of the Yiddish writers had grasped the ugly facts about the Jewish elite under Communist rule. If this elite wanted to protect themselves and their families, they had to publicly accuse their former friends and colleagues outside the Soviet Union.

Wherever Kadya went, that correspondence went with her. It traveled with her from Warsaw to New York in 1935. She lived in 6 different places in New York between 1935 and 1950, and each time she moved, that correspondence went with her. It traveled with her from New York to Israel in 1950; and then it traveled back to New York in 1952. Clearly, this correspondence must have meant much to her.

If Kadya did not mention her deep emotional bond with Bergelson in her memoir, that is understandable. By the time she wrote her memoir, her relationship with Bergelson was more of a might-have-been affair in her life than a genuine one; after all, Bergelson was the man she did not marry. More painful yet, for all his intelligence, Bergelson walked right into the lion's den of Soviet Russia, and might be said to have brought his murder upon himself. It was so horrible a fate, that Kadya simply fell silent.

In 1930, Kadya published the first of 3 poems that had in it the words "Paper Bridge(s)"[21]. It is not surprising that she seized upon this metaphor. During the formative years of her life, from 1914, when she was a young adult of 20 years old, to 1924, when she returned to Warsaw at the age of 30, she had been on the run. First, she needed to stay ahead of the waves of violence brought on by WWI; then she needed to stay ahead of the violence brought on by the Russian Revolution and the pogroms that came in its wake. Life was indeed a "paper bridge"[22]: a precarious thing; one could never be certain one would cross over to refuge in safety.

In the 1930 poem, entitled "My Paper Bridge", Kadya speaks of a time, clearly a time in the past, when "…the sun was a golden wheel on its own path/That led to my feet straight and true." At this, obviously happier, time, the poet "…contemplated a household and a bed/And golden days and nights bursting with stars,/I contemplated a husband and a child,/And green springs and brown summers". This is the one of the few times that Kadya allowed herself to speak openly and publicly of her sorrow at not having children of her own. She admits in this poem that while she was on this precarious bridge made of paper, she did have such a dream. And she dedicated this poem, full of admitted longing for a child that never was, not to her husband, but to Dovid Bergelson!

Simche Lev: The Man She Did Marry

While Dovid Bergelson is the man Kadya did not marry while she was in Kiev, Simche Lev is the man she did marry. Once again, the memoir that Kadya

Chapter Two: Kiev, Two Men Enter, One Man Leaves   45

left behind tells us far less than we know from other sources. Still, before continuing, it is worthwhile considering Kadya's official version of this story:

"In Kiev I met Pu'ah's sister, Levita (Rokhl)...And through Levita, I met a man from Lekhevitch, also a teacher, a sharp-witted man, and I had issues with him– in discussions with me, he always won out. I actually married this young man, Simche Lev, and thank God, till now we have not divorced; may things continue as they are."[23]

In the next paragraph, she talks about the new shoes she bought for her wedding. It was winter and the couple had to walk through deep snow to get where they were going:

"There was then a deep snow [on the ground] and it seemed to me as though the street was strewn with a white carpet in honor of the new shoes I was about to buy. We slipped on the snow, fell a few times- and we were happy. We returned with a new pair of shoes for me, and I was certain that the Rothchilds didn't have shoes like mine."[24]

This is all she tells us about her wedding day. There is no mention of the wedding guests, no mention of the music played, no mention of the meeting and mixing of families, no mention of a rabbi who married them. All we have is a light-hearted segue into the present time, when the two are still married. The reason for this silence becomes clear when the archival material is examined.

What is the story Kadya was glossing over and doing her best to hide? Simply that her marriage to Simche in Kiev was not a Jewish marriage, but a civil marriage.

We know from the papers left in the Makhon Lavon archive in Israel that in 1937 it was crucial for Kadya and Simche to prove that they were married. That was the only way Kadya, who had been naturalized as an American citizen, could get Simche out of Europe in the late 1930s. From the correspondence between the two of them, the picture becomes clear: Kadya and Simche were married in a civil ceremony that winter day in Kiev when the snow was deep. They did not have a Jewish wedding ceremony until they arrived in Belarus and met each other's parents about a year later.

Oddly, Simche seemed to have believed they were married in Brisk/Brest; that is apparently what he told Kadya in a letter that has not been preserved. We know about this letter because of a response of Kadya's that has been preserved. In this response, Kadya insists that they were married, not in Brisk, but in Lekhevitch. As she says there: "I seem to remember we were married the 20th of May in 1921 in Lekhevitch" (Simche's home town).

While it is true that when Kadya wrote this letter (in 1938), 17 years had passed since the day of their (supposed) wedding, it is a bit odd, to say the least, that Kadya is not entirely sure of the date and place of her own wedding: she only "seems to remember" the date and place. If in fact Simche and Kadya had had an elaborate wedding in Lekhevitch on that date, one with the meeting and mixing of the two families, both Simche and Kadya would have remembered it. But that is not what happened. Instead, in Lekhevitch, Simche's home-town, a rabbi performed the religious ceremony for the couple that had been living together as man and wife for approximately a year.

A civil marriage between Jews presents something of a problem. Not all Jewish authorities see it as binding under Jewish law. When Kadya and Simche met and decided to marry in Kiev, neither was moored to a traditional, religious community. It is not as though the two were against having their families at their wedding, but that was impossible under the circumstances. In the political chaos of the time, the roads were dangerous and their families could not have gotten to Kiev safely. Besides, these were the heady days of revolution and sweeping change, when the young Jews of Kadya's and Simche's milieu truly believed that a new system would replace the outdated traditions of the Jewish religion. It would seem that neither Kadya nor Simche felt the need for a religious ceremony. But once they were in Simche's home town, the couple decided not to antagonize their traditional parents. It was then that they found a rabbi who performed the traditional Jewish service. Perhaps they were asked to bring Simche's family and friends, though we are never told that this is so. Whatever they did, it was enough to get them registered in the Jewish registry of married couples. For all we know, the two were able to pre-date the marriage certificate at the local (Lekhevitch) rabbinate. After all,

Simche's family was well-known in the town, and the two had gone through a civil ceremony.

Once we realize that Kadya and Simche were married civilly in Kiev, we understand why Kadya suggests in her memoir that she and Simche were a married couple before they met their prospective in-laws. They had indeed been married civilly, and it is true that the "couple" wanted to introduce their partners to their families: Simche wanted to present his wife Kadya to his parents in Lekhevitch, and Kadya wanted to present her husband Simche to her parents in Berze.

It is understandable that Kadya keeps the picture fuzzy in her memoir. By the time she wrote that memoir, the Socialism/Communism the two had put their faith in had proved to be a disaster, and the Jewish traditions the two had spurned, were looking a bit more acceptable.

In her memoir, Kadya tells us that after she and Simche left Kiev, they wanted to go back to their homes to see their respective families, but they were unable to do so immediately. First, they stopped off in Minsk. It is clear they arrived in Minsk around 1921, but it is not clear from Kadya's memoir how long they stayed in Minsk. It would seem that they stayed long enough to meet old friends and make new ones.

In her memoir, Kadya says about Minsk of the inter-war years: "Minsk was not Kiev. Minsk was a thoroughly Jewish city. You heard Yiddish spoken in the street. I felt that the entire city [was filled with-ZKN] relatives of mine"[25] What Kadya was getting at was more than just the familiar dialect. While it is true that the dialect she heard in Minsk matched the one she knew from home (there is a comfort to be had in being surrounded with folks who sound like you), Kadya was getting at something deeper. In Kiev, the Soviet hold on the Jewish population had become a grip that could not be avoided. From the fact that Kadya was delighted to hear Yiddish spoken in the streets of Minsk, we realize that the situation there was different from what it was in Kiev, where it had become dangerous to speak Yiddish on the street.

As Elisa Bemporad has shown[26], a retrospective view of social upheavals often muddies the picture. The Soviet/Communist revolution was not all of one piece, and changes did not take hold all at once. While Jewish life was constricting in Kiev, in Minsk, post-revolutionary life went on as it had in pre-revolutionary times. This era may be seen as a brief interlude in hindsight, but for Jews who lived in Minsk in the inter-war years, life continued as it had been before the revolution. Kadya and Simche rented the teeniest of rooms in Minsk, but the kindness of a neighbor who shared her soup with them every day, staved off their hunger and made them feel welcome.

From Minsk they traveled northwards, till they were stopped at the border. Their home-towns had once been part of Czarist Russia, but after the wars, the two towns were part of the newly independent Poland. One needed the right papers to enter this new part of Poland. Kadya and Simche were held in a border detention camp for a short while, where their few possessions were disinfected and their papers were examined. Only after all of this, were they on their way to see their families.

There is a marvelous story in Kadya's memoir about her "dowry". When Kadya and Simche married in Kiev, she was 27. She had seen advancing armies and the chaos of war, she had traveled solo and nearly penniless from one town to another in chaotic times, she had been held-up in a "lite" pogrom and kept her cool, and she had supported herself throughout all her travails. By the time she found a husband and married, she had not only been self-supporting for years, she was also a recognized poet. She was, in short, a modern woman of the world. And yet, her mother, still rooted in the world of the *shtetl*, imagined that the rules of behavior had not changed. Shortly after Kadya and Simche arrived in Simkhe's home-town of Lekhevitch, Kadya's mother visited her new in-laws unexpectedly. In a tete-a-tete that she had with Simche's father, she offered to give her respectable, Jewish daughter a proper dowry: the rent money that was owed the family from the income of two small shops. It never occurred to her that neither her daughter nor her son-in-law wanted this dowry. Nor did it occur to her that the institution of a dowry was anathema to them and to their friends.

Kadya tells us that her mother stayed in Lekhevitch only one day, long enough to make this offer. For all that Kadya realized the offer of a dowry was a "heartfelt" gesture of love, she tells us in her memoir that she felt her mother had come from "another planet"[27].

Modernity had not reached Simche's mother either. In her memoir, Kadya tells us that in Simche's home, the Sabbath was observed just as it was in her home. All weekly chores were put aside, the woman of the house lit candles, the best food was served and eaten, and all worldly cares were forgotten as the Sabbath peace and quiet settled on the home. Apparently, Kadya did not light Sabbath candles, as her mother-in-law did. The mother-in-law, Kadya tells us, remonstrated very gently. She said to Kadya: "Aren't you lighting candles? When you light candles, your home fills up with angels. If you don't light candles, when will the angels come?"[28] When she reported this conversation in her memoir, Kadya was more than seventy. She looked back at that incident with a mixture of wonder and skepticism. She said in her memoir: "That Sabbath remained in my memory and I almost believe that angels arrived in that household."[29]

The few sentences quoted above are all Kadya tells us about her husband and their relationship in her memoir. This is no confessional autobiography. Indeed, it hides the crises, the reversals of fortune and the reversals of roles that beset their marriage.

To know more about Kadya's marriage, we need to rely on archival sources. In the Makhon Lavon archive in Afeka, Israel, Kadya left two sorts of evidence that speak volumes: one, a small card tucked into Simche's Polish passport, the other a series of letters written over a period of three years. The card tells us something about their marriage when Kadya was living alone in Warsaw; the correspondence tells us about their marriage while Kadya was living in New York, and Simche was still in Warsaw. Because the correspondence ends once the couple is reunited, that is where our survey will end. Here is the arc of Kadya's relationship with Simche as it appears in these documents.

Kadya and Simche lived primarily in Warsaw after their marriage. The photo of Simche as a young man in Poland, with an upturned overcoat collar, and a cigarette poised at an angle, suggests a pensive, but self-confident Humphrey-Bogart-like character. It would seem that unlike Kadya, who was taught at home, and even so had only a gymnasium [academic high school ZKN] equivalency degree, Simche had a university degree, although the source of this degree is unclear. He was accepted as a student in the Sorbonne after their arrival in Warsaw, a rare and coveted honor, especially for a Jew. When they married in 1921, Kadya had published only two short poems in a journal that became defunct after a short period. But a mere eight years later, in 1929, Kadya had already put out a book of highly praised poems, and she was a regular contributor to *Literarishe Bleter*, the most acclaimed Yiddish literary journal of its time.

Was it Kadya's success and popularity that propelled Simche into leaving Kadya in Warsaw, and agreeing to going to the Sorbonne alone? Did he want to earn a name for himself that would measure up to hers? Or did their marriage have difficulties of another sort? There is no way of knowing. We do know that Simche took up this offer to study in Paris. He left Warsaw, and Kadya, and traveled there to study. But did he only study in Paris? It would seem not.

In the Israeli archive, tucked inside Simche's Polish passport, (one that he had no intention of using after the Holocaust), is a small note in French, addressed to Simche by a French woman-friend. It suggests that she enjoyed his company and was looking forward to seeing him again soon. Whoever his woman was, when she sent this note to Simche, she was writing to a married man. Possibly Simche had an affair with this woman; there is no way we can know now for certain. But from the poetry that Kadya wrote then, it is clear that her marriage/love life had reached an impasse.

In the April 1929 volume of *Literarishe Bleter*, Kadya had a poem entitled "Between You and Me There Are No Longer Any Words". As Fishman Gonshor puts it, this is "a poem of love that is no more".[30] At this point, Kadya was an abandoned married woman, alone in Warsaw, and everybody knew her plight. With a sort of cruel glee, A(ha)ron Zeitlin, no friend of Kadya's, called Kadya "a professional, certified *agune*/deserted-wife".[31] Most frank is the title of another poem: "You Leave- And I No Longer Recognize Your Street". This, from its title alone, is a poem of "love that is no more".

Chapter Two: Kiev, Two Men Enter, One Man Leaves

In the spring of 1929, Kadya followed Simche to Paris. From the documents that are found in the Israeli archive it would seem that while she was there, she took the opportunity to study Friedrich Froebel's philosophy of child psychology. Ostensibly, she was in Paris to do this and to look for "an illustrator for her planned book of children's poetry."[32] It is more likely, though, that she used these activities as a cover story for her trip. In Paris, she joined Simche, and did what she could to save their marriage. She spent the years 1929-1931 with him in Paris, and she got what she came for. Simche did in fact leave Paris and return with her to Warsaw.

It is probably not an accident that the note from this woman-friend to Simche was left in Kadye's Israeli archive. It is almost as though the two of them, Kadya and Simche, had decided to bury that part of their life. They had had difficulties, but their marriage had survived. Leaving this note behind was equivalent to saying "that's behind us; now let's go on and not think about it anymore".

What Kadya left in which archive, tells us much about her emotional state. The letters she got in Europe from Bergelson followed her wherever she went. The man had disappeared from her life, but his letters stayed with her. The "incriminating" note that indicated Simche's dalliance early in their marriage, was buried in an archive that Kadya left behind her. The man stayed with her; the evidence of his affair was abandoned.

Just as Simche left for Paris and left Kadya behind in Warsaw, so Kadya left Warsaw for New York a few years later. In 1935, Kadya got a visitor's visa to the US, where she was invited to tour and give readings of her works as well as to help start a Yiddish children's journal. That visitor's visa was only for her. While she advised and toured and spoke, Simche was left to fend for himself in Warsaw.

One might suggest that Kadya's departure was a "tit for tat": just as Kadya had been deserted by Simche, so she deserted him. But, as will become evident, Kadya had personal reasons, in no way connected to her life with Simche, for wanting to get out of Warsaw in 1935. Besides, there is an enormous difference between the two "desertions". When Simche "deserted" Kadya in Warsaw in the 1920s, the lives of the Jews in Warsaw were not in immediate danger. But when

Kadya left Warsaw for the US in 1935, Hitler had already risen to power, and most Jews in Poland were very aware that it was only a matter of time till Hitler made good on his promise to "solve the Jewish problem".

In her memoir Kadya reports feeling guilty as she watched Simche run after the train that took her to safety and left him alone and seemingly deserted.[33] But Kada did not desert Simche at all. As soon as she acquired US citizenship, two years later, she began working on getting Simche out of Poland and over to the US. In a letter that she wrote to her friend Ida Maze during this period, she confessed her fear that Simche's "crazy behavior in Paris" might backfire on him and prevent the US authorities from issuing him a visa.[34] It is highly unlikely that the US State Department cared much about an individual's dalliances out of wedlock. But they most certainly did care about allowing potential Communists into the US. This was the time of the "Red Scare" and Jews were the usual suspects. As we have seen, many Jews had in fact sympathized with the Communists when the Czar was overthrown in Europe. And an affiliation with known Communists or with public activities in a Communist cell was almost certainly enough to disqualify a potential immigrant from being granted a US visa. A far more likely explanation for Kadya's fears, then, is that Simche got involved in some sort of Communist activity while he was in Paris. Had the US immigration authorities caught wind of that, they would indeed have refused him a visa. But that didn't happen.

The inter-war years in Poland were a time of ever-worsening economic and social conditions for Jews. Under Wladyslaw Grabski, who served both as Prime Minister and Treasury Minister of Poland in the 1920s, discriminatory laws were passed requiring extra taxes and licensing permit fees that essentially targeted only Jewish merchants. In the wake of these laws, thousands of Polish Jews, who were barely eking out a living even before these laws were passed, emigrated to what was then Palestine. In deference to Grabski's role in pushing these Jews into emigration, Zionists called this wave of immigration the "Grabski *Aliyah*".[35]

But laws targeting small businessmen were by no means all the bad news. The *numerus clausus* that restricted the number of Jewish students who could be enrolled in institutions of higher learning, was extended during those years to an ever-increasing number of institutions. That is almost certainly why Simche did not continue his university studies while he was in alone in Warsaw in the later 1930s. The smaller numbers of Jewish students who did attend university, were forced to sit on "ghetto benches" and were occasionally assaulted by their fellow Polish students.

Jews were forbidden from employment in the Polish civil service or in government jobs and the Polish *Endecja* Party advocated not only a boycott of Jewish merchants, but also the confiscation of Jewish businesses. The Jewish community's self-help institutions, overburdened by the orphans and homeless victims of World War I, then the Russian Revolution and the civil war that followed, and finally by the Polish-Russian war of 1920-21, were hard-pressed to ameliorate the grinding poverty of so large a needy population.

While Simche was in Warsaw witnessing the misery of his fellow Jews, he got part-time work doing type-setting. He never planned to make this his profession; he intended to become a historian or a writer, perhaps even a writer-intellectual. Later, when Kadya was an editor, she did give Simche a forum for his own writing. But that earned the two of them no real money. In fact, type-setting became Simche's profession, even if only by default. Because labor issues and fair labor practices were always of primary concern for him, he joined the type-setters' union in Warsaw. When he needed to earn a living in later years, he found himself uniquely qualified to be a type-setter. He had the knowledge of written languages that it required; he had already been a member of a type-setters' union, and type-setting provided a solid and steady income.

The Israeli archive contains tens of letters that Simche and Kadya wrote to each other during the three years (1935-38) they were separated. Some of them concern Simche's uncertainty over his own professional future. Others are about rescue efforts, for Simche as well as for Leibl, Kadya's brother and his family. A review of them gives us a close-up of the couple's relationship.

Kadya saved some (but by no means all) of her responses. Here is one in which she addresses his future and her role in determining it:

"Now about business. You write asking why I am silent on your making your way into the American press as well as the Warsaw press. I'll give you the truth. I'm of the opinion that I do you no good by offering my opinion. On the contrary, I'd like it better if you'd do as you wish, what you consider necessary, what you feel like doing. I won't hold you back but I also won't goad you into doing it. If not for my advice, you might or might not be in the same predicament as [name unclear- ZKN]. But in any case, I [will ZKN] have that on my conscience."[36]

She continued:

"...It doesn't look good if I recommend your articles. I can recommend anyone else's, but I can't recommend my husband's if I don't want to come out looking ridiculous."

Most of Simche's letters border on panic. As the regime in Poland became increasingly hostile to Jews and the social climate made it amply clear that the Socialist bonds of brotherhood between Poles and Jews was a figment of the imagination of self-deluded Jews, an element of despair crept into Simche's letters. All over Warsaw, Jews lost their jobs and could not afford even the low-rent apartments that were available. Simche himself had to move, and needed money. Knowing that Kadya was living and working in the US, Simche's family appealed to him for help, and Simche passed on their appeal.

Kadya felt overwhelmed. She barely knew English, and in the US, she could not get by on her Yiddish alone. For the first two years of her stay, even her legal status was uncertain. She needed to renew her visa from time to time, and there was no certainty she would eventually get citizenship. Especially galling was her financial dependency. She had been financially independent in Europe for years, but now she was dependent on the generosity and financial backing of her sister, Dora. Recognized and famous as she was, she was asked to do public "readings" of her work in different cities in the US and Canada. She traveled everywhere and spoke everywhere, Chicago, Detroit, Cincinnati, Toronto, Montreal, and Winnipeg, but still, her earnings were meager, and her income, such as it was, was not steady.

In response to Simche's request for funds for himself, she mentions the requests she got from Simche's family and her own cousins in Poland, and says:

Chapter Two: Kiev, Two Men Enter, One Man Leaves   55

"During the twenty-two months that I have been in America, I have not had <u>one</u> day of rest. [The underlining is there in the original. ZKN] I have worked very hard to support myself and I've been unable to do more about arranging the [visa] papers. I don't understand why you complain that you have not got enough money. The [Jewish] community has always been behind in payments about 2-3 months. That was a normal procedure even in my days."[37]

She goes on to say that she will be giving lectures in Chicago and Detroit and she'll be earning a bit from these gigs. But then she adds:

"I would like to have a steady job and be rid of these happenstance earnings. I don't know if you can understand how difficult this is."[38]

All through his years in Warsaw, Simche continued to do archival work in preparation for the writing of a magnum opus. When he told Kadya that he'd given up working as a teacher and taken on type-setting, she replied with:

"How is your archival work going? And how are you living now that you've given up teaching? Are you getting enough work from the printers' union?"[39]

Despite her economic independence, as long as she lived in the US without Simche, Kadya did not have an apartment of her own. She confessed in one of her letters to her friend Ida that she did not like living alone in an apartment. But as soon as it seemed that Simche might join her in the near future, she began to think of finding an apartment for the two of them. She confessed to him that she was considering looking for an apartment for them both:

"By the way, I am awfully tired of wandering and even more tired of living without an apartment [of my own- ZKN]. Just having a room [of my own] would be a great comfort."[40]

It is fascinating that Kadya speaks of having "a room of her own". Whether or not she knew of Virginia Woolf's book of that name, there is no doubt that she suffered greatly from being a constant guest. We learn from the YIVO archive that immediately before Simche's visa came through, Kadya was so very fed up with being a guest, that she even contemplated taking a job as a teacher in a Detroit Yiddish school. One Shloime Bercovich offered her this job, and had she taken it, she would have had the room of her own that she so coveted. The deal must have been very tempting. It offered her $40 a week for 40 weeks work a year.[41] But before she could accept or refuse it, Simche's visa came through, and she quickly gave up all thought of leaving New York. The man she married in Kiev supported her, financially and morally, and was "her man" for the rest of her life.

While the inter-war years were the worst of times for Polish Jews from an economic perspective, they were, paradoxically, the best of times from the perspective of Jewish creativity. In these years, there was an outburst of literary activity. In Warsaw, Kadya had been an active member of the Writers' Union. The members fought over every possible intellectual issue, but the arguments were real and of great import to all. Jewish parties of every sort were active: Zionists and Anti-Zionists, Folkists, and Anti-Folkists, Bundists, and Anti-Bundists, Communists and Anti-Communists, and religious parties like Agudas Yisroel and Mizrachi. For the first time ever, some of these parties had representation in the Polish parliament. Jewish newspapers of all ideological stripes flourished. None of this was present in the US. From the standpoint of cultural creativity, the American Jewish scene was a wasteland. Kadya may have suspected this was the case from afar, but experiencing it was nothing less than a culture shock. In New York, where Kadya settled after a short stay in Philadelphia, Jews tended to have more money than the Jews of Warsaw, but they also had far less affinity with things Jewish. It was not simply an issue of a lost language, though there was that. Most American Jews seemed to have replaced their lost Jewish tradition with empty organizational trappings. There were "[Jewish] ladies' clubs" and synagogue clubs and *landsmanschaft*[42] meetings, but these provided only the superficial comfort of meeting with fellow sufferers. The younger generation of Jews, born in the US, had no need of these, and no reason to seek out fellow Jews. In Europe, Kadya and her fellow Yiddish writers had envisioned a secular Judaism based on secular Yiddish culture. What they saw in the US was simply secularism. It had little affinity with Yiddish, and only a tenuous connection with anything Jewish.

The crass materialism, the empty organizational trappings, the loss of Yiddish and its culture, all make their appearances in Kadya's written works and in the letters she wrote to her friend Ida Maze. But she does not mention these issues

Chapter Two: Kiev, Two Men Enter, One Man Leaves 57

in the letters to Simche that are preserved from this period. Instead, she collapses the whole troubled package into one mass of discontent and tells Simche that her first year in the US was "the most difficult year"[43] she had ever had in her life.

She can and does discuss the lack of the camaraderie that she had known in Warsaw. That camaraderie had no American counter-part, and she made no genuine, close friends. As she told Simche:

"I have so to speak paper friends, literary friends, not really open, genuine friends."[44]

In her letters to Simche, Kadya did her best to try to see things from his perspective. He was begging for help in getting out of Poland, and she was truly doing her best to help him. She wrote:

"I understand that you are tired and that you are almost certainly confused and bitter, but you and God are my witnesses that I am doing my best to help you. And I deserve more frequent letters from you."[45]

Kadya was clearly lonely. And this was so, despite the genuine help she got from her former friends and her European acquaintances. She told him:

"When you will arrive in America, you will see how utterly a person is left to himself...A pity we didn't stay in Western Europe [France- ZKN], there it is more humane"[46]

In a similar vein, she says in a different letter:

"I would like you to be here already so I could creep a bit out of the loneliness that is nearly unbearable in New York. And this despite the many friends and acquaintances that I have." And here she adds: "This must stay absolutely between us".[47]

From this last letter it would seem that the two really did reconcile in Paris. Here we see Kadya confiding in Simche, and confessing that only his presence will alleviate her loneliness.

Kadya made inquiries on Simche's behalf. She reported to him that she'd been told the most important thing for a potential immigrant was to have work when he arrived. She told him she could get a letter from a printer saying that a linotype-setter who knew Hebrew, Yiddish, Polish and German, could easily find work.

Apart from teaching at a summer camp, where she improved her English, Kadya also took upon herself to teach young children in school. She worked as a part-time teacher: three times a week for four hours each time. And for that she was paid $20 a week. In a letter to Simche, she made it clear that she remained at her teaching position only because of him:

"I would have long ago spat on them, but because of your arrival, I must have an official job."[48]

Kadya was very aware of the very real danger that hovered over her loved ones in Warsaw. As she told Simche:

"I am often uneasy over you[r fate]. I worry about you and about Leibl and [his wife] Lola and everyone."[49]

The stress of trying to get Simche out of Poland and the worry over the fate that awaited her brother and his family took its toll on Kadya. In a letter she wrote to Simche, she informed him that she'd lost 15 pounds since she'd arrived in the US.[50]

In response to her letter telling him that she has lost 15 pounds because she was working so hard, he says:

"Earn a few dollars less, but take care of yourself."[51]

In her memoir, Kadya omitted all mention of Simche's family. But her resentment was reserved only for his unreliable, American-based family, who did nothing to help him while he was impoverished and uncertain of his fate in Europe. She had nothing against his parents. They lived in Poland all their lives, and like most Polish Jewry, were murdered by the Nazis. During the late 1930s, when Kadya was in New York and Simche was still in Warsaw, she recommended that he share with his father some of the money she sent him. "He needs it",[52] she told him.

If Kadya empathized with her father-in-law, Simche felt truly close to his father-in-law. Tucked away inside Simche's Polish passport (in addition to the card from his lady-friend in France) is a small New Year's card. It is an inert item that speaks volumes. The card has only a few printed words: the traditional Jewish New Year's greeting, and it is dated 1937. It was signed:

"Your father, Aizik"

Chapter Two: Kiev, Two Men Enter, One Man Leaves

1937 was a year of approaching terror and grave trepidation for Simche. The Nazis had not yet moved on Poland, but they were clearly bent on expansion and ridding Europe of its "Jewish problem". His wife, Kadya, was living safely in New York, while he was trapped in Warsaw. His own immediate family in the US showed no interest in helping him escape Poland, Kadya was complaining about her own problems of adjustment, and no one knew which exit, if any, would be best for a potential immigrant. Trapped as he was, and doubtful that he would ever escape, Simche must have drawn great comfort from that little card. His own father was trapped in Poland, as he was. But Kadya's father, Aizik, lived in safety, and for Aizik, Simche was a son. Aizik had confidence in the future and Aizik cared about him. Simche did eventually leave Europe, and he did join Kadya. That card traveled with him to Israel in 1950, and fifteen years after he received that little card, he deposited it along with his passport in Kadya's Israeli archive. But the fact that he held onto it that long, and its presence in his passport, testify to its powers. When he was at the edge of despair, Aizik, Kadya's father, sent him that card, and it buoyed his spirits.

Two years after her arrival in the US, Kadya got her permanent US visa. As soon as that happened, she told Simche she was off to HIAS to arrange for his emigration, and for the arrival in the US of her brother and his family. But that turned out to be far more complicated than she'd imagined. She needed to post $500 bond just for Simche. The two of them needed to provide the authorities with their birth certificates, marriage certificates, medical reports, and moral recommendations. If the potential immigrant had family, the family needed to provide proof of financial liquidity.

While Simche was in Warsaw, word got out that the American consul in Poland was a difficult man. So Kadya was advised to consider applying to the Belgian consul for Simche's visa. This began a back-and-forth correspondence between Kadya and Simche over which to prefer: Poland or Belgium. Each state's consul had his detractors and his defenders, and these were weighed carefully. After all, Simche's life could well have hung in the balance.

For his part, Simche's nerves were strained. He did his best to understand Kadya's difficulties, but as far as he could see, the culture shock that Kadya suffered paled in comparison with the danger he was facing. He told her how he felt and tried at the same time to keep calm:

"My nerves are taut and at edge. How do Jews put it? As long as one is healthy, there are no lack of troubles."[53]

He continued: "I'm anxious to see the day when we see each other and reach a shore. Visas and troubles and afflictions. Especially when you're on one side of the ocean and I'm on the other side, and we see no end to it. I try hard not to think about it; otherwise I'd be paralyzed and unable to take a step."

In response to her money complaints, he reminds her that they have never been rich and nevertheless they always managed:

"In any case, we never had money and we never made a fuss over it. We always found a way to manage. Just let me get my visa and let us be together, then all will be well, even without money. "[54]

In a later letter he writes:

"From the tone of your last letter I get an awful sense of your edginess, a deep sense of resentment that almost borders on bitterness. From that I understood that you, poor thing, feel bad in America, that you are suffering and are upset. And I feel very upset about that."[55]

He continued: "I tell you, Kadyele, that the day when I will tear myself away from here, when we will finally reach a shore and will be able to live together, however long it is destined for us to live, [that day] will be a holiday for me."[56]

In the years he was alone in Warsaw, Simche, like all other Poles, suffered from the run-away inflation that plagued the country. About his own financial state, he tells us that he gives private lessons in addition to his other work, but:

"No matter how much I work, there is never enough."[57]

A genuine sense of mutual concern emerges from these letters. Kadya is determined to rescue Simche and bring him safely to the US, while Simche worries that Kadya is overworking herself on his behalf. Simche confesses his uncertainty over his next move, while Kadya confesses her disgust with her dreary job. This is

Chapter Two: Kiev, Two Men Enter, One Man Leaves 61

the conversation of good friends, friends who are lonely and miss each other and are comfortable enough with each other to share their true feelings. Kadya does tell Simche she is lonely without him. And Simche ends his letters with "I kiss you". But that seems more of a pre-prepared formality, than a spontaneous confession of longing.

Nowhere in this correspondence do we find the impassioned dialog of lovers who sorely miss each other's physical presence. Indeed, there is not even the faintest trace of an erotic spark here. Can the absence of Eros be attributed to their ages? That does not seem likely. When these letters were written, Kadya and Simche were just about forty years old. While this is no longer the age of raging hormones, it is also not the age of a de-activated id.

From the correspondence between Kadya and Rokhl Korn, we learn that Simche had a way of making women feel liked, even when they (and he) were middle aged. Twenty years after Kadya arrived in the US, in 1955, Korn wrote to Kadya telling her how she felt in Simche's presence:

"Give Simche a kiss from me. …At least once I want to feel like a Czarina. Till now no one made me feel this way."[58]

As for Kadya, we know from the evidence of her friend Melekh Ravitch, that she, too, exuded a sort of magnetic charm. Here is how he put it:

"While still in Warsaw, and then later in New York, I saw healthy young men run over to Kadya, as though they were [her-ZKN] sons."[59]

Admittedly, Ravitch is not speaking of an erotic charm necessarily, but of a sort of personal magnetism. But Korn, in a letter from as late as 1969, went even further:

"I am willing to bet with everyone…that you, yes, I mean you, would be able to handle a kingdom no worse than King Solomon, and also with a harem of 1,000 men. But you would make do with your Simche."[60]

It is apparent, then, that both Kadya and Simche, separately, if not together, were capable of great charm. For all of that, in their correspondence that is preserved in the archive, we find a couple, who, when left to themselves, generated a kind of comfortable companionship, but one bereft of erotic ardor.

Interestingly, in the late 1930s, while she was writing these good-pal letters to her husband, Kadya was imagining what her life would have been like had she been twenty years younger. In a Walter Mitty-like fashion, she functioned and corresponded like a responsible forty-year old, but fantasized an alter-ego that was twenty years younger, fresher, and sought after by all available, and some unavailable, bachelors. This younger alter-ego will emerge in a few years as a character named "Rivke Zylberg".

When Simche was still in Europe, both he and Kadya wrote to his brother, then living in the US, and apparently a US citizen, asking him to sign an affidavit of moral rectitude in Simche's favor. He never answered. Had Simche depended on this brother, he never would have gotten out of Poland.[61]

It was Kadya's family that rescued Simche. The archival records show that Kadya had over $700 in the bank when she was attempting to get Simche out of Poland.[62] It seems clear that Kadya herself could not possibly have saved up that sum in the two years she was in the US. Indeed, she had so little money that was truly hers, that she wrote to Simche in 1938 telling him not to send her a box of books because she would be asked to pay for it, and she did not have the money to do so. In that same letter, she told him she had put money in the bank that she could not touch.[63] There is no doubt, then, that her sisters helped her accumulate the relatively large sum in that bank account, and it was not hers to use.

Simche did eventually get a visa, and he was originally supposed to land in Canada in 1937. From the letters that Ida Maze saved and left in an archive in Montreal, we know that Simche was sent a ticket for a ship that sailed to Montreal. Because Kadya was unable to meet that ship in Montreal, Ida promised to do so.[64] Kadya sent Ida the name of the ship, and the name and contact information of a friend of Simche's who would be able to identify Simche coming off the ship. And Ida promised to wire her friend Kadya just as soon as Simche landed. But that landing never took place.

At the very last second, Kadya was told that the Canadian authorities had the right to ship her husband back, and if they did so, he might not get another chance to emigrate. As a result, that plan was shelved and Kadya got to work on purchasing a different ticket that would land Simche in New York.

And she succeeded. Simche finally arrived in New York on the Aquitania on July 21, 1938. There is no doubt that he owed his escape from Poland to the concerted efforts of Kadya and her family. Kadya did the paper work, her sister Dora put up the necessary funds, when legal help was necessary Lina's husband came to the rescue, and their father Aizik provided moral support.

It has been suggested that Kadya supported herself as a writer.[65] But that is simply not so. It is true that between 1935, when she landed in the US alone, and 1938, when Simche joined her in the US, Kadya supported herself. During those three years, she even sent some of her earnings to Simche. But once Simche found a job as a type-setter in the US, and after that, for approximately fifteen years, he was the true bread-winner. Kadya's earnings brought fame and public acclaim, but Simche's earnings were greater and far more dependable.

NOTES

[1] *Svive*, no. 33, January, 1971, p. 54.
[2] Ibid.
[3] David Bergelson: From Modernism to Socialist Realism, Joseph Sherman and Genaddy Estraikh eds., Leeds, 2007, p. 23.
[4] *Der Nister,* (which translates as 'The Hidden-one"), is another Russian writer of Yiddish who perished at the hands of Stalin. See http://en.wikipedia.org/wiki/Der_Nister
[5] Op. Cit., p. 55.
[6] See: https://en.wikipedia.org/wiki/Der_Nister
[7] Ibid.
[8] Ibid.
[9] Ibid.
[10] Op. Cit., p. 57
[11] This poem appeared in *Kheshvendike Nekht*, p. 60. The translation is my own.
[12] *Svive*, no. 33, January, 1971, p.57.
[13] Sherman and Estraikh, eds., p. 65. See also: http://rachelkorn.com/text/articleyiddishcultre.htm
[14] Sherman and Estraikh, eds., p. 52.
[15] Sherman and Estraikh eds., p. 30.
[16] Entitled "*Ikh deroykh mayn sigaret*", I smoke my cigarette, it can be found on p. 108.
[17] As I understand it, this means the 29th of May.

[18] Sherman and Estraikh, p. 50.

[19] The poem appears on pages 16 and 17. The heading is obviously on page 16. It has been suggested that the heading of this poem was switched from Warsaw to Berlin because Kadya did not want to openly admit that she had been hassled by the Polish police. By now there is no way of knowing where the truth lies.

[20] I am grateful to Amir Shomroni for sharing this letter with me. He found it in the YIVO archive among the letters Kadya wrote to Opotashu.

[21] The book this poem appeared in was published in1933, but the poem itself is dated 1930.

[22] We should note that there is a famous Hassidic saying, attributed to the Hasidic Rebbe, Nachman of Breslav, which says: "The entire world is a narrow bridge..." There is every reason to believe that Kadya knew this saying. It may well be that she was echoing and elaborating on it when she used the phrase "paper bridge(s)".

[23] *Svive*, no. 33, January, 1971, p. 59.

[24] Ibid.

[25] *Svive*, no. 33, January, 1971, p. 59.

[26] See Elissa Bemporad's Becoming Soviet Jews: The Bolshevik Experiment in Minsk, Indiana University Press, 2013.

[27] *Svive*, no. 33, January 1971, p. 62.

[28] *Svive*, no. 33, January, 1971, p. 63.

[29] Ibid.

[30] See Anna Fishman Gonshor, https://www.collectionscanada.gc.ca/obj/s4/f2/dsk2/ftp01/MQ43878.pdf, p. 57.

[31] This was said in a letter that Zeitlin wrote to Joseph Opotashu. See Natan Cohen, *"Mekoma U-Fo'ala Shel Kadya Molodowsky Ba-Sviva Ha-Sifrutit Ha-Yehudit Be-Varsha"* p. 168. In *Bikoret U-Farshanut*, no. 40, Bar Ilan Press, spring 2008.

[32] Fishman Gonshor, p. 55

[33] *Svive*, no.36, April, 1972, p.63.

[34] This letter is found in the Ida Maze archive in the Montreal Jewish Public library.

[35] *Aliyah* is the Hebrew term for immigration to Israel. Literally it means "elevation". Immigration to Israel by Jews is considered a spiritual "elevation" since Israel is the Land of the Holy Sanctuary. When Zionists called the immigration of Polish Jews to Israel "Grabski's Aliyah", they were not suggesting that Grabski was a Zionist. They merely meant that Grabski was the unwitting agent of this migration of Polish Jews to (what was then) Palestine.

[36] In a letter date January 30th, 1937, found in the Makhon Lavon archive.

[37] Ibid.

[38] Ibid.

[39] In an undated letter, written some time in 1937, found in the Makhon Lavon archive.

[40] In a letter dated June 6, 1937, found in the Makhon Lavon archive.

[41] This, in a letter dated August 24, 1938, found in the YIVO archive. Apparently this Bercovich was the school administrator.

[42] See: https://en.wikipedia.org/wiki/Landsmanshaft

[43] This in a letter written in May 20th, 1936, found in the Makhon Lavon archive.
[44] An undated letter written in 1937 in the Makhon Lavon archive.
[45] In a letter dated February 23, 1938, found in the Makhon Lavon archive.
[46] In a letter written while she was in camp Nayvelt, written August 5th, 1937, found in the Makhon Lavon archive.
[47] In a letter written November 18, 1937, found in the Makhon Lavon archive.
[48] In a letter dated March 8th, 1938, found in the Makhon Lavon archive.
[49] In a letter dated March 23, 1937, found in the Makhon Lavon archive.
[50] In a letter dated May 23, 1937, found in the Makhon Lavon archive.
[51] Ibid.
[52] In a letter dated November 30th, 1937, found in the Makhon Lavon archive.
[53] In a letter dated June 22, 1937, found in the Makhon Lavon archive.
[54] In a letter dated July 14th, 1937, found in the Makhon Lavon archive.
[55] In a letter dated August 10th, 1937, found in the Makhon Lavon archive.
[56] Ibid.
[57] In a letter dated October 12, 1937, found in the Makhon Lavon archive.
[58] See Zelda Kahan Newman "The Molodowsky–Korn Correspndence". In *Women in Judaism*, vol. 8, No.1, p. 14.
[59] Ibid.
[60] Kahan Newman, p. 15.
[61] See Kahan Newman, endnote 14.
[62] In September 30, of 1937 Kadya's bank, located in Philadelphia, where her sister and father lived, sent a formal letter to the American Consul General in Warsaw informing him that "Mrs. Lew maintains an account with us since June 1936, and …the balance in her account as of the close of the business day today is $711."
[63] In a letter dated March 8, 1938, found in the Makhon Lavon archive.
[64] This, in a ltter dated April 24, 1936, found in the Ida Maze archive in Montreal.
[65] See Kathryn Hellerstein's introduction to Paper Bridges, 1999, p. 17 She says there: "In New York City, she supported herself by writing for the Yiddish press and founded a literary journal, *Svive* (Surroundings), which she edited for nearly thirty years." As I will show, she supported herself for three years while she lived in the US, and again three years when the couple lived in Israel. The rest of the time, her income was a sometime thing, and the couple depended on Simche's earnings.

CHAPTER THREE: WARSAW, KADYA BECOMES FAMOUS

"A writer should have the precision of a poet and the imagination of a scientist"
Vladimir Nabokov

The Pre-Warsaw Period

While it is true that two of Kadya's poems were published in *Eygns*, the literary journal put out in Kiev, her name reached the Jewish public at large only after she began publishing in the Warsaw journal "*Literarishe Bleter*". When that journal began appearing in 1925, she made her genuine debut. She continued publishing there for a full decade, until she left for the US in 1935. But she did not always live in Warsaw.

Once they had visited Simche's parents in Lekhevitch, Kadya and Simche spent a few months with her family in Berze. For Kadya it was a relief to be home, away from the poverty and misery of the orphan homes she had known in the big cities of Europe. Nevertheless, even as an older woman, she remembered that period in her life with mixed feelings. Her mother took such a liking to Simche, she reports in her memoir, that his was the preferred opinion whenever there were questions to be resolved.[1] And her mother's preference for Simche's opinion over hers rankled her, apparently for the rest of her life.

The couple naturally gravitated to Warsaw. That was where the jobs were, and more importantly, that was where the literary talent of Jewish Europe gathered. There was probably never so vibrant a Jewish community in the Jewish Diaspora as the inter-war community of Warsaw. As is common among Jews, there were vehement disagreements about the ideal way to conduct private and public Jewish life. At the Warsaw literary club there were proponents of Folkism, of Socialism, of Communism, of mystical rabbis and anti-mystical, rational rabbis. There were secularists and anti-secularists, Zionists and anti-Zionists. All gathered at the literary club and argued, and all were bound together by the solidarity of their serious interest. What's more, across all of Europe, writers knew that if they wanted a hearing, they needed to pay a visit to the literary club of Warsaw. Kadya reports that in those inter-war years, Peretz Markish visited from Russia; Moshe Broderzon visited from Lodz; Moshe Kulbak visited from Vilna. Yet more surprising, the literary meetings were popular social events: the lecture hall, Kadya tells us, was always packed beyond capacity. As she depicted the club in her memoir:

"Each one [was] there with his own world, and each one felt there [that he was] under a cozy roof."[2]

In a memoir chapter headed "We Become Rich", Kadya explains why she and Simche left Warsaw for the city of Brisk/Brest for a year, despite the unparalleled intellectual excitement that Warsaw provided. In the depressed economic climate of inter-war Poland, it was hard, if not impossible, for Kadya and Simche to save money on their meager salaries. However, teachers who agreed to go to Brisk, where there apparently was a shortage of teachers, were promised a salary equal to the salary given to Warsaw teachers, but with extra benefits: their rent was paid by the Joint Distribution Committee.[3] Such an arrangement allowed Kadya and Simche to save some money for the first time in their married lives. Kadya continued to write poetry during the year she was in Brisk. Some of the poems she wrote that year, were printed a year or two later when *Literarishe Bleter* began its publication. The year in Brisk was a fateful year for Kadya. First her mother died (at the relatively early age of 45), and then she herself was diagnosed with a mild case of tuberculosis. Her doctors recommended a stay in a sanatorium in the country town of Otwock. Kadya stayed there for a few months, recuperating and writing about her mother, and about the world of patients and life in Otwock. It was clear to her that life for a woman in the shtetl was harsh and punishing. Her pity for her mother as well as her sense of how difficult life was for the peasants she saw, made its way into the poetry she wrote in this period. This may explain why, in the early years of Zionism, when it was fashionable to extol the pure life of farmers/pioneers, Kadya never felt tempted to opt for rural life.

While she was in Otwock, Kadya composed a poem laying bare her awareness that the most womanly of experiences, child-bearing, would never be hers to enjoy. But she did her best not to begrudge her friends their happiness:

"My woman-friends already have little babies in white prams

May they be healthy."[4]

Kadya's stay in Brisk was a brief interlude. Both she and Simche much preferred Warsaw, and they returned to Warsaw after the school year in Brisk was up.

Kadya Appears in *Literarishe Bleter*

Once she was in Warsaw, Kadya joined up with old friends. Nachman Mayzel was there, and he knew Kadya from Kiev, where he had co-edited *Eygns* with Dovid Bergelson. Mayzel first tried editing a new literary journal, *Literarishe Bleter*, Literary Pages, together with I.J. Singer, Peretz Markish, and Melekh Ravitch. But when team editing did not work, he became the journal's sole editor.

Nowhere in her memoir does Kadya discuss her feminist poetry in *Literarishe Bleter*. And yet it is her feminist poetry in that journal that first brought her to the attention of the Yiddish world. Kadya's debut there was with a poem that was untitled. It is known by its first line: "*iz nekht azoyne frilingdike do*", There are spring nights like this one. The poem acknowledges the sacrifices of women who suffer, and perhaps even die, so that the next generation can go on. There is a natural cross-over here between nature, which ensures survival and renewal, and the need of humankind for women who will do what they can to ensure the survival of their children.

If she hints at her barrenness in this poem, in a later poem, she makes an analogy between nature and humankind, and admits outright that she herself is barren. Kadya confessed in that later poem that her hands, too, would like:

"to embrace a warm trusting body",

but that is not to be. She

"will remain a wintry tree, shorn of its leaves."[5]

While Kadya never spoke publicly about her barrenness, its causes or its etiology, she did make it quite clear in her early poetry that she knew she would/could not have children. Kathryn Hellerstein, who translated Kadya's poetry into English,[6] asked Kadya's niece and nephew for more details, but they could give her no family lore on that issue. I, too, questioned Ben, her nephew, but got no answer. If Kadya's sisters knew exactly what the problem was, they never revealed anything. Apparently, they respected Kadya's privacy on this matter. Hellerstein is of the opinion that Kadya "apparently chose a writer's career over motherhood".[7]

While neither Hellerstein nor I can be certain, I disagree with her conclusion. In a small pocket note-pad that Kaya apparently took with her whenever she traveled, one that she left behind in her Israeli archive, Kadya noted that she longed "for the feeling of a child in her lap". That does not sound like the thought of a woman who chose childlessness willingly.

As Fishman Gonshor points out, Kadya's debut "whether by her own or her editor's choice, was with a "women's poem", thus identifying her in the mind of the public as a "woman's poet.""[8] The above-mentioned poem was only the first of her "women's poems". Kadya examined and re-examined the fate of women and their role in the world in general and in the Jewish world in particular.

The next time Kadya's name appeared in *Literarishe Bleter* (henceforth L.B.), it was attached to a collection of four poems. The first of these appeared later in her first book as the lead poem of a cycle entitled "*Oreme Vayber*", Poor Women.

The focus here it is the grinding poverty of the Jewish women in Warsaw. Kadya does not speak as an outsider. She, too, knows all too well what poverty is like:

"Just like all impoverished women, who scrub burned pots
I too have yellow boney fingers
Which carry a basket.

And one next to the other, we manage to carry our heavy burden
Like dumb, yoked mules."[9]

The next poem in this cycle begins with the line:
"At night when I am awake..."

Its first stanza is devoted to Kadya's mother, whose
"...life, stretched in heavy, mundane days"[10]

This pious, virtuous woman prays to God at the end of the first stanza, and her night-time prayer has words tinged with anger that are:

"like fiery coals that are embers".

The mother cries as she prays, and:

"And her tears come streaming down like a stingy drizzle."[11]

The second stanza of this poem begins with the line: "I, too, am a woman". And here Kadya points out that although she is unlike her mother in many ways (her hair is not covered, and her neckline is open), she, too, has known sorrow. Like her mother, Kadya recites a quiet plea to God at night. And, as was the case with her mother, Kadya's tears:

"come streaming down like a stingy drizzle."

That last line of the second stanza, which echoes and parallels the last line of the first stanza, clearly suggests that we draw the inevitable conclusion: modernity has changed much, but it has not changed the ultimate sadness of life. A woman's heartache stays constant despite the changed social climate.

In the third poem of this cycle Kadya was brazen enough to broach the subject of the widespread prostitution of poor Jewish women of her time. Like women everywhere who have no other resources, desperately hungry Jewish women were forced to sell their bodies to get enough to eat. This poem begins with the line:

"Is bread that costly here?"

Unfortunately, the answer to that question was apparently: yes. Kadya saw these women, friendless and lonely, on the street, and by describing them with empathy, she bestowed on them a dignity they otherwise lacked.

The fourth and last poem of this cycle was unique for its time in its choice of style: it is constructed as a modern *tkhine*. *Tkhines* are/were prayers for women written, not in Hebrew, the traditional language of Jewish prayer, but in Yiddish, the language that most East European Jewish women knew and understood. Unlike the Hebrew prayers which use the "we" of the Jewish people, *tkhine*s are personalized. Women address God as "Dear, sweet God" and speak of themselves as "your servant". These prayers are very specific in their wishes and can be customized. A woman might pray for the welfare of her very sick child, or for the safe return of a husband who was traveling unsafe roads. Like traditional *tkhines*, Kadya's poem makes a very personal plea. Its first line says: "Do not let me perish". But unlike traditional women's lives, Kadya's life was not bound up with ritual and tradition. Her prayer makes no mention of her husband (which she had) or of her children (which she did not have). Instead she asks for strength as she says:

"Plant in me your breath of life

Just as you plant a seed in the earth."

In addition, she asks not to be:
"The last fly, that quivers frightened on a pane of glass."[12]

Kadya's willingness to embrace the repertoire of traditional Yiddish prayer was an unusual phenomenon for its time. Jewish women-poets of the inter-war years tended to see Jewish tradition and ritual as limiting shackles that needed to be discarded.[13] And when these women poets cast off Jewish ritual, they cast off all forms of traditional prayer as well. Kadya was unique in this respect. She adopted the traditional form of Jewish/Yiddish prayer in her poetry without embracing traditional Jewish rituals in her life.

The next poem to appear in L.B., entitled "*Di Imo'es*", (the Biblical Matriarchs), again reprises the *tkhines*. Unlike the traditional men's prayers, which occasionally ask God to remember the merits of (ungendered) Jewish martyrs, understood to be male, or even of young Jewish children who "learn Torah" in school, the *tkhines* invoke the memory and merits of known Jewish women. Underlying these prayers is a sense of sisterhood: women need other women for support and only women who have suffered, will understand the plight of other suffering women.

In this vein, the *tkhines* mine Jewish history for Jewish heroines who can be relied on to understand the straits of the praying woman. The woman who says the *tkhine*/prayer then appeals to these Jewish women to intercede with God for her. The prototypical woman to appeal to is the Biblical Hannah, who was falsely accused of being a drunkard by Eli, the High Priest. For the honesty of her prayer and as a reward for the slight she suffered, God awarded the childless Hannah with a son, Samuel, the well-known hero/ prophet of the Jewish Bible.

Kadya was the first secular Yiddish poet to grasp the strength of sisterhood underlying these *tkhines*. The understanding that women must lean on other women for support underlies her poem "*Imo'es*". This feeling was first voiced in her early poetry. It underlay her involvement in the women's labor movement when she lived in Israel and her concern with feminist themes in the short stories and novels that she wrote in her later years.

In *Imo'es* the Biblical Matriarchs are invoked, but these are *tkhines* with a punch. The women who need the intercession of the Biblical Matriarchs are not the usual pious, upstanding women of the Jewish community. They are the women-outliers of Jewish society. The four Matriarchs of this poem are asked to intercede for four different kinds of unfortunate Jewish women: 1) lonely street walkers, 2) impoverished brides 3) married women who are barren and 4) unmarried women. To each of these unfortunates a different one of the four Matriarchs comes and offers comfort.[14] Each Matriarch, in turn, does what she can to comfort the contemporary women with whom she can identify. If this poem did not actually comfort the women-outliers of Warsaw, it at least highlighted their genuine grief. And that was clearly Kadya's aim.

Kadya's attitude toward the traditional Jewish world is a complex one. There is no doubt that she was not Orthodox, or in any way observantly bound to Jewish ritual. On the other hand, she was respectful of that world and mindful of the comfort it brought to those who were bound to ritual. That is obvious from a poem she wrote in the inter-war years entitled "*A Tkhines Sider*", a prayer-book of *tkhines:*

"An old *tkhines* prayer-book lies before me
With yellowed pages bent in corners
At the prayers for rain and dew
At the story of the binding of Isaac
And at the fiery furnace of Nimrod.
Quiet tears fell there,
And softened the page

As a heart softens with a *tkhine*
And all the "May it be...s" have been marked by a finger.
And now who will carry the fear of God
Under his arm?
Perhaps in fact I should take it to my green covered table
Place it in the middle
And when a dryness falls over my heart
Take it to my burning lips.[15]"

It's important to note the difference between genuine respect for tradition and an intent to conform to traditional behavior. Kadya did not say she *would* take up that prayer-book, only that she might be comforted were she to pick it up and take it to her lips.

Ageing and the fear of ageing is one of the subjects that surfaced early in Kadya's poetry. Already in 1927, when she was only 31, she raised the issue. In a poem she wrote that year, she said:

"And with the first snowfall
My head will turn gray
And my upper lip will begin to wrinkle."[16]

Fishman Gonshor's opinion is that "the poverty and hardship which surrounded her, which she sees in the women and which she herself endured- greatly affected her".[17] Fishman Gonshor perceptively noted that the grinding poverty of those times brought on premature ageing.

Kadya was unflinchingly honest in her willingness to see this and describe it. In a poem she wrote during those Warsaw years she said:

"The women deny two or three years
And get crooked lips from telling lies…"[18]

This may be a reference to Pinocchio, who got a long nose from telling lies, but it may point to something else entirely. In Warsaw of the inter-war years, much of the Jewish population suffered from malnutrition, and malnutrition can cause a loss of teeth. Since a wrinkled lip is often a result of tooth loss[19], perhaps what Kadya was reporting was not a result of ageing, but the effect of widespread malnutrition.

Kadya did not shy away from pointing out that society views ageing men differently than it views ageing women:

"I wear bright socks and girlish lacquered shoes
But I am still pursued by the early middle age of a woman…
Men have strong legs…
And stand anchored, fixed against time."

In a review of a book that she wrote in these years she wrote witheringly of the ways in which ageing affected women:

"This is a tragedy of ageing for a woman- of losing the natural powers of youth and beauty. Women barricade themselves behind the family; chain themselves to a husband…and thus armored, the woman marches sadly towards old age, secure in the knowledge that she will not be abandoned and will be respected."[20]

Fishman Gonshor claims that in the above passage, Kadya "seems to project her own musings and fears."[21] As we have seen, Kadya was herself abandoned for a short time, but that was in her youth, not her old age. One thing is certain. If she was respected, and she was, it was not because of her married status. She did not take on her husband's family name as a writer; she retained the name "Molodowsky" for all public and publication purposes.

Interestingly, she did not object to having her husband's family name "Lew" supplant her maiden name for non-professional uses. Thus, in her medical records archived in Israel, she is "Kadya **Lew**", (pronounced "Lev"), and she appears under that name in the official document that was given to her as an immigrant to Israel. Nevertheless, the public knew her solely as "Kadya Molodowsky/Molodowska[22]". The respect she was given by the public was something she earned. Her friends and family respected her gestures of genuine friendship and her readers were grateful for her literary gifts.

It is ironic in the extreme that Kadya spoke of "chained" women in this review. In the parlance of Jewish law, as Kadya undoubtedly knew, a "chained woman" is one whose husband has abandoned, but not divorced, her. As such, she is "chained" to this recalcitrant man, and cannot according to Jewish law, take up a relationship with a different man. Worse yet, according to Jewish law, if such a chained woman has a child whose father is not her legal husband, that child is considered a *"mamzer"*/bastard. And the legal consequence of this bastardy is dastardly: Jewish law does not allow that child to marry another Jew under any circumstance. In later years, when Simche left her in Warsaw, and went to Paris alone, the wagging tongues of Warsaw called Kadya a "chained" woman.

1927 was a fateful year for Kadya. In that year she had a very public and heated argument in print with Melekh Ravitch, then the head of the literary club in Warsaw and one of the leading figures, if not **the** leading figure, of secular Yiddish culture in Warsaw. In that year, she published her first book of adult poetry, as well as the first of the children's poems for which she is still known. It was the children's book that won Kadya her first award: the award given jointly by the Warsaw community and the Warsaw Yiddish PEN club.

Kadya's argument with Melekh Ravitch is important for two reasons. It reflects on how feminism was understood then and is understood now, and it started a life-long relationship between the two that began in anger and mellowed over their lifetimes into a genuine friendship.

Melekh Ravitch published an essay in L.B. about women and women writers and poets. He claimed in that essay that there were no serious woman poets of Yiddish and there could be no woman writer of note until women would "desist from being chaste and so tied to tradition."[23] This brought out the fight in Kadya. Although her first book of poems had not yet been published (It was published later that year), she had published individual poems in L.B. for two years by then. She felt personally attacked by Ravitch's essay and she was incensed with what she saw as Ravitch's condescension. She scolded Ravitch for "trivializing the works of women poets and for having the audacity to predict that there would never be a significant female poet of Yiddish."[24] She reports that Ravitch confided in her his intent to edit an anthology of women poets, an intention that belied his stated belief in the worthlessness of women poets. In an attempt to counter his comment about the piety and lack of sensuality in women poets, she added "I am certain that through mediocre editing, it [Ravitch's book of women poets] could be quite a piquant book."[25] She also attacked Ravitch for lumping all women writers into a group when each writer deserved to be judged individually and on her own merits. Finally, she came to Ravitch's dismissal of all future women poets and to the aspersion that it was casting on her soon-to-be-published book:

..."My small book has not yet crossed your desk, but you have ensured that even those works not yet published and those that will be published seven years hence will also have no merit. God! How can a person be so evil."

Kadya's habit was to argue long and hard with an adversary until the original enmity melted into a feeling of camaraderie. It is worthwhile remembering that Kadya reported in her memoir that this is what drew her to Simche: the two of them argued, Simche often won, and that drew Kadya to him. The issue, it would seem, was not so much who won and who lost, but how serious and worthy the argument was. So it was with Kadya and Melekh Ravitch, and so it was with Kadya and other writers. We will have occasion to see the older Kadya and Melekh remembering the forgiven, but not entirely forgotten, early enmity.

The notion of "women's poetry" was an issue then and it is an issue now. Is all poetry written by women to be judged together just because all the poems have been written by women? Does it even make sense to speak of "women's poetry"? Kadya didn't think so. She didn't like the label and didn't want it used on her. As she saw it, just as individual women greatly differ from each other, so their poetry differs. The label of "women's poetry" was therefore meaningless for her; it was, she believed, based on "an absolute misunderstanding"[26]:

"[A] woman can arrive through her femininity at certain artistic truths, which, must perhaps, remain hidden from Man. But the results must be measured by purely human standard. As to the means by which one conveys these truths, they are different for all poets, whether man or woman. Therefore, one must conclude that the same criteria must exist for the poetry created by women as for the poetry created by men. Every attempt to define the difference between the two 'types' of poetry would be no more than trivial hair-splitting and could not be honestly or artistically sound".[27]

Kadya did not change her opinion, and Melech Ravitch did not change his. At the time, the two simply agreed to disagree.

Kadya's First Book: *Kheshvndike Nekht*

Kadya's first book was *Kheshvndike Nekht,* Late-Autumn Nights. The Hebrew month of *Kheshvn* is called in rabbinic Hebrew *Mar-Kheshvn*, or bitter *Kheshvn*, ostensibly because the month contains no Jewish holidays.[28] Kadya did not put the word "*mar*", bitter, into her title, but it lingers, unspoken, in the background. There is an aura of anomie in the poems of this collection. Autumn is waning, and so are Kadya's youth and high spirits. Indeed, the good cheer of the entire city of Warsaw is ebbing. Perhaps Kadya's choice of a secular life put her into a funk; perhaps it is simply the passage of time. The reader is free to choose among the possibilities.

This first book was reviewed favorably in L. B, the artistic arbiter of its day. Shmuel Zaromb[29] in his review of this book said:

"Her tenderness and compassion…are akin to a humble simple psalm from a deep suffering female personality, speaking with fine subtle images and metaphors."[30]

For all that Kadya feigned indifference to the critical responses that her first book received, saying in her memoir, [after all] "a book is [merely] a book",[31] that is more a pose than an honest admission. Kadya's Israeli archive contains a detailed list of every one of the critical reviews she got. This includes the names of the papers/journals and the dates of all reviews on just about every continent: North America, South America, even South Africa. Again, we repeat the caveat: one has to distinguish between the public face an author presents, and her more private self.

While *Kheshvndike Nekht* contained one poem she had written (and published) in Kiev, and one poem she had written in Minsk, the majority of the book consisted of poems she had written in Warsaw. These poems often chronicle her anguish at the unremitting poverty and misery of life in that city. But the poem she composed in Minsk is of an entirely different nature:

"When I will arrive
The cemetery will rejoice.
I'll knock-over the grave-digger
And mock the mourners…"[32]

Chapter Two: Kiev, Two Men Enter, One Man Leaves 81

Looking back on her career in her memoir, she says of the latter poem: "That was an up-beat poem. I couldn't write that kind of poem now. One can only understand that I was young then."[33]

In that book, heading a cycle of poems entitled "*Froyen Lider*", Women's Poems" is a fascinating poem that is both more and less than what critics have traditionally made of it. It is more revealing of the poet's inability to have children and less of a critique of religion than of social norms:

"The women of our family will come to me at night and say

We have carried a pure blood across generations

Bringing it to you like well-guarded wines from the kosher cellars of our hearts"[34]

The secular critics, unaware of the fine details of Jewish law, did not know, that there is indeed such a thing as women's blood that is ritually "pure" in Jewish law: it is the blood of a woman who has given birth. The time that she continues to bleed after giving birth are called "*yemei tohar*", the days of purity, and that blood is called *dam tohar*, the blood of purity.[35] In fact, in Deuteronomy 17/8, we are told that judges need to distinguish "between [ritually impure] blood and [ritually pure] blood". Now that we know that only the blood of childbearing can be (ritually) "pure blood", we understand what that poem was saying. Because the women of Kadya's family bore children, they personally experienced having "pure blood". They carried it within themselves and discharged it when they gave birth. Just like wines need to be kept away from impure hands to be kosher[36], so this "pure" birth-blood is considered precious in the poem, and it is guarded carefully. But Kadya knows that she will not give birth; she will therefore never have "pure blood". And she is made to feel guilty for her barrenness. That is why she laments:

"And why should this blood without impurity

Be my conscience, bound like a silken thread

On my brain."[37]

In the Bible, a scarlet thread/cord is a symbol of sinfulness. The prophet Isaiah (18/1) promises the sinners of Israel: "If your sins will be like scarlet, they will be whitened like snow". There is yet another inter-textual Biblical allusion here, one yet more telling. The story of Rakhav, the Cana'anitic prostitute who lodged and then protected the Israelite spies in Jericho, records another use of a scarlet thread/cord. Here Rakhav is told to hang a scarlet cord from her window (Joshua 2/17) to guarantee that no harm will befall her and her family inside her house when the Israelites capture her city.

What has happened in this poem, then, is that Kadya's lack of "pure blood" has become objectified; it presses on her like a scarlet thread. While the scarlet cord saved Rakhav, the prostitute, the scarlet thread around Kadya's head does just the opposite: it weighs on her mind/her brain, and causes her pain.

It is not as though the law or any one individual is actively accusing her; this is not the Jewish equivalent of the Scarlet Letter "A" of Hester Prynne. There is no Jewish law forbidding bareness among women and there is no Jewish institution that will pursue her for not having children. It is Kadya's own conscience that is condemning her, and that is a product of social and cultural norms.

Kadya Continues to Publish in *Literarishe Bleter*

For all that she considered herself a poet by profession, Kadya earned her living by teaching young children. For their amusement, she wrote stories and poems. Two of these poems, "*A Hintl un a Hunt*", A Puppy and a Dog, and "*Kits, Kats, Ketsele*", Kit, Cat, Kitty-Cat, appeared as "*kinder lider*", children's poems in L. B. in 1927, the same year her first book was published. Both poems, delightful in their alliteration, rhythm and paregmenon, were instant favorites. They were incorporated into the children's book that Kadya published in 1931: *Mayselekh*, (short stories), or, *"Geyen Shikhelekh Avek Vu Di Velt Hot an Ek"*, Little-Shoes Walk to the End of the World.

The book of women's poetry that Melekh Ravitch spoke about with Kadya was in fact published in 1928, but he was not the one to edit the book. Its editor was Ezra Korman, and his book *Yidishe Dikhterins,* Yiddish woman poets, was the first anthology of women poets ever to be published. As Fishman Gonshor says: It "continues to this day to be a source of scholarship on women in Yiddish literature."[38] Ravitch did review the book, however. In this review, which was featured in L.B., we can see the beginnings of a rapprochement between Ravitch and Kadya. In a move that almost makes him a penitent, Ravitch says that Kadya was "the virtual princess of the entire anthology", and that Korman could have given her three times the space because "her poems are good, perhaps the best in the anthology."[39]

Modern feminist critics have taken umbrage with the tone of critics like Ravitch and Korman[40]. But with the publication of Korman's book, even the male-dominated establishment realized that women had been writing Yiddish poetry for years.

As we saw earlier, in 1929 Kadya left Warsaw for Paris. She may have been in Paris, but her poems appeared in Warsaw. That year, the poems that Kadya wrote appeared as a full-page feature in L.B. under the heading: "(*"Naye Lider"*, New Poems) Kadya Molodowsky/Paris". Among the love poems she wrote then, is a poem that says much about the poet's turn of mind in general. Entitled *"Kh'bin oyf der Velt Gekumen"*, I came into this World, it shows the poet unable to dwell solely in her own personal world. For all that she was born for love, she says, she cannot forget that the world "is full of inequality and injustice". This is what the Hebrew writer Yakov Fichman noted about her in her earlier, supposedly carefree years in

Odessa. This inability to ignore the suffering of those around her followed her throughout her life.

In what seemed naïve after the Holocaust, Kadya wrote a poem in 1929 entitled "*Goyim, Yidn, Rasn*", Non-Jews, Jews, Races. Here she announced her belief in the "brotherhood of Mankind", the Socialist refrain of those years. The sad truth, as was clear to all after the murderous decimation of Europe's Jews, was that this feeling of brotherhood went one way only: Jews felt a brotherhood with gentiles, but that feeling was not generally reciprocated.

In that same year, Kadya was admitted to the prestigious Yiddish PEN club of Warsaw. Since there were only two women-members of a total of 33 club members, Kadya's admission was a formal recognition of her abilities.

In the beginning of 1930, a full page in L. B. was dedicated to the poems of two woman-poets: Kadya Molodowsky and Esther Shumiatcher, the wife of the poet Peretz Hirshbein. Esther Shumiatcher must have been a good friend, for five years later it was she, along with another woman-friend of Kadya's, who arranged the details of Kadya's lecture tour to the US. And that lecture tour saved Kadya's life.

In 1930 Kadya published the first of her 3 poems, all entitled "*Mayn Papirene Brik*", My Paper Bridge. Fishman Gonshor points out that the first 3 lines of this poem as the poem first appeared in L.B., were later deleted in her second book of collected poems, "*Dzhike Gas*", Dzhike Street. Here are the deleted lines:

"And who needs even me? And my poem?

And my silent madness?

Unless 'tis the snow of my home"

In light of these lines, Fishman Gonshor believes that Kadya's "experience in Paris clearly held out no hope for improved opportunities."[41] But it is best to remain skeptical. We have no record of what was said then between Kadya and

Chapter Two: Kiev, Two Men Enter, One Man Leaves 85

Simche. We do know that Simche did not stay in Paris, but returned to Warsaw, and we do know that the note from his woman-friend in France was, eventually, put to rest. While it is true that a mere five years later, it was Kadya who left Simche, it is also true that Kadya and her family went out of their way to rescue Simche when the Nazis were nearly at the gates of Poland.

It was in 1930 that two of Kadya's most famous children's stories in verse were published: "*A Mayse mit a Mantl*" A Story of a Coat, and "*Olke mit der Bloyer Parasolke*", Olke with the Blue Parasol. Both stories are rhymed and both have a delightful rhythm. In the former story, a coat/jacket is sewn for the first child in the family. The boy makes good use of it, but after a few years, he outgrows it. The coat then is handed down to the next child of the family, this time a daughter. She too, wears it for years, till she outgrows it. The third child also wears it for years, but he falls while wearing the coat, and the buttons fly off. But the coat lives on. It is handed down to the next child of the family, again a daughter. She, like the others, gives the coat years of wear, but finally rips it when she coughs. The last child to get the coat is a climber of trees and a lover of cats and dogs. He tears the coat at its sleeves and at the knees and finally donates the holes to a cat.

Here is the final stanza of that poem in transcription and a loose translation:

"Vert a tuml a geshrey.	So there's a din, a hue, a cry
Akh un okh, un vund un vey!	Oh so, oh no, oh me, oh my!
Aza mantl, aza mantl	That such a jacket, such a jacket,
Falt arayn tsum takhshet Pantl".	Should've been worn by Pantl hack-

it.

While later generations may not have experienced the need for or the custom of hand-me-downs, the rhythm and the rhyme captivate readers and listeners of every generation.

The second story, "Olke with the Blue Parasol", tells the story of a six-year old girl, the day-dreaming daughter of a poor, hard-working couple. Olke would like to play with her parasol, fly high with the geese she sees, and live in her dream world. But her parents, who need her help around the house, call her back to reality. Olke is constantly reminded that she needs to learn to read and write.

Here is an English translation of this portion of the poem:
"There's washing and mending
And housework to do.
And don't forget
Your reading and writing, too."[42]

Olke helps care for her brother, does some wash, brings in some water, and helps chop wood, just as she is asked to do. But when she is given some buttons to sew, she drops them. Instantly, she imagines the buttons are vehicles that will take her away.

Here is an English translation of this section:
"One popped under a barrel
At Olke's feet
Two formed a bike
To ride down the street.
Three carried a board
For tipping and sliding
Four made a cart
For pony riding."

In the poem, Olke announces her intention of escaping her parents, her home and its chores. She wants to go to a place where she can play all day.

There is no question that Kadya's own experience as a child served as a model for Olke and her *parasolke*. In her book of poems entitled *In Land Fun Mayn Gebeyn*, In the Land of My Bones, she tells the reader she's taking us back to the time when she dragged or pushed the wagon for her mother's home-brewed kvass:

"That place where my lacquered shoes shine

There indeed where my foolish nightingale sings…

As she is doing what she's been told to do, she day-dreams, rhymes nonsense rhymes to herself and imagines what she'll do when she's free to do as she pleases:

"*Hayde-rude, Shemelke Tsalke*

On Purim I'll dress up as Esther *Ha-malke*/Queen Esther"

"*Hayde*" is what one says to a horse in Yiddish to get him to go faster. One might say it is the Yiddish equivalent of the English: "Giddyap!" Of course, there is no horse here. But that does not stop the young Kadya from imagining one. The word "*rude*" by itself is not a word, but there is a Yiddish word "*ruder*"; it is the Yiddish for the English word "paddle". Once again, there is no paddle here. But that does stop the young Kadya from imagining there might be. As for "*Shmelke Tsalke*", this is a nonsense phrase. While "*Shmelke*" is a fine Yiddish name given to a Jewish man or boy, there is no Jewish male here; there is only the non-Jewish young boy who is the family helper. As for "*tsalke*" it is totally meaningless. It is there in the line simply because the poet wanted a word to rhyme with "*malke*", the Yiddish word for "queen."

Traditionally, little girls love to dress up as Queen Esther once a year, on the holiday of Purim. That is the only time little girls get to wear their mother's jewelry and pretend they are grown-ups. But as the young Kadya loses herself in these lovely thoughts, the wagon she is pulling gets stuck in the mud:

"And with Queen Esther in golden shoes
The wheels get stuck grooz and grooz..."[43]

Once again, it's of no import if modern children need to help their mothers, as Kadya did, or were expected to do house-hold chores, as Olke, the heroine of her poem did. All children live in a world of make-believe and all would escape the responsibilities of the grown-up world if they could. The appeal of this poem is universal. That is why both this story and "The Story of a Coat" were anthologized over and over again. And the story of the coat has the dubious distinction of being "redone" (perhaps plagiarized is a more accurate word) over and over again.

In 1931 other children's stories of hers appeared. They too, like the first batch of stories, captivated Yiddish speaking children, in Warsaw and indeed wherever else Yiddish was spoken. The most imaginative of these has got to be "*A Mayse Mit A Balye*", The Story of a Washtub. Here the hero, one Khontshe, buys a basin for kneading dough. For some reason, however, the dough refuses to rise in the basin. Not wanting to waste his money, Khontshe decides to convert this basin to a wash basin. And, wonder of wonders, the basin washes the clothes that are put into it- all by itself! How does that happen? Here's her answer:

"*Vi Azoy?*
S'git a hemdl dray mol a drey, vi a rayf
Vert a balye zayf.
Links a rod,
Rekhts a rod–
Shoyn fun bod".[44]

How? / A shirt turns thrice, like a hoop / And the basin becomes soap. / Turn once to the left/Turn once to the right/ They're clean and bright.

Chapter Two: Kiev, Two Men Enter, One Man Leaves

Now as one can imagine, the entire town wants a piece of the action. Mothers with many children and loads of laundry, ask for the visit from the basin. And the basin obliges; it goes from household to household. It knows where it is needed, and it goes to each household on its own. This happens day after day, every day of the week, until Friday. What happens on Friday?

"Fraytik geyen kinder in klorn vesh,
Fraytik vert di balye zeyer frum
Un vasht zikh gor aleyn arum".[45]

Friday all children wear laundered clothes. / Friday the basin becomes pious / And washes itself all round without bias.

The elite of the Yiddish-speaking world may have been secular, but every Jew in Warsaw knew that in preparation for the Sabbath, Jews clean their houses, wash their clothes and then bathe and clean themselves. If this wash-basin is so animate that it knows who needs to have clothes laundered, it obviously is animate enough to be obligated to bathe itself in preparation for the Sabbath. And so, following that logic, the poet tells us that on Friday, as the eve of the Sabbath approaches, the basin "becomes pious" and washes itself all around in anticipation of the Jewish Sabbath!

The First of Kadya's Children's Books

"Mayselekh,", (Short Stories) *or "Geyen Shikhelekh Avek Vu Di Velt Hot an Ek"*, (Little Shoes Walk to the End of the World)[46], Kadya's first book for children (but her second altogether), published in 1931, was a perennial favorite of the children who were exposed to it. In poems like the story of the wash-basin, there is whimsy, delightful rhythm, charming rhyme, as well as a flight of fancy worthy

of a science fiction writer! It was not till the 1950s that households knew about "automated" washing machines. And yet, for Kadya that was an idea that was waiting to happen. It is not for nothing that Kadya was the darling of households with children from the 1930s onward.

"*Mayselekh*" won Kadya a prize jointly offered by the Yiddish Writers Union and the Warsaw Jewish Community Council. In her memoir, Kadya says she was not entirely happy with the prize:

"It upset me that I got the prize for my [book of] children's poems and not for my book "*Kheshvndike Nekht*". I considered the children's poems part-mischief, and here I was getting a prize for my writer's mischief-making…" [47]

This is one of the best examples of a writer's inability to judge her own best work. While there have been other Yiddish poets (even woman poets) who have written moving poetry for adults, no Yiddish writer, before Kadya or after her, ever wrote works for children that even approximate the lilting rhythms, the delightful word-play and the soaring imagination to be found in Kadya's children's stories and poems. In her work for children, she "pulled all the stops". She imagined a washing basin which would, miraculously, turn around on its own, and wash clothes without any effort on the part of humans. She knew the comfort to be had in the world of imagination and she opened that world up and invited children to join her inside it. Even the title of her first poem for children: "*Kits Kats, Ketsele*" shows her innate sense of rhythm. After all, every musician who gets ready to play her instrument says: "one/ two/ one-two-three", as this poem does. There is a universality to be found in Kadya's children's poems that is simply lacking in her adult poetry. Not every adult (Jewish or non-Jewish) has known grinding poverty personally. But every child known to humankind has found solace in the world of the imagination. And like a fine magician, Kadya conjured up that world and made it seem alive. The title poem of the collection, the story of shoes that wander, was so popular in Europe, that it was among the first to be translated into Hebrew when the State of Israel was still quite young. In its Hebrew translation, it was made into one of the first Hebrew-language films ever made.[48]

Another indication of the timelessness of these children's works is their lasting popularity. Many of these poems and stories were re-printed in Kadya's second collection of children's poems, *Afn Barg*, (On the Mountain), in her third collection, entitled *Yidishe Kinder* (Jewish Children), and in her fourth volume of children's poems, "*Martsipanes*", Marzipans. While not every poem in the original collection found its way to the re-issued books, the favorites are there, and they are still appreciated all over the Yiddish-speaking world nearly eighty years after they first appeared in Warsaw. In fact, a book of Kadya's children's poems is still selling today on Amazon[49].

Enemies and Friends

There is no question that the success of these children's poems/stories brought Kadya to the attention of a wider audience than her adult poetry did. Her success, as well as her inherent personal charm, made her a magnet for those who met her.

But not everyone was charmed by her. In that same year that these two poems appeared in print, Kadya shared a half-page of poetry in L.B. with her nemesis, A(ha)ron Zeitlin. One wonders what the two of them thought of this forced co-existence. A(ha)ron Zeitlin was the very embodiment of everything that Kadya was not. The son of Hillel Zeitlin, a revered religious writer and thinker, the younger Zeitlin was born into privilege. He received a full-fledged *yeshive* education, not an interrupted, somewhat haphazard Hebrew education like Kadya's. He had a university degree, something Kadya never got. Unlike Kadya, he did not have to scrape to make ends meet. Moreover, in the lingo of pre-war Warsaw, he was considered a rightist, while Kadya was considered a leftist. As things seem now, neither Melekh Ravitch nor A(ha)ron Zeiltin deserved the snide remarks she made about them. But while Ravitch was quick to appease her, Zeitlin had no intention of condescending to appease a writer who, he felt, was intellectually and artistically his inferior.

As we will have occasion to see, their relationship changed radically over the years. But it never lost the acrid taste of their early encounter in Warsaw.

A second writer with whom Kadya shared a page and a half in L. B. that year was Rokhl Korn. This pairing was far more natural. The two women were friends even then. Their friendship lasted their entire lives, throughout their changes of address and their changes of fortune. Of all her friendships, (and Kadya was a famously good friend), the friendship with Rokhl Korn was among the most meaningful for Kadya.

The early 1930s witnessed a concerted effort by L.B.'s editor, Nachman Mayzel, (along with other prominent writers), to root out "*shund*", trashy, sensationalist Yiddish literature, and promote quality literature. There was a genuine problem. Because of the world-wide Depression, many Yiddish publishing houses had folded. For writers desperately seeking cash, novels that were serialized in journals and newspapers became especially attractive. And serialized novels that were sensationalist and erotic sold very well. Kadya joined the fight against "trash", but in doing so she made a few enemies. She accused the highly placed Kh Kazdan, a leader of the Bund in Warsaw, of being unable to support literature that did not have the requisite party "buzz words" in it.[50] In addition, she suggested, apparently on the basis of too little evidence, that A(ha)ron Zeitlin also supported trashy literature.[51] She therefore refused to contribute to the journal that Zeitlin edited.
Kadya reviewed a book of H. Leyvik in 1932. Given that Socialism and Marxist materialism were the reigning ideologies of the day, it was brave of Kadya to rally to the defense of Leyvik, a non-ideological adherent of Jewish mysticism. What she admired, she said, was his "search for human purity". The way she put it:

"Real poets write the poem of their lives and carry the poem in their teeth, like wolves."

And for her, Leyvik was one such wolf.

In that same review, Kadya made a backhanded, somewhat unflattering, reference to Zeitlin's own brand of mysticism. The mere hint of criticism from some one (a woman, no less) far less learned than he, stoked Zeitlin's fury. In a private letter he told Leyvik that Kadya's grasp of this literature was "the grasp of a true ignoramus".[52]

It is hard to know now whether the issues between Kadya and A(ha)ron Zeitlin were a matter of constitutional differences or simply a matter of mutual misunderstandings. Given the fact that the two were both members of the rather small Pen club, it is unlikely they were able to avoid conversing with each other, even if only cursorily. But there is no doubt that they disliked each other. Now that we have access to Zeitlin's correspondence, we know that his open criticism of Kadya was relatively mild. In a letter he wrote to Opatashu, Zeitlin reports that word has it that Kadya believes he [Zeitlin] is jealous of her. He most certainly is not, he says in this letter:

"After all, why would Rockerfeller care if a poor man got a few tarnished pennies"?[53]

In 1931, L.B. published an index and analysis of the writers whose work appeared in the first 5 years of its publication. In its 52 issues, 5 of the 49 Yiddish writers were women. And when calculating the number of times a single poet was published during the year, Kadya ranked second from the top. She was bested only by Itsik Manger; his work was published six times in the same time period.

In 1931 and 32, the poems that would eventually appear in Kadya's second book, *Dzshike Gas*, Dzshike Street, surfaced bit by bit. Some of these were about contemporary issues that have since been forgotten. Her poem *Chako*, for example, is about the ship of that name that carried political exiles from Argentina. The ship sailed the seas, but its exiles were offered a haven by no country. This scenario repeated itself before the outbreak of WWII, when Jewish refugees escaping Germany on the MS St. Louis sought entry to any country in the world, but were essentially rejected by all.[54] And once World War II began in earnest, the Jews of Europe, those who managed to escape the Nazi armies, were wanted nowhere. Similar, but "lesser" events of an earlier age have faded from memory. But they live on in Kadya's poems

If we remember that Kadya had switched from the pro-Zionist/Hebraist orientation of her early years to a Communist-leaning/Yiddishist orientation of later years, we can see why she spoke (in one of the poems that was later included in *Dzshike Gas*) of the friends she used to have, but no longer had:

"Because my heart is heavy
As a sinking ship
Wanting to lighten its burden
I avoid friends of my youth
Not wishing to see, to feel,
The gruesomeness of their hidden glances
And silent tongues."[55]

Dzshike Gas and Its Reception

The nastiness that had been voiced in private had an opportunity to find its public voice when Kadya's second book for adults, *Dzshike Gas*, Dzhike Street, was published in 1933. As expected, the reviews of *Dzshike Gas* in L.B., Kadya's natural stomping-ground, were flattering. Both Nakhman Mayzel and Rokhl Korn praised it. But this praise was by no means endorsed by all.

Kazdan, Kadya's secular-Yiddishist/Bundist nemesis, disapproved of this new book because it was too "esthetic" and not political enough, while A(ha)ron Zeitlin, Kadya's religious nemesis, disapproved of it because it was too political and not esthetic enough. In both cases, there was more than a slight dose of payback involved. Kadya had insulted both of these men, and when they reviewed her book, they found an appropriate opportunity for revenge.

Unlike her first book, which for the most part, was lyrical in tone, *Dzhike Gas* had poems whose tone was sarcastic and/or ironic. The opening lines of this book, one critic feels, were bordering on sarcasm so sharp that they lost a sense of poetic worth:[56]

"The unemployed live here

Communists

And also- poverty...

Jews live here-

A nation that can make you die of laughter..."

Critics of the 1930s have been joined by modern critics who feel that the latter tone is strident, and does not show off the best of Kadya's talents.[57] In this volume Kadya mixed levels of usage- High Register Hebrew-derived Yiddish words mixed with Slavic-derived, curse words. This was the trend of those years, but it is not one greatly admired in modern times. Avrom Novershtern feels that these linguistic trends were a natural concomitant of Kadya's "proletarian" orientation. The individualism of her earlier work, he says, was replaced by a nationalistic, near-ideological commitment.[58] Indeed, for a short time, both Rokhl Korn (who had given *Dzhike Gas* a glowing critical review) and Kadya worked for the short-lived daily newspaper "*Fraynd*", a newspaper unofficially connected to the Communist party.[59] Kadya was a member of the literary editorial board, while Rokhl Korn contributed occasional poetry and prose to the paper.

While *Fraynd* was supported by the Communist party, Kadya's work as a literary editor of Fraynd by no means proves that she was a member of the Communist party.[60] Just as in the US, Kadya wrote for the openly religious newspapers, *Der Tog* and *Morgn Jurnal* without subscribing to their religious ideology, so in Warsaw, she oversaw the literary production of a newspaper whose ideology was not necessarily, or entirely, hers.

More Skirmishes

As is often the case when one feels strongly about something, Kadya was vigilant in her defense of Jewish Warsaw when it was attacked by others. But that didn't stop her from criticizing nearly every faction within the city herself.

Late in 1933, she wrote a major essay in L.B. entitled "About the Vogue of Negating Warsaw"[61]. This was a response to an earlier article by am émigré who had left Poland twenty years previously. In his absence, the writer said, the state of cultural life had deteriorated. Whereas previously cultural life had bloomed, now it was in decay. Always one to rally when she felt attacked, Kadya responded by counter-attacking. She was outraged, she said, by the false and unwarranted nostalgia. She retaliated with specifics. The numbers of schools, libraries and unions had increased in twenty years. What's more, there were more literary weeklies. She did admit that trash literature was a problem, but that was something intellectuals were aware of and were attempting to control. There was no gainsaying the dire economic conditions all over Poland, she said, but that had nothing to do with Jews per se; it was a world-wide issue. As for cynicism in Warsaw, she said, it was the writer who was contributing to it with his unwarranted accusations.

That year she participated in a general strike of school-teachers against the religious party, Agudas Yisroel. The party, the strikers claimed, paid its teachers poorly, and too late. Worse yet, it wanted to close down the schools run by the

Chapter Two: Kiev, Two Men Enter, One Man Leaves   97

secularists and open religious schools in their place. The strike did not succeed in changing the working conditions of teachers, but it succeeded in keeping the secular schools from closing down.

Fishman Gonshor says that the gentle tone of Kadya's memoir belies the "acerbic manner"[62] in which she attacked her enemies, or her perceived enemies, in those years. There is no question that she was then quick to attack. We saw earlier that Kadya also had a run-in with Kh Kazdan, a leader of the Bund. That, it turned out, was a mere skirmish. In the years 1934-35, that feud mutated into an all-out battle between Kadya and one Y. Khmurner, the head of the Bund. But this interpersonal battle was part of a larger war that was fought between three parties: the (pro-Yiddish) Bund, the left-leaning (pro-Hebrew) Po'alei Zion Party and the Communists. All three factions together formed TSYSHO, the Yiddish school system. Here is Fishman Gonshor's take on the story:

"The articles in the *Literarishe Bleter* provide only a glimpse into the smear campaign that developed around the secular school issue and the role of the press connected to it. In this debate, Kadye Molodowsky is far from the "non-joiner" she pretends to be."[63]

Kadya attacked Khmurner's "fat, disgusting"[64] leadership for the way it treated workers who could not afford to pay union dues. This subject surfaced again later in her life. On this issue, she was naïve in the extreme. For some reason, she supposed that a union should and would protect even those who had not joined. She neglected to explain how this was feasible; she simply assumed it was so.

Kadya expanded her attack to Yankev Patt and Sh Mendelsohn, both respected, upstanding community members with reputations abroad as well as in Warsaw. She accused them of personally benefiting from the funds that American supporters donated to the secular Yiddish school system. In an open attack on Bund leaders she said:

"One does not have to be your political enemy to bitterly oppose you and hate you. One need only be an honest person."[65]

Because Kadya said she had "swollen legs"[66] from working in such abominable conditions, the ongoing war between her and the Bund was commonly known as the "swollen legs affair."

While Kadya apparently never joined the Communist party, her husband, Simche, was a full-fledged member of the Communist party. It is quite likely, then, that the advocacy for Communism of her mentor, Dovid Bergelson, together with Simche's outright identification with Communism, affected her own opinions. That may well be why, in the internecine war between the rival Jewish factions in Warsaw, Kadya tended to side with the Communists.

It seems in retrospect that the Communist faction in TSYSHO exploited the legitimate grievances of the Yiddish school-teachers to drive a wedge between the teachers' union and the Bund. The accusations and counter-accusations of each of the three factions in TSYSHO were personal and nasty, and often based only on the slimmest threads of factual evidence. In their dire straits, all were hurting, and every faction needed someone to blame. In desperation, they blamed each other.

Kadya's Fourth Book

Right before she left Warsaw, Kadya published her fourth book, (after *Kheshvndike Nekht*, *Mayselekh*, and *Dzshike Gas*). Entitled *Freydke* (1935), it was a 16-part poem and its heroine was a Jewish, working-class woman. Considered the most didactic of her poetry books, its concern with social reform was so prominent that Kadya's playful imaginative powers could not come to the fore.

The heroine of this book, an impoverished young woman, might have gained the reader's sympathy were her conditions presented differently. As it is, the reader is told that in her low-ceilinged room "there hangs a picture of Rembrandt (ha-ha)".[67] It is a bit surprising to find so skillful a poet as Kadya doing what writers are warned not to do: telling rather than showing. But the fact is that's what Kadya does in this long poem.

This poem is by no means the finest of Kadya's poetic achievements, but it does give a snapshot of what life was like in Warsaw for some Jews during those awful interim years between the ascendency of Nazism in Germany and the German invasion of Poland.[68] Like I. B. Singer's Black Dobbe in his story "The Spinoza of Market Street", Freydke walks the streets of Warsaw selling eggs, a thankless, poorly paying business that barely keeps together body and soul. In Kadya's poem we get to know the store-keepers Freydke has to deal with; we see where and how her children play, and we hear how she anxiously awaits letters from her husband, a political exile of Socialist/Communist persuasions. We also hear in this poem about Birobidzan, the Soviet "haven" for Jews that was supposed to provide autonomy and self-respect for Russia's beleaguered Jews.[69]

Not all of the characters in Freydke live in Warsaw. Others, like Freydke's husband, apparently looking for "action" on the Socialist/Communist front, live in Paris. This collection contains portraits of migrant Jewish Communists who land in Paris, and, via a kind of underground-railroad, exchange information about the agitation necessary to effect political change. The run-down inns, the shifting, shallow human relationships, the whispered, shared information among agitator-conspirators, all seem too detailed to have been imagined. It is worth remembering that Kadya herself was in Paris when she followed Simche there just a few years before the publication of Freydke. We will never know whether Kadya saw these inns and these migrants herself, (a likely scenario), or simply heard about them from Simche. But like her pictures of the impoverished souls in Warsaw, these portraits of the Jewish Socialist/Communist migrants of Paris are so closely observed, and so carefully detailed, that they have the ring of authenticity.

There were many sorts of Jewish communities in Europe before the Nazis destroyed the Jewish civilization that had existed for centuries. To read Chaim Grade's *Talmidei Khakhomim in der Lite*, Lithuanian Torah Sages[70] is to get a close-up of one sub-group (the world of scholars in *muser yeshives* in Lithuania) of pre-WWII Jews in Europe; to read Kadya's *Freydke* is to get a close-up of an entirely different sub-group. While the two sub-groups lived in the same time period, neither one fully represents pre-WWII European Jewry. To create a complete picture of Jewish life in pre-WWII Europe, one needs to take into account the various sub-groups in all their particularity.

The last poem in *Freydke* is an unexpected marvel. After the descriptions of a variety of social outcasts, detached from the workaday world and hiding out in a hotel for exiles while plotting world revolution, we get a very powerful, personal poem.

Entitled "*Dem Tatns Pelts*", My Father's Fur Coat, this poem is as close as Kadya ever got in her poetry to an examination of her professional self and her relationship with her father. When Kadya wrote this poem, her father had already immigrated to the US and was living with her sister Dora in Philadelphia. Her older sister, Lina, was also living in the US. Obviously, someone had to clean out the family house; obviously that someone was Kadya. She finds an old pair of her father's glasses in one of the pockets of his fur coat, and then says:

"They [the glasses ZKN] consider me philosophically

And murmur piteously: Kadye, Kadye

How come you're not tired of wandering under the fur-coat

And writing a *khad-gadye*, a *khad-gadye*"[71]

It can be assumed that all children want parental respect. But for Kadya, the respect of her father was especially crucial. Kadya saw her father as a soul-mate: she trusted his judgment more than she trusted anyone else's. "*Khad-gadye*", the folk ditty that is traditionally recited at the Passover table, is a seemingly mindless round, with repetitive sections telling the story of a goat that gets eaten by something that is eaten/killed by something that is eaten/killed, and so on, until God Himself kills the Angel of Death. *"Khad-gadye"*, the Yiddish dictionary tells us, is also slang for "jail".[72]

What, then, is Kadya saying here? Why should she be pitied? Could it be that her father sees her work as not worthy of respect? As a writer-child, she had not earned the respect of her mother. Did she worry, then, that her father, too, would not think much of her efforts? Are his glasses his "true" sight? Perhaps; in that case, she stands reprimanded even when her father himself will not reprimand her. Is her work itself a jail for her? Perhaps; after all, it locks her in and doesn't allow her "out in the world". Worse yet, her father's glasses are accusing her of "wandering under the fur coat". Are they suggesting that she has not freed herself from her father's influence? That is another possibility. Perhaps these glasses are telling her that her work is an escape from reality, rather than a confrontation of reality? That, too, is a possible reading of this passage.

There is more to this poem. The glasses wander off, at least in Kadya's imagination, and she is left to do as she pleases, without being subjected to their scrutiny. Here is what happens:

"Seeing that the glasses were off on the road
I crawled with both ears under that fur coat.
But even in that quiet hide-out
I still hear the murmur of my father's glasses."[73]

Psychiatrists speak of the wish of an adult to "return to the womb", where all is safe and one is nourished and protected by one's mother. Here we find an adult wishing to return to her father's embrace and the protection of his warm, fur overcoat. There she can escape from her problems and find protection and safety. But there is no returning to the pre-adult world. Even in the furry, warm world under that coat, she stills hears the gentle admonishment of her father's glasses.

An Escape Hatch Opens

By 1935, Kadya had alienated herself from nearly all the factions in Warsaw: the religious party, at whose school she had once worked, the Bund and the Socialist party, to which all her friends belonged, and the non-political, upstanding leaders of the Warsaw Jewish community, whom she had wrongly accused of misconduct. That is why, when she received an invitation from her friends in the US to tour and lecture in the US and Canada at the expense of the North American Jewish communities, she was delighted. Leaving for the US seemed the best way out of her friendless impasse.

She undoubtedly wanted to see both of her sisters, as well as her father, who were in the US. What's more, by then Hitler's plan to rid the world of its Jews was known to all, and Polish Jews seemed especially vulnerable.[74] But few Polish Jews had an escape hatch. By agreeing take up the invitation to tour the US, Kadya was able to get herself out of a nasty environment (albeit one of her own making), get a chance to visit with her dearly beloved father and her sisters, and perhaps, only perhaps, eventually obtain American citizenship. If she could do that, she might save herself, and maybe even her husband and her brother.

On her way to the boat in Hamburg, Kadya stopped off in Paris, where she stayed with Simche's sister.[75] In an interview she gave then to the Parisian Yiddish newspaper, *Naye Presse*, she said:

"Yiddish literature in Poland does not express the suffering and heroic struggle of the common folk in Poland. It is lacking in talent, intellect, and even heart...Yiddish literature in Poland does not see this, the hero of the era, the unclothed, the homeless, the seekers of work and bread. It doesn't even see the shopkeeper who's become impoverished, or his shop which is howling with emptiness. It creates the same types over and over again of cheap literature. The literary atmosphere/milieu is shallow. It has not become the living breath that hovers over life, enhances and glorifies, that grows of its own over the heights of this atmosphere and becomes its highest expression."[76]

It is ironic indeed that only a short time after she arrived in New York, Kadya was pining for this very atmosphere: the "literary atmosphere of Warsaw and its PEN club". For all that she had only criticism for it as she left Poland, she spent the rest of her life trying to create this "atmosphere". And she memorialized this "atmosphere" in the literary journal that she edited for the last two decades or so of her life, the journal that was itself named "*Svive*", or "atmosphere/milieu".

The Unmentioned "Special Friend"

There is one relationship that Kadya had in Warsaw that she never mentions in her memoir. It is her friendship with Sarah Dubow.

There is no doubt that the two women knew each other in Warsaw. Melekh Ravitch, the most influential man of the PEN club in Warsaw, was in touch with both these women once the three of them had gotten out of Europe. In his letters, he often gives one news of the other.

Recall that Simche left/abandoned Kadya and went off to Paris alone. Perhaps Sarah and Kadya spend some time together then, when he was gone. That certainly seems possible. Another possibility is that Sarah and Kadya knew each other when both women were single and Kadya was rooming with room-mates. Sarah may have been one of Kadya's room-mates then; we have no way now of knowing how or when they met.

We know for certain that Kadya left for the US in 1935, but we do not know when Sarah left. We do know the date of the first preserved, archival letter. It was sent by Sarah to Kadya in 1936, when Kadya lived in New York and Sarah lived in Chicago.

Recall that Kadya left the note that "incriminated" Simche in her Israeli archive. In a similar manner, she left in her Israeli archive the "revealing" letters sent to her by Sarah Dubow. The other, more neutral, letters that Sara sent, traveled back with her to New York, and were left in her New York archive.

We will soon see how Kadya's relationship with Sarah was reflected in her creative work. What's more, we will see how the relationship between the two changed over time. There is no question, though, that without the archival material, we would never know about the special friendship between these two women. Because the evidence for that relationship only surfaces when Kadya was in New York, that story will be told in the next chapter.

NOTES

[1] *Svive*, no. 34, August 1971, p.38.
[2] *Svive*, no. 35, December, 1971, p. 57.
[3] For more about the Joint Distribution Committee see: http://www.jdc.org/
[4] *Kheshvndike Nekht*, pp. 106-107.
[5] Op.Cit., 86-87.
[6] Her book of translations, Kathryn Hellerstein, Paper Bridges, was published by Wayne State University Press in 1999.
[7] See Kathryn Hellerstein's A Question of Tradition, Stanford University Press, 2014, p. 334.
[8] Anna Fishman Gonshor, https://www.collectionscanada.gc.ca/obj/s4/f2/dsk2/ftp01/MQ43878.pdf, p. 28.
[9] The poem appeared in *Kheshvndike Nekht*, p. 90. The translation is Anna Fishman Gonshor's, which I have altered slightly. For the slight differences between the original poem as it appeared in L.B. and the poem as it appeared in *Kheshvndike Nekht*, see Fishman Gonshor, p. 30
[10] Fishman Gonshor, p. 30.
[11] These last two lines are my translation.
[12] See Fishman Gonshor, p. 32.
[13] There were two women poets of the inter-war years who did not cast off Jewish tradition: Miriam Ulinover and Roza Yakubovich. Hellerstein devotes an entire chapter in her book to these two poets. See Hellerstein, 2014, pp. 169- 242.

[14] Hellerstein, 1999, p. 16, claims that "by narrating rather than expressing the substance of the *tkhines*, Kadya "calls into ironic question the very efficacy of prayer". That is her opinion. However, whoever holds this opinion has to explain how it is that Kadya herself has six pages of poems (pages 144-45, 146-47, 148-49) that she herself entitled "*tfiles*", prayers, in this very same book: *Kheshvndike Nekht*.
[15] *Kheshvndike Nekht*, p. 21.
[16] Op. Cit., p. 30.
[17] Fishman Gonshor, p. 40.
[18] *Kehsvndike Nekht*, p. 61.
[19] I owe this insight to my husband, David Newman, who is a dentist.
[20] Fishman Gonshor, p. 57.
[21] Ibid.
[22] It was traditional in Poland to give a woman the family named suffixed by an "a".
[23] Fishman Gonshor's translation, p. 41
[24] Fishman Gonshor, p. 42.
[25] Ibid.
[26] Fishman Gonshor, p. 55.
[27] Fishman Gonshor, p. 56
[28] See http://www.daat.ac.il/he-il/hagim/hodashim/marheshvan/sarshalom-marheshvan.htm
[29] A pseudonym for Moshe-Tsvi Fayntsayg.
[30] Fishman Gonshor, p. 44.
[31] *Svive*, no. 35, December, 1971, p. 62
[32] For that poem and its translation into English, see Hellerstein, 1999, pp. 112-113.
[33] *Svive*, no. 33, January, 1971, p. 61.
[34] *Kheshvndike Nekht*, p. 11
[35] To be exact, this time, 33 days after the birth of a boy, and 66 days after the birth of a girl, begin only after an initial period of a week in the case of the birth of a boy, or two weeks, after the birth of a girl, when the blood of a childbearing woman is indeed "impure". The details are not critical here. What is crucial is that according to the Bible, only a child-bearing woman ever has "pure blood". The Biblical proof-text can be found in Leviticus 12/4-5.
[36] In Jewish law, wine that has been touched by idol-worshippers is called "*yayin nesekh*". This wine may not be drunk by Jews.
[37] Ibid.
[38] Fishman Gonshor, p. 49. Hellerstein, 2014, devotes the first two and a half chapters of her book to Korman's anthology. See Hellerstein, 2014, pp. 15-143. A detailed discussion of the poems that Kadya wrote in her Warsaw years can be found on pp.107-142.
[39] See Fishman Gonshor, p. 52.
[40] See Fishman Gonshor's reference to Hellerstein,1999 in her note on p. 54.
[41] See Fishman Gonshor, p. 68

[42] This translation is from a small book called <u>Olke and Her Blue Parasol</u>, published by *Heym un Shul Farayn,* Montreal, 1976. The few lines that were translated above these are my own translation.
[43] *In Land fun Mayn Gebeyn*, p. 9.
[44] *Mayselekh*, p. 21.
[45] Op. Cit., p. 24.
[46] A more revealing, though less literary, translation would be: "And-so Little-shoes Go/Where the World Has An End". No one has ever seriously suggested this title, but it hints at the word-structure and rhyme scheme of the original Yiddish.
[47] *Svive*, n. 36, April, 1972, p. 58. The three dots of the quote are in the original.
[48] The Makhon Lavon archive contains the correspondence between Kadya and her Hebrew-language translators as well as the (rather poorly maintained) reel(s) of this early movie.
[49] These are published in a dual-language, Yiddish-English, edition.
[50] See Fishman Gonshor, p. 70, and Natan Cohen, *"Mekoma U-Fo'ala Shel Kadya Molodowsky Ba-Sviva Ha-Sifrutit Ha-Yehudit Be-Varsha"* p. 168. In *Bikoret U-Farshanut*, no. 40, Bar Ilan Press, spring 2008.
[51] For more on this see Natan Cohen, p. 165 ff.
[52] Natan Cohen, p. 168.
[53] Ibid.
[54] In the case of the St Louis, The Dominican Republic agreed to take in some Jews, but no other country followed its example. For more on this see, http://en.wikipedia.org/wiki/MS_St._Louis as well as http://archives.jdc.org/educators/topic-guides/the-story-of-the-ss-st.html. See also: Richard Breitman and Allan Lichtman's <u>FDR and the Jews</u>, Harvard University Press, 2013.
[55] *Dzshike Gas*, pp. 56-7. This is Fishman Gonshor's translation.
[56] Avraham Novershtern, "*Ha-Kolot Ve-Ha-Makhela: Shirat Nashim Be-Yidish Beyn Shtey Milkhamot Ha-Olam*", p. 136. In *Bikoret U-Farshanut* no. 40.
[57] Avraham Novershtern considers this "a turn to radicalism", p. 115.
[58] Avraham Novershtern, pp. 137-39.
[59] Avraham Novershtern, p. 120.
[60] Amir Shomroni seems to believe that her association with *Fraynd* necessarily implies membership in the Communist party. See *Ha-aretz, Musaf,* March 9, 2018, p.42. I have found no evidence that proves Kadya's membership in the Communist party.
[61] Fishman Gonshor, pp. 78-80.
[62] Fishman Gonshor, p. 81.
[63] Fishman Gonshor, p. 86.
[64] Ibid.
[65] Ibid.
[66] Ibid.

[67] *Freydke*, p 9.
[68] Already the characters in this poem hear "Heil, Heil!" in the streets. See *Freydke*, p. 67
[69] In *Freydke*, Birobidzhan is a sort of Jewish Never-Never land, where all the problems that Jews encountered in the Diaspora evaporate. That can be seen in the poem *Kinder*, children, p. 41, which tells of a bear in Birobidzhan who is so tame, that he helps the children with their house chores. Recall that the symbol of Russia is a bear. Can the author be suggesting that the Russian government helps with household chores? Is this a case of sly humor, or perhaps, irony? That is for the reader to decide. For the history of Birobidzhan, see: http://www.yivoencyclopedia.org/article.aspx/Birobidzhan
[70] This epic poem, written in Yiddish and never translated, appeared in the journal *Di Goldene Keyt* in the 1970s in three parts: in volumes 90, 94, and 96. Reading this poem is like seeing a Breughel painting: the details of life are minutely depicted. There is no literary picture of the world of Jewish scholars that compares in depth or breadth to the one found in this poem.
[71] *Freydke*, p. 98.
[72] See Uriel Weinreich's Modern English-Yiddish Yiddish-English Dictionary, New York, 1968, p. 183.
[73] *Freydke*, p. 70
[74] Recall that the Jews of Poland had suffered from Anti-Semitic edicts even before their country was invaded by the Nazis. I. B. Singer's book The Certificate gives a superb sense of the tensions felt by Polish Jews at this time.
[75] I know this from the doctorate of Amir Shomroni. I am grateful to him for sharing this with me.
[76] This interview was quoted in LB July 12, 1935, p. 451.

CHAPTER FOUR: THE US – (1935-1950)

Culture is… an inward condition of the mind and spirit, not… an outward set of circumstances.

    Mathew Arnold

First Impressions

In a gesture that was apt for a woman who famously championed the sisterhood of women, Kadya was greeted and feted upon her arrival in the US by two women-friends: Bertha Kling and Esther Shumiatcher. Women-poets that these two women were, they felt a sense of camaraderie with Kadya. They advised her in advance which travel plans were preferable, and they did their best to make her comfortable when she arrived.

Shortly after she arrived in the US and was living in New York, Kadya was contacted by Ida Maze, a Montreal-based Yiddish writer, and a woman known as "the den mother of Yiddish writers."[1] Ida invited Kadya to Montreal to give some talks there, and in her usual fashion, she offered to be useful in any way she could be.[2]

Careful to address Ida as "Dear Ida Maze" (they had not yet met in person)[3], Kadya told Ida that she could not travel outside the US (to Canada) because she did not yet have US citizenship. She was grateful for the kind offer of assistance, she said, and she might travel to Montreal at a later date. Then, in what seems like a response to a query, Kadya told Ida how surprised she was at the "frightful assimilation" (of American Jews) that she saw all around her.

At this point, Kadya had not yet realized that most American Jews were delighted with the assimilation that had taken place. Indeed, they fervently wished the process would deepen and speed up. This must have been a persistent topic between them, because five years later, in 1940, Kadya reverted to this topic once more. This time she said that while others might believe American Jewry was in the "dry-bone" state (the state that precedes rebirth and redemption, in the story made famous by the prophet Ezekiel), she herself did not believe the dry bones of American Jewry would ever come to life.

In that same first letter to Ida, thinking like the multi-lingual European that she was, Kadya confessed it was "a pity"[4] that Jewish Americans had acquired so many Anglicisms, that their Yiddish had become a mixed Yiddish-English jargon. This mixed Yiddish-English was something that Kadya and her father loved to mock. But, as far as I can tell, Kadya never shared that mockery with anyone but him.

Like most immigrants, when Kadya first arrived in the US in 1935, she stayed with family. Her father lived with Dora, and Dora was the sister she was closer to. Accordingly, Dora was the natural choice for a first stop. Nevertheless, it is her sister Lina's reaction to her threadbare clothes that she records in her memoir:

"My older sister Lina was simply shocked when she saw a patch on my dress. From her reaction I understood that in America one does not wear patched clothes. She looked at me as though I had, God forbid, gone naked. In the morning she bought me three new dresses: two cotton, and one woolen. When I saw her three dresses, I became confused: What's this, three dresses?! At home in Poland we sewed three dresses for a bride [and gave them to her] at her wedding. That was her dowry. But just like that three dresses– that was beyond my comprehension. My sister told me to throw out the patched dresses and put on a new one."[5]

After telling us this in her memoir, Kadya admits that despite the fact that this event took place long ago, and she has spent much time in NY since then, she has still not ever bought three dresses at one time. Kadya may never have been rich, but she was also not poor, at least not in the US. If she never bought three dresses at one time in all the years she lived in the US, that was not because she could not afford to do so. Just as men and women who lived through the near-hunger years of the Great Depression could never allow themselves to throw out edible food, so men and women who knew the sort of abject poverty that Kadya knew in the inter-war years in Warsaw, simply could not ever allow themselves the seemingly outrageous luxury of buying more than one necessary item of clothing at one time. The years of want left their mark on Kadya long after the want was gone and was replaced by comfort.

If Kadya never became fashion conscious, as her sister Lina apparently was, she did realize over time that the social norms of her new home dictated a different sort of outfitting. Even before she met Ida Maze, her benefactor in Montreal, she let Ida know at the end of her first year in the US how her socialization was progressing. She reported:

"I know some English, I wear American clothes, and I look like an ordinary person".[6]

A year later, she reported that she'd (finally) given away her "gypsy dress".[7] It would seem, then, that while it was not important to her to wow others with her fashion statement, it most certainly was important to her that she not be seen as aberrant.

Kadya did not stay long with her sister in Philadelphia. Explaining her decision to move to New York, she told Ida Maze that New York was the hub from which everything radiated out and was interconnected.[8] And she wanted to be right in the middle of that hub.

The Appearance of Rivke Zylberg

Three years later, when Simche had arrived safely in the US, and Kadya was able to look back at her traumatized beginnings in her new-found home, she began writing a fictive biography of one Rivke Zylberg, entitled "From Lublin to New York: The Diary of Rivke Zylberg". We know from her memoir, that Kadya finished this novella around 1940, not so long after Simche arrived in the US. However, it did not see the light of day till 1942, when it found a publisher. It is clear, then, that while she was writing this novella, Kadya was dredging up still-fresh memories of herself as a new immigrant.

The novella was published in book form in 1942, broadcast as a radio play on the Yiddish language radio station, WEVD, in 1943, and later re-worked into a play entitled "The House on Grand Street". But that happened only in 1953.

I am convinced that "Rivke Zylberg" is Kadya's feminine persona. There are two bases for this claim. The first is the exact match-up of Rivke's "rags" scene and Kadya's "rags" scene. This can be viewed as their "outer" lack of attractiveness. The second is the exact match of Rivke's and Kadya's most winning physical feature. This can be viewed as their shared inherent attractiveness.

In the passage from Kadya's memoir quoted above, we are told how Lina behaved when she saw Kadya's patched dress, but not how Kadya herself felt. In the "Diary", however, we get that scene replayed "from the inside". Now we get to see how 'Rivke' feels when she is looked down upon as a clueless vagabond in need of charity:

"My aunt...and Selma laughed at my socks, my blouses and my dresses. In Lublin I was well-dressed. Will they always laugh at me in America? My aunt picked up all my clothes and said: Rags! [*shmates*]! We must buy her a dress and a hat. I had a hard time keeping back tears..."[9]

For all that Kadya never tells the readers of her memoir that she cried when Lina humiliated her by mocking her beggar-like clothes, she does admit to one case of deep hurt as a child. Recall how Kadya's age-mate, Malke, humiliated the young Kadya when she took a stick and ran it over the bottles holding the Molodowsky family's drink. When she was past seventy, Kadya admitted that she called the sound of the kvass bottles "Malke's Melody". She then said: when others humiliate her in the same way, she calls the humiliation "Malke's Melody". It would seem that Lina's reaction to Kadya's "rags", qualified as "Malke's Melody". Whether or not Lina realized it, when she pointed with derision to Kadya's rags, she was playing Malke's Melody.

It is obvious that this topic plagued Kadya long after her sister Lina "played Malke's Melody". Towards the end of 1935, Kadya told Ida Maze:

"By now I know some English, I walk around in American clothes and I pretty much fit in."[10] Here, then, is the exact, external, match-up of Rivke and Kadya.

Now to the inherent match-up. What is the most crucial part of Rivke's feminine identity as she appears in The Diary? Put differently, what, in everyone's opinion, makes her attractive? The answer, unquestionably is: her hair in general, and her braids in particular. Here are the facts that substantiate this claim.

In a book of a little more than three hundred pages, there are as many as sixteen references to Rivke's hair. All either suggest or unambiguously state that Rivke's hair is her "selling point" as a woman. And the last reference is the clincher: it wins over her in-laws-to-be and brings her the love and comfort of family that she so desperately wants.

The first time Eddy, the fiancé of Rivke's cousin Selma, meets Rivke, the newly arrived refugee from Europe, all he says is: How do you like America?"[11] That is quite civil and natural. But the second time the two of them meet, things go differently. It is true that all Eddy says is: "Hello *grine*"[12], but as he says this, he also runs his fingers through her hair.[13] This is the first indication the reader has that Eddy is attracted to Rivke.

This gesture does not go un-noticed. As soon as Selma's mother sees Eddy's hands move, she finds a reason to take Rivke out of the house and safely out of Eddy's way.[14] But this does not have the desired effect. The very next time the two meet, Eddy whispers to Rivke: "You know, you're beautiful".[15]

Later on, Rivke tells us that her cousin Selma spends hours (and presumably lots of money) on doing her hair at a beauty parlor. Rivke, on the other hand, does not have money for a beauty parlor, and in any case, does not want fancy hair-dos. She simply takes her braids and winds them around her head. When she meets Rivke, Mrs. Shor, a neighbor, says: "Believe me, Rivke doesn't need a beauty parlor".[16]

For all of Eddy's attentions, though, the man in Rivke's life is not Eddy, but his friend Larry, also called "Red". Once this young man starts paying Rivke some attention, Mrs. Shor says to Rivke: "I think it's because of your braids; the boys have seen enough of girls with odd hair-dos."[17] Rivke's hair is not only beautiful, then, it is also naturally so. And this, Mrs. Shor says, is attractive in and of itself.

A short while later we hear Rivke musing. She says to herself: "I think Mrs. Shor was right that the boys like me because of my braids." And as proof of this fact, Rivke continues "because Red actually kissed me first on my throat and then on my hair".[18]

As the novella progresses, Rivke gets herself embroiled. Her cousin's fiancé is clearly taken with her and that displeases her aunt and uncle. As she muses over her problems, she tells herself: "Mrs. Shor says everything is due to my braids....In such a large city as New York they feel crowded because of my braids. It's a strange city, New York..."[19]

It was Mrs. Shor who first noticed Rivke's feminine graces, and it is she who nurtures it. As Rivke gets ready to go to a "ball", Mrs. Shor gives her a satin flower and tells her the flower will maintain her luck.

When Rivke asks: "What luck?", Mrs. Shor answers: "That you please the boys". And as she says this, she pins the flower to Rivke's hair.[20]

And it was just as Mrs. Shor said. As Red continues to court Rivke, he brings her flowers. And to show just how much she means to him, Red takes out a flower from the bunch he brought with him, and sticks one in her hair.[21]

Till now we have seen how others perceive Rivka's femininity and the way it is linked with her hair. We have also seen Rivke reflect on the opinion of others. But there is one passage in the novella where we get Rivke's own self-directed view of herself as a woman, and it revolves around her hair.

As she strolls outdoors, Rivke tells us that "a breeze blew from heaven, and my hair was drawn to the sky. It's a pity my beret hides this."[22] Here Rivke is walking alone. She need not please anyone in particular. Nevertheless, a woman outdoors is never unaware of potential onlookers and her effect on them. And for Rivke this appreciative gaze of others is brought on by her hair.

As we have seen, Leyzer, Rivke's European beau, managed to escape to Palestine. Throughout the novella he continues to write to Rivke, urging her to join him. We see no impassioned lover's angst on Leyzer's part. But he does tell Rivke he would like to see her. Indeed, as he sees it, Rivke's life would be more meaningful if she would join him in Palestine.

In one of his letters, he speaks of a mutual acquaintance of theirs, now also in Palestine, and says: "Imagine, he remembers your braids." Leyzer reports that this acquaintance asked him: "Does she still have those long braids?" He then reiterates his opinion that Rivke's place is in Palestine, and he says: "The Land of Israel needs your braids."[23]

One of the secondary characters in this novella is a woman called Mrs. Rubin. Among other things, she tells Rivke stories about herself and her family. While reminiscing about her sister (who did not parlay her feminine wiles into an opportunity to marry when she could), Mrs. Rubin says: "And that immediately reminded me of your braids."[24] The suggestion here is clearly: If you have the braids, you can get the man. And you should get the man you want while you can. Otherwise it may be too late.

For most of the novella, Rivke's mind wavers. Whom should she choose? She did care for Leyzer when the two of them were in Europe. But he has left Europe and gone to Palestine, and there is no longer a way to reach Palestine. She is not about to steal her cousin's fiancé, although that young man seems willing enough to ditch her cousin for her. And for a while, she is unsure of whether or not she wants Red. When she discusses her predicament with Mrs. Shor, the latter tells her: "I'm telling you, Rivke, everything is due to your braids. With those braids… you can turn everyone's head."[25]

Later on, during this same conversation, Mrs. Shor says to Rivke: "That's exactly what I'm telling you. You always keep your braids high up, like a crown, as though all of New York was about to pay you a visit."[26]

We come now to the last of the mentions of Rivke's hair. By the end of the story, Red has asked Rivke to marry him and she has agreed. But she has not been formally introduced to his parents. To this crucial meeting Rivke comes imagining that her father-in-law and mother-in-law to-be are bears and that her world will overturn when the two will swing their paws at her. The first thing her father-in-law to-be says to her is: "How many hours did you spend today in the beauty parlor with those braids?"

Rivke is flummoxed and cannot answer. But Red comes to her rescue.

What do you mean?" Red says to his father, as he removes the four pins clasping Rivke's hair together. Then, Rivke tells the reader, "…my braids fell down, one in the back and one in the front." Red's mother says: "Larry[27], you're crazy?" But Red's father looks at Rivke's braids and says: "She is the real thing, your girl."[28]

This is the validation Rivke was seeking. She is so overcome, that the room turns and she loses track of what exactly is being said. Nevertheless, she asks Red affectionately as they leave: "Red-Shmed, what did you do to my hair?" Red laughs, announces that the engagement was wonderful, and gives Rivke a kiss.[29]

With this climax, Rivke's hair has done what it needed to do. Under its spell, Rivke has found love and family, and the reader is supposed to believe that all will be well.

Now to Kadya and her "winning feature". There is no question that Kadya herself had braids as a young woman. The photo of her stannding between Simche and Arvohom Sutzkever, taken in Poland, clearly shows her with a braid wound around and on top of her head.[30]

For Kadya, it was just her hair, not her whole body, which brought her to the attention of others. In one of the letters that Kadya left in her Israeli archive, there is a

Chapter Four: The US – (1935-1950) 117

letter from one Tania, apparently a friend from their days together in Europe. She was upset with Kadya for not having written. In her mock anger, she says:

"Listen, Kadyenke, If I'll find you somewhere, I'll tear out your braids, or your shortened braids [in Yiddish: *tsepelekh*, ZKN] (Do I know how you're wearing your hair now?") [31]

Even more crucial than the fact that Kadya herself had braids, is the fact that for Kadya, hair grooming is coupled with erotic attention. We mentioned Sarah Dubow earlier, it is time now to see how her real-life relationship with Kadya was reflected in the fictional story of Rivke Zylberg.

Recall that in her memoir, Kadya tells us that the first trip she took outside of New York was a trip to Chicago where she was hosted by Sarah and Yakov Dubow.[32] There is no hint there that there is anything special about Kadya's relationship with Sarah. But the archives tell a different story.

One of the strangest letters that Sarah wrote, can be found in Kadya's Israeli archive. It arrived after Kadya's first cross-county lecture tour. Here are segments from that letter, dated February 27, 1936:

And who are all the men of Chicago in love with?	With Kadya
! ! !	
And who has the most beautiful voice?	Kadya
[and 8 more exclamation points]	
And who has the most beautiful smile?	Kadya
And who has the most beautiful legs?	Kadya!!
And who got a prize for the most beautiful legs in Paris?	Kadya!!
Who made the greatest hit in Chicago?	Kadya!
[and 7 more exclamation points]	
Who is great?	Kadya!!!
Who is powerful?	Kadya!!

Who is smart?	Kadya!!!
Who is beautiful?	Kadya!!!!
Who writes the best poetry?	Kadya!
Who is the best high-pressure salesman?	Kadya!!!
So proclaims/shouts all of Chicago"…	

If Sarah was Kadya's age (and there is every reason to assume the two were age-mates), then Sarah was more than forty years old when she wrote this letter. For all that she is middle-aged, she sounds in this letter more like a teen-age groupie high on grass, than a sedate, married woman of over forty. One can see why Kadya chose not to take this letter with her to New York when she left Israel.

There is another letter, this time one that was left in the YIVO archive of New York, that is dated 1937. At this point, Kadya was still alone; Simche was to join her only in 1938. Sarah says:

"I love you still more [for this] and when you'll be here I'll give you a good Russian kiss. But I'm waiting; I'll give you this when you come to Chicago. And you must come to Chicago."[33] She goes on to plan with Kadya the details of Kadya's next cross-country trip, after the upcoming printing of Kadya's first book put out in the US. She will, Sarah says, get in touch with the appropriate folks in Cleveland, and Detroit. What's more the Sholem Aleichem schools will be apprised of this tour and they will do their part to invite Kadya and do what is necessary to make the tour a success. Then she says:

"I am happy at the thought that we will soon see each other and I truly miss you.

I am telling you now that I will wash your hair and give you a real "permanent"' and I'll make you into a true beauty [in the original: *ikh vel dikh makhn far a krasivitse*]. You will look so beautiful, that the men will stand you up in the street and beg you to

Chapter Four: The US – (1935-1950) 119

return with them to their rooms. And not only they, but all [the men of] of the Bronx will fight over you and will want to rent out a room for you."

This last bit about renting a room was apparently in response to a refusal that Kadya had met with. A landlord on Clinton Street had refused to rent a room to her because she was not the "right type"; they were looking for a different sort of renter. In an attempt to comfort Kadya, Sarah said:

"They are certainly Fascists, Nazis or Hilterites. Or perhaps they're actually Polish spies?"

Kadya had apparently promised to discuss a set-back she had with her colleagues. She had not given more information in her letter, but she promised to do so when they met. Sarah told her she was looking forward to their upcoming person-to-person talks.

Here there is evidence of a deep friendship. When something troubles Kadya, she confides in Sarah, And Sarah does her best to comfort her friend. She tries a bit of humor and a bit of fantasy, hoping that something will work.

For our purpose, the crucial point here is the promise that Sarah makes to wash Kadya's hair and make her into a beauty. The groomed hair that will make Kadya a beauty, will, in Sarah's imagination, bring Kadya many suitors.

There is yet another, later, letter that Kadya left behind in Makhon Lavon. This letter, written in 1939, (when both women had husbands living with them), clearly links hair grooming and a physical relationship between the two women. In this five-page letter, Sarah says:

"If I could grab you in my hands now I would give your hair a good combing. (It's been a long time since I combed your hair and you need it a lot.) …"

Sarah goes on to say she has a new warm shawl and finds it very comfortable. Then she says:

"I would like to wrap you around close to me in this warm shawl so you, too, could feel the same pleasant warmth that I feel now. And I long for your warmth. I miss you very much and I would like to see you…"[34]

It is noteworthy that this outright reminder of their former physical relationship does not prevent Sarah from saying:

"And give your Simche a good kiss from me. And you, too, [make sure you] feel my kiss…"

For all that the two women were both married and lived far apart, there seems to have been a homoerotic nature to their relationship. It is apparent, too, that they had once shared some sort of physical intimacy. And hair grooming was, to all appearances, an erotic spark.

We see now, that what is true for Kadya, is true for Rivke Zylberg. Both were initially unattractive in their rags, and both were inherently attractive because of their hair. For both, hair sparked an erotic interest.[35] It is this identity, I maintain, that makes Rivke into Kadya's feminine persona.

While there is no way to know now when the friendship between Sarah and Kadya began, we do know that it lasted all their lives. In the 1939 letter mentioned above, Sarah tells Kadya that she and Melekh Ravitch share their affection for Kadya, and that the two of them, Sarah and Melekh, discussed Kadya when they met. It would seem that the former friends of Warsaw re-grouped in the New World and, though they were dispersed, they networked through their mutual correspondence.

Apparently, everyone in Warsaw knew of the closeness between Kadya and Sarah. This can be seen from another letter that Kadya saved in her Israeli archive. Here there is a letter from Ezra Korman asking:

"Did *Sarah Bas-Toyvim* come to visit you at all? Did she at least help you get a green card? One must have some decency [in Yiddish: *derekh erets*]!"[36]

The use of the phrase *Soroh Bas-Toyvim* is an interesting one. This may be the name of a(n) historical figure, or perhaps, a pseudonym that men used when they composed *tkhines* for women.[37] In colloquial speech, the phrase "*bas-tovim*" is used to mean "of good parentage", or "respected". It is hard to know if the Warsaw crowd used this term for Sarah Dubow out of true respect, or with a dose of irony. Since we are missing the clues to their inner lives, we cannot know for sure.

Recall that in the letter Kadya wrote to Simche when she was new in the US, she said that in the US she had "...so to speak paper friends, but few genuine friends".[38] What she meant, it would seem, was she had made no deep friendships, nothing akin to her friendship with Sarah Dubow, whom she had known in Europe.

It is clear that Kadya confided in Sarah when she was troubled. Another one of the undated letters in Makhon Lavon reveals that one Mr. Bercovitch[39] accused Kadya of stealing his books. Upon learning of this accusation, Sarah was full of righteous indignation. She says:

"I would not speak with anyone who could accuse you of such a lowly deed. It's no small thing to get accused of stealing books!

But you need not worry, I will go straightaway to my nephew the lawyer, and he will go to the lawyer who took your fingerprints, and the two of them will telegraph the consul and tell them not to believe Bercovitch. And whom do you think they'll believe, a lawyer and a detective or a Yiddish teacher?"

For all the genuine closeness between the two women, Kadya did not necessarily run to Sarah when called. In an undated letter, apparently written the summer before Simche arrived in the U.S.,[40] Sarah invited Kadya to spend vacation time with her in the mountains. Sarah wrote:

"I would pay you as much as they pay you in camp...I would like to share my good-times with you, but what can I do. You do not let me share with you.

You would do everything in the world, you would break plates and tear muscles, but you will not allow yourself to share my good times with you in the village."[41]

In this letter Sarah hit upon a crucial character trait of Kadya's: pride. Not for Kadya the free-loading gift of others. She wanted to earn her own way in life, if she could. And at this point, she still could.

Although Kadya's friendship with Sarah explains the allure of Rivke Zylberg's hair, it would be misguided to look for other correspondences between Kadya and her fictional creation, Rivke Zylberg. Indeed, superficially, there are many differences. Kadya's father was living safely in Philadelphia when Kadya arrived in the US, while Rivke's father was living in a barn in Lublin. Kadya's's brother fled eastward and left his daughter with his wife, while Rivke's brother fled westward to Paris with his wife and child. When she arrived, Kadya stayed with her sister and father, while Rivke Zylberg stayed at her aunt's house. While Kadya was a bit more than forty years old and a married woman when she arrived in the US, Rivke Zylberg was a mere twenty years old, and definitely unattached. Kadya arrived in the US as a publicly known (and loved) figure in the Jewish world, while Rivka is a simple young woman with no celebrity status whatsoever.

One of the struggles that Rivke does share with Kadya is the struggle to acquire control of English. For both Kadya and Rivke, Yiddish is the preferred language, the one that reminds them of home and its bygone comforts. But on US soil, they both find a monolingual English-speaking Jewish population, one that has no use for the language and the ways of the Old Country. However, the effects of this Jewish monolingualism in the US were radically different in the two cases. For Kadya, this was an especially crippling handicap. A writer depends solely on her language expertise. If she cannot express herself orally in the language of those who surround her, her writerly abilities melt away. But Rivke is not nearly as linguistically frustrated. She does not understand much of what is said around her, and there is no doubt that she is especially upset when she senses that folks around her are speaking of her, but on the whole, she accepts her status as a non-native speaker. She asks when she doesn't understand something, but the reader never feels that the language issue is a burning concern for her.

In The Diary, Rivke signs up for an evening course to learn English. But sometimes she goes, and other times, she doesn't. When she is "down", she cuts classes. Kadya, who didn't work in a garment shop and was not the needy young woman of her novella, made every effort to acquire English as soon as she could. She taught in a summer camp "in the mountains"[42] not only to earn money, but also because she wanted to be around children who would tolerate her mistakes in English. She knew that immersion was the best way to acquire a language. That is why she placed herself squarely in the midst of English speakers. So anxious was Kadya to acquire a good grasp of English, that six years after she arrived, she completed a seven month, 200-hour program of "English for Foreign Born".[43]

Unlike Kadya, Rivke/Rae was able to marry a native-born American, and thereby gain a sliver of normalcy in America. Kadya, married to a man who was an immigrant himself, never knew that comfort. The diary-woman, then, is Kadya's attempt to imagine what her life would have been like had she arrived as an immigrant in the US, young, unattached and unknown, and not the older, married celebrity that she was.

In The Diary, Rivke gets letters from a beau named Leyzer, who courted her in Europe. It is clear that the two were not formally engaged, but it is also clear from Leyzer's letters that he was hoping they would marry once Rivke joined him in Palestine. He is the "someone" who is waiting for Rivke in that last paragraph of the "Diary". Rivke/Rae holds onto his letters and hides them from her fiancé. We are not told much about this man. But we do know that Rivke could not possibly join him: Italy had entered the war, and the sea route to Palestine was cut off. In fact, right before she agrees to marry Larry, her American-born fiancé, Rivke asks her laundress-friend to hold onto Leyzer's last letter. She knows that the laundress has a drawer of "might-have-been" love letters and keepsakes, and she wants Leyzer's last letter to rest there. If she cannot have him, she can at least hold onto a letter from him.

It is tempting to look for a parallel between this part of Rivke's life and Kadya's own life. To be sure, Kadya never tells her readers that she would have preferred anyone to Simche. As we saw earlier, Rokhl Korn certainly believed that Simche was "her man" by choice. But she did carry Dovid Bergelson's letters, sent in 1928 and 1930, with her to Israel twenty years later, and she did bring them back with her to New York when she returned in 1952. And she kept those letters for more than twenty years after that. Like Leyzer, Bergelson was unreachable. A prisoner in the Soviet Union, he was allowed out of the Soviet Union only when he was given official permission, and then his family remained captive in the Soviet Union while he traveled.

Once again, we are dealing with a fantasy-world. We have no reason to believe that Bergelson would have given up his family for life with Kadya had she been foolish enough to leave the US and travel to the Soviet Union to be with him. But a writer can indulge in fantasy. In her fantasy world, Kadya can imagine that the man she adores is waiting for her, just as in her fantasy world she can imagine she is about to marry a handsome young man who feels totally at ease in his American skin.

A good deal of the plot in The Diary is taken up with Rivke's suitors. Rivke nearly steals her cousin's fiancé, but she moves out of her cousin's home in time to leave that young man for her cousin. Interestingly, when this fiancé approaches her on her doorstep, and visits her in her new apartment even after his engagement to her cousin, she does not openly and forcefully reproach him, as she might do. Instead she gently reminds him that when he visits her, he should, by right, take his fiancée, her cousin, along with him.

One can't help wondering if Kadya had something on her conscience. Did she, perhaps, nearly "steal" a beau of a friend of hers? Perhaps; that is something we cannot know now. If this incident did not in fact have a real-life model, it is yet more interesting. That suggests that what we have here might be sheer fantasy: the imaginings of a woman honest enough to admit she might have liked the thrill of sweeping a "taken" man away from his recognized, rightful woman, and playing with him for the excitement of the catch. A fantasy world may be something we all indulge in, but only writers are courageous enough to give that world voice.

By the end of The Diary, Rivke is engaged to an American-born young man, but she has paid a price. For one thing, she has agreed to change/Anglicize her name. As far as we know, Kadya was attached to her given name, and did not for a moment ever think of changing it. But Rivke is not Kadya; Rivke is the every-(Jewish)-woman of Kadya's imagination. And of course, most American Jews then did not keep their European/Jewish names; they changed/Anglicized their names. Rivke simply did what everybody was doing. In fact, Rivke makes no open issue of this name change. She almost slides into it, despite herself.

But Kadya does not let her fictional character get away with this supposedly easy switch. She makes it quite clear that this sloughed-off identity does not simply disappear. It lingers in the memory, and it haunts the immigrant, no matter how easy the switch has seemed. She has this simple young woman say to herself in the book's final paragraph:

"It seems to me that Rivke Zylberg is no more. Soon a person with the name of Rae Levit will start to walk around in New York. Rivke Zylberg remained in Lublin. Someone is waiting for Rivke Zylberg in the Land of Israel, and Rae Levit lives in New York."[44]

"Rae", as we have seen, is the Anglicization of "Rivke". "Levit" is the family name of Rivke's husband-to-be, the family name she will assume after marriage. Just as Rivke of The Diary changed her name when she married, so Kadya herself was not averse to taking her husband's name on formal documents. While it is true that Kadya did not want her professional name to be tied to her husband's family name, in The Diary she is imagining herself an ordinary young woman, shorn of her professional self. In this case, assuming one's husband's family name is the most natural thing imaginable.

Interestingly, Kadya had a relative with that exact name: "Rae Levit".[45] One wonders if this relative knew enough Yiddish or enough about the Yiddish literature of the day to realize that Kadya had "borrowed" her identity, or at least her name, for the novella that was written in Yiddish.

1935-1938: The Stressful Three Years

In the three years between Kadya's arrival in the US in 1935, and Simche's arrival in 1938, Kadya did support herself. She needed to save up money to rescue Simche, and she hoped to be able to rescue her brother Leibl and his family as well. All this, in addition to her own needs.

As soon as her American visa had been extended, she made the trip to Canada, as Ida Maze had suggested. A lecture tour to Montreal and Toronto brought in some cash, but Kadya did more than just lecture. She left behind books of hers, to be sold to any and all lovers of Yiddish. Ida took this job upon herself; she was instructed to send the funds from the lecture and the sales of Kadya's books to Dora, Kadya's sister. This remained a pattern for the rest of their lives: Ida, in her role as Kadya's enabler, was the sales person, and Dora, in her role as Kadya's banker and financial advisor, was the account manager and accountant. One can imagine just how many books Kadya needed to sell to accumulate the thousands of dollars she would need for her rescue operations: she told Ida to price her books at "forty cents unbound and fifty cents bound".[46]

But Canada was only one stop of many. In her ceaseless effort to support herself and acquire the funds that she would need to rescue her loved ones, Kadya traveled to and lectured in Cleveland, Detroit and Chicago. It was an exhausting schedule, and Kadya confessed to Ida, as she had to Simche, that she'd lost 15 pounds during these rounds. She attributed her anxiety in part to the visa issues Simche was having, and in part to the overwhelming sadness that she felt watching the destruction of Jewish life in Poland.[47] It may well be, though, that this treadmill-like travel schedule kept her mind off the worries she mentioned to Ida.

Always a staunch friend to those whose friendship she valued, Kadya found out in 1937 that her fellow writer and friend from Warsaw, Rokhl Korn, had been arrested. She immediately wrote to Ida Maze, informing her of the bad news, and urging her to sell Rokhl's books so that the money could be forwarded to Rokhl.[48] As it turned out, once the war began, Rokhl was on the run. It would be another decade before she found her way to a Displaced Persons camp in Stockholm. But she did eventually make her way to Canada, and she became a Montreal resident, just like Ida. All the while, Kadya and Ida did their best to exchange news about her fate and see to it that her books were kept in circulation.

For all that she had left Poland after alienating nearly every Jewish faction in Warsaw, Kadya felt herself longing for "home" once she had settled into life in the US. It was not Poland and its natural beauty that she missed. It was Warsaw. But even that is not precise enough. It was Jewish Warsaw that she longed for. And when she spoke with others of her longing for Warsaw, she admitted that her nostalgia was bound up not with anything material, but with the atmosphere of the place in general, and with the atmosphere of the Yiddish Writers' Club in particular. She called this missing ingredient *"Svive"*, a word derived from the Hebrew component of Yiddish that literally means "surroundings". More generally, it means "atmosphere".

Kadya and I.B. Singer

A fellow writer of Kadya's who happened to immigrate to the US in 1935, just as she did, was Isaac Bashevis Singer. There is a fascinating overlap in their experiences. Both had flourished in the Warsaw Writers' club and both looked back at it with the pained realization that it could never be replaced. Both looked at their fellow American Jews with horror as they realized its Yiddish speakers, few as they were, were not actively working to ensure the future of Yiddish in the US. In a letter that Bashevis wrote to his (and Kadya's) friend Melekh Ravitch, he said:

"...it's sad because here in New York I see even more clearly than in Poland...that there is no one to work for. There is a crazy Jewish people here which keeps slightly kosher and peddles...and awaits Marx's vision for the people of the world. But it doesn't need Yiddish literature."

And then Bashevis uses the metaphor that Kadya herself used three times in three different poems to indicate an exercise in futility. He said:

"We built on a paper bridge."[49]

For the two writers, Bashevis Singer and Kadya, life in the US seemed devoid of any promise: there simply was no serious mass audience for Yiddish literature in the New World, as there was in Warsaw. The two of them knew each other from the Warsaw writers' club. She was the first woman to be offered membership in the Yiddish branch of PEN, while he was the youngest writer to be admitted to the writers' club. How much either of them had to do with each other while the two of them were in Warsaw was not recorded.

They spoke different dialects of Yiddish (she, the North-eastern dialect known to the folk as "*Litvish*", and he, the Central Yiddish dialect, known to the folk as "*Galetsiyanish*"), and had very different backgrounds. Bashevis' father was a community rabbi with Hassidic leanings, and Bashevis himself had the strictly religious education for boys that was de rigueur for a rabbi's son. Kadya's father, on the other hand, was far more open to modernizing tendencies in Judaism. He read a Zionist Hebrew-language paper, and was not averse to secular education for his children.

We also do not know if Kadya and Bashevis ever spoke to each other about methods of obtaining citizenship in the US. Whether by accident or by way of the same legal advisor, both ended up taking the very same pathway to citizenship. They took a bus to Detroit, and from there crossed a bridge to Windsor. Once in Canada, they received a permanent visa to the US.[50]

Like Kadya, Bashevis felt the need for a serious literary journal that would take the place of the literary journals they knew in Poland. Once WWII began in earnest, it was patently clear to both of them that a literary world, an immaterial world that was to replace the physical Writers' Club of Warsaw, would have to be created in the US, if Yiddish was to have any future at all. In an attempt to create this literary world, the two of them co-edited a journal called *Svive* (Surroundings/Mileu) from 1943-1944. But as the war progressed, Kadya found herself unable to continue with her editing duties. The two of them put out seven issues of the journal, and without her help, Bashevis soon gave up on the idea.

It is not as though Kadya was professionally unsuited to be an editor. On the contrary; as we will see later, she was supremely suited for editorial work. But the timing was not right. The pain of waiting to hear of the fate of her brother and friends caught up by the Nazis, and the pain of her helplessness, drove her to creative work, not to nurturing work. It would be years before she resumed editorial work again.

It would seem that the role of editor, a coaxer and an advisor, suited Kadya far more than it suited Bashevis. That may be why Bashevis himself did not ever become an editor. Alternatively, it may be that the role of editor was not financially remunerative. Bashevis could not afford to take on many hours of unpaid work; he had no sugar Mommy. But Kadya had a Sugar Daddy in Simche. Once he was their source of steady income, she was free to take on the creatively rewarding, but financially profitless, work of literary editor.

Kadya's First Book Published in the US

Kadya's fourth published book, written after she had settled in New York, dealt with life in Poland and the US, and was entitled "*In Land fun Mayn Gebeyn*", In the Land of My Bones/Skeleton". Published in 1937, that book showed that Europe in general, and Russia/Poland in particular, may have been where Kadya was born and where she thrived, but once her Jewish home base was under the siege of Anti-Semites, the land itself was merely where her physical frame had taken shape. It was by no means a longed-for homeland. Unlike the earlier books of poetry that she published in Warsaw, *In Land Fun Mayn Gebeyn* has no strident calls to social action. It goes as far back in time as the plight of the Jews in Germany with the rise of Nazism, and as far forward as Kadya's arrival in the US and the party her uncle made for her upon her arrival.

In a poem entitled "*A Mayse She-hoyo*" "A True Story", the narrator relives an incident that (she says) occurred in Germany when the Nazis had already taken over. The narrator sits next to a Jewish man on a train and strikes up a conversation. The Jewish passenger tells the narrator about a possible project he will undertake:

"*She-ken efsher makhn mir a krom*
(Fun rozhinkes mit mandlen)
Efsher makhn mir a krom
Bizn nekstn pogrom?"

And so perhaps we'll make a store/(With raisins and almonds)/ Perhaps we'll make a store/ Until the next pogrom"

The author puts the phrase "raisins and almonds" in parentheses for a reason. Just like the phrase "almonds and raisins", when used in a well-known Yiddish lullaby to lull young children to sleep, is a stand-in for an impossible but longed-for reality, so this passenger is pretending he can proceed with business as usual in the new reality of Nazi Germany. But in fact, the passenger is not as unaware as he might seem. After the narrator continues to pester him, he breaks his silence and says:

Ikh ken fun der khad-gadye a shir
Dem shir mitn nekomedikn khalef".

"From the *khad-gadye* I know a song/ The song with the vengeful knife."[51]

Chapter Four: The US – (1935-1950)

The passenger knows the song "*Khad Gadye*" from the Passover seder. In that song, a father buys a goat which is eaten by a cat. The cat in turn is bitten by a dog, and from there on, each animal or thing is eaten by or harmed by another animal or thing. The cycle continues until God Himself intervenes and slaughters the Angel of Death. Like all the animals and objects of the song, the passenger on the train is in the grip of a reality over which he has no control. Only God Himself can save him. And that, it appears, will happen only after the Angel of Death is vanquished.

Kadya got a lot of mileage from this popular Passover song.[52] Earlier, obviously referring to the structure of the song, she used it as a stand-in for a senseless round of repeated actions that seem to have no purpose. Later on she will use it again to speak of an action done over and over again. Here she is interested not in the structure of the song, but in its message. It is a grim message indeed: there is no escape from death unless God Himself will intervene.

In Poland, Kadya supported a revolt of the people. In this book, published in the US, not only is there no call for an uprising of the people, there are, instead, the beginnings of doubt, doubt about the ideological truths she had so deeply held while she was in Warsaw:

"And I ask myself:

The essence of the mistakes– is this by chance or does it always happen?

I ask myself:

Which is truer–

The fist of Cain

Or Jacob's ladder?[53]

It is interesting that she dedicated this poem to her then-absent husband, Simche. While he was clearly a Communist in Europe, she had maintained a skeptical approval of Communism. It is as though she were now asking him in absentia to reconsider, as she herself was re-considering, the inevitability of the Socialist revolution on one hand, and the viability of Jewish tradition, on the other hand.

Another poem in this collection entitled "*In Likui Khame*", In the Solar Eclipse, speaks of "the sad land of the solar eclipse", but does not mention the Soviet Union by name. There was no need then to mention the Soviet Union by name. It was common knowledge that the state emblem of the Soviet Union was "a sickle and a hammer on a globe **depicted in the rays of the sun** and framed by ears of wheat".[54] These were years when there was no communication between Soviet Jews and Jews in the rest of the world. If the Soviet Union was a land of the rising sun, then the Jewish blackout was a solar eclipse. There is every reason, then, to assume that all Kadya's readers knew that in this poem she was referring to the plight of her fellow Jews in the Soviet Union.

It is fascinating to note that a mere three years later, Arthur Koestler used the very same metaphor, an eclipse of the sun, when he wrote his searing criticism of Communism, and called it "Darkness at Noon". Neither author named the Soviet Union outright, but by the late 1930s, both had come to realize that the strongly ideological men who fought for Communism, were often tried for treason by the very authorities they themselves had supported.[55]

The major part of *In Land fun Mayn Gebeyn* is a clear-sighted backward glance at the types of men and women Kadya knew in the home that no longer was her home. Writing about the book and her former home in 1937, she told Ida Maze that Lithuania/Poland was her "unhappy home" and she did not yet feel like an American.[56]

At this point in her life, already 43 years old, Kadya could afford to look back and think of her past as her inheritance. In a poem entitled just that, *Yerushe*, Inheritance, she characterizes herself mockingly as "half-comic, half pauper":

"*A himel iz do– zaynen shtern faran,*
Un kih– halb a badkhn
Un halb oreman."

Chapter Four: The US – (1935-1950)

There is a sky– and there are stars/And I'm – half comic/And half pauper. She goes on to say:

"Ver veys tsi a shvindler, ver veys– a po'et
In antliyene shikh–
In farblondzhiter bet."

Could be a swindler, could be– a poet/In borrowed shoes–/In a wandering bed.

As we saw earlier, Kadya was painfully aware that her European wardrobe did not measure up to expected standards in the U.S. It may well be that she was borrowing shoes from others even two years after her arrival. Most probably she had learned that in the US a well-dressed woman was expected to wear shoes that matched her outfit. Since this is not something she had done in Warsaw, it is quite probable she could not bring herself to do so this early in her acculturation to life in the US. As a result, when she needed to make a public appearance and appear "well-dressed", it is quite likely that she borrowed shoes. What is certain is that she wandered from one apartment to the other until Simche joined her in the US.

It is doubtful whether Kadya ever felt at home anywhere in the world. She was never fully at home once she emigrated from Europe. Nevertheless, she was fully aware that only in the US was she free as a Jew. In the book *In Land fun Mayn Gebeyn*, in a poem entitled "In Der Fremd", In An Alien Place, she gives voice to her ambivalence. The poem may call the US "an alien place", but she says:

"Un s'hot zikh mir gevolt
Aniderfaln oyf di kni
Un zogn tsu der zun
Vi its tsu berg–
Mode ani."[57]

And I felt like/falling to my knees/and saying to the sun/As now to the hills/*Mode Ani* [Hebrew for "I Thank-you, God"- ZKN]

"*Mode ani*", I Thank you, oh God, is the first prayer a Jew is supposed to say in the morning. It is said upon awakening, and it indicates the individual's awareness that her/his life, always in God's hands, is pulsing, and waiting the start of a new day. For Kadya, life in the US may have seemed alien, but she was also acutely aware that the US was her refuge. Without it, her fate would have been no different from that of her friends and family still trapped in Warsaw.

As was true for her book of poems *Freydke*, the last poem in this collection appears to be out of place. It seems to have walked away from her previous book and lodged itself, unpremeditated, in this book. One of the fully-fleshed characters in the book *Fredyke* was a traveling woman-Communist named Sheyndl Kanarey. We get to see her one final time on the last page of *In Land fun Mayn Gebeyn*: there we see what might have happened to her had she lived in a carefree era.

Simche's Arrival in the U.S.

Simche arrived safely in New York, in July, 1938, and that brought with it new issues. For one thing, now that she had her own apartment, Kadya had house-hold duties to perform. For another, she needed to attend to her husband as well as to herself. Here's how she explained things to Ida:

"Now that I have an apartment, I need to clean and dust and cook and make the beds. I need to quarrel a bit with my husband, and make-up a bit – and then, there you have it; the day is over."[58]

By the end of 1938 Kadya was able to report to Ida that Simche was already working as a part-time typesetter.[59] This must have been a relief to Kadya who had worked so very hard for the three years the two were separated. By 1940, a mere two years after he arrived, Simche was the bread-winner for the two of them. We know this from a letter Kadya wrote Ida in 1940, telling her that Simche made a living, but she did not.[60] Three years later, in 1943, she told Ida outright that Simche supported her.[61]

Perhaps because Kadya found an understanding soul in Ida, perhaps because Ida lived far enough away so that confidences could be easily kept, Kadya found herself confiding in Ida and revealing to her changes of heart that she did not reveal to others. In a letter written in December of 1939, she told Ida about her disillusionment with Socialism. She had once "believed in the working man", she said. But she no longer did. That belief had dissipated. What's more, as she saw it, her generation was "shattered". Was it, perhaps, time to consider lighting (Sabbath) candles, as her mother had done? She doesn't say that she has decided to do so, only that she might reconsider her position on tradition. Then she asks Ida: "Do you also think of lighting candles?"[62]

When Simche arrived in the US in July of 1938, he brought with him the first volume of a multi-volume magnum opus he had been working on in Europe. Kadya tell us that this was entitled "Chapters of Jewish History", and that it encompassed the social and national changes that overtook the Jews in Poland and Russia between 1897 and 1903.[63] What she does not tell us, but we know from their correspondence, was that this book viewed Jewish history in a Marxist light. The trajectory of history was supposed to be "forward" from primitive religion and tradition, through liberating Socialism, up to secular nationalism. Kadya does tell us that this volume of the magnum opus was published in 1941, and she made a small party to celebrate the book's publication.[64]

Simche was in the midst of writing this magnum opus in the early 1930s, when the Nazis came to power in Germany. His book, "The Role of the Russian Czar in the Formation of Jewish Nationalism"[65], was not finished when he had to flee Poland for the US. On this issue, Simche was what is known in Yiddish as a *"shlimazel"*: a man defeated by fate. In the US, Jews did were not interested in Jewish nationalism, and the Czar was passé. It was Communism that concerned Americans. In Russia, Jews considered themselves, and were considered by others, a nation. There one was either a Jew, or a Russian; there were no "Russian Jews". In the US, on the other hand, a Jew could be an "American Jew". In fact, there was nothing that Jews in America wanted more than to be integrated into the general public and become "American Jews". To make matters worse, Simche envisioned a non-assimilationist Jewish nationalism that would be founded by and dependent on a Jewish form of Socialism. Most American Jews were quite happy to assimilate. But Socialism, while appealing to a small minority, was anathema to most Americans, and to a great majority of American Jews.

Kadya's First Published Play

In 1938, the same year that Simche arrived in New York, Kadya published a play in Warsaw. Entitled "*Ale Fenster Tsu Der Zun*", All Windows Facing the Sun, it is a play intended for children, and written in rhymed verse. The verse and plot are charming. Its language is Kadya at her most lilting, but its plot displays Kadya at her most didactic moment.

The single mother of the story is hard-working, and the plot's true hero, an architect and a dreamer, wants to build a tower where "All windows face the sun". What's more, in this tower, all doors are kept unlocked and all rooms are gardens. Clearly with this tower, we are in Utopia.

The play that begins on a light note, gets bogged down in propaganda. Towards its end, the troubles of the Jewish proletariat are given voice, and a land is found where this tower can be built. Where, in fact, can this dreamer-architect get his tower built? The country is not given a name, but we are told that it is the land where "all the windows face the sun". We can suppose at this point that the land not mentioned by name was the Soviet Communist Utopia.

It is probably not surprising that Kadya never mentions the publication of this play. She undoubtedly prepared it for publication while she was still in Warsaw. By the time it was in fact published there, she had been in the US for three years. In those three years, as we have seen, she had had begun to reconsider her views on the Communist paradise.

Rescue Attempts

The Nazis invaded Poland approximately a year after Simche's arrival in the States, in September 1939. No sooner, it seemed, had the Molodowsky family managed (through a concerted effort) to rescue Simche, than they were confronted with the need to rescue Kadya's brother, Leibl, and his wife, Lola, stuck in Warsaw. In December of 1939, Leibl and his wife had a baby daughter, Ilana. By 1940, then, there were three souls that needed rescue. These were tense years for the entire family.

Ever since the pre-World War I days, when Kadya roamed northern Europe just a bit ahead of the moving front in a wild attempt to save her brother from army duty, Kadya felt personally responsible for her brother's safety. Now that he was trapped in Poland trying to shield his wife and baby daughter, she felt yet more obligated to try to rescue him. So concerned was she to do something, anything, that might work, that she even turned to her former nemesis: A(ha)ron Zeitlin. The two had been open enemies in Warsaw. But now with the Nazis as the open enemies of all the world's Jews, these petty rivalries seemed to fade, though they did not altogether disappear.

Zeitilin was in New York, where he had been invited to oversee a production of a play, when the Nazis invaded Poland. His wife and son in Warsaw were trapped, just like Kadya's brother Leibl and his family. Without a permanent US visa, Zeitlin was unable to stay in New York. Once his visa expired, he went to Cuba, as many other Jewish refugees of that time did. News of the fate of Yiddish writers traveled, and

Kadya knew of Zeitlin's stay in Cuba. Knowing that he, too, must be trying to get his family to Cuba, she wrote and asked him what it took to get Jews from Poland to Cuba.

Whereas just about everyone addressed Kadya as "Kadya", or even "Kadyele", when A(ha)ron Zeitlin wrote to Kadya, he addressed her as *"khoshuve kolegn"*[66], a stiff, rather formal, address that is best translated as "Dear (literally, important) Colleague". Clearly, neither he nor she had forgotten the old rivalry. But he did give her the information she asked for. One needed a $500 deposit in cash for each person. But that was just for starters. In addition, one needed approximately $2,000 for the proper documents. And to top it all, one needed ship's tickets. The sums were astronomical; Kadya just didn't have that kind of money. Nor did she feel she could ask her sisters to come up with those sums.

Zeitlin's response is among Kadya's papers, but we see no mention of it in any of the letters she wrote her father or her sister. Apparently, she kept it as a sort of proof to herself that she did investigate the possibility, even if there was never the slightest chance that she could round up sums of that sort.

In the Makhon Lavon archive in Israel there are twenty-three postcards, sent by Aizik to Kadya during the war years. There are, in addition three letters, one in Yiddish and one in Hebrew. One can imagine that other cards were written during those years. But these are the ones that Kadya chose to preserve. Often these cards contain what seems now to be trivial information, best left for a quick phone call. But phone calls, at the time, were expensive and were intended to convey crucial information that could not bear delay. Letters were reserved for more reflective musing, as well as for conveying information that was not of immediate import. It was the role of postcards, then, to convey information of the middle time-span: information that was of import, but in the not-so-immediate future. For example, Aizik will sometimes devote most of a postcard to telling Kadya and Simche that he plans to visit them the following week. Alternatively, he occasionally devotes most of a card to inviting them to visit him the following week. However, because these years were war years, it is rare that a postcard contains only timely information. Indeed, one imagines that Kadya looked over these cards and chose them for the non-timely, value-added information they contain.

Many of these post-cards are about their efforts to save Leibl and his family. In the years 1940-1941 American Jews were well aware of the plight of the family and friends they had left behind in Poland. Letters came begging for help, from nearby relatives, from distant relatives, from friends who were desperate.[67] And those living in the US did their best to help. From Aizik's letters to Kadya it is clear that packages were sent and delivered. Naturally, their first thoughts were of Leibl and his wife, Lola.

In a card postmarked April 19, 1940, Aizik suggests that Kadya visit him in Philadelphia so that, among other things, they can go to the Red Cross together:

"It would be a sensible thing for you to come to us on Sunday. First of all, you'd be able to attend to making/arranging the papers on Monday.[68] Secondly, we'd be able to visit the Red Cross. Perhaps they'd be able to find a way to somehow bring food to Lola."

In that letter Aizik goes on to speak of a trip to Washington:

"About [the trip to] Washington we'll consider it further. Perhaps you have a different understanding about Washington. Then you'll be able to go without me."

It's impossible to know exactly why the two of them were considering a trip to Washington. Perhaps it was to join a demonstration? Perhaps it was to see about the possibility of finding ways to bring Leibl to the US?

In a card postmarked October 22, 1941, Aizik speaks again of sending packages to Poland:

"When I noticed that my last package to Lola was sent the third of September, I shuddered. It'll soon be two months since I sent anything or wrote anything. I'm waiting till we see each other. I saw an announcement in the [Yiddish newspaper called] *"Der Tog"*/The Day that packages and money are still being sent from New York to Poland."

It appears from this correspondence that HIAS was in the habit of informing the American senders of packages that their packages were received. However, Aizik was not easily reassured. He compared the dates of the reception of the packages according to HIAS with the dates he sent out the packages, and the dates of the letters received from the family in Poland, and decided something was not right. Here is his comment:

"Through HIAS I received a notice from Lola that they are all well, and that they received 5 packages and another one from HIAS. So they say. But this notice tells me nothing, because the notice was sent from Lisbon on July 25th, and I heard about them [the packages] from Lola on September 11th, 7 weeks later."

For all his suspicions about what was in fact getting through and whether he was getting a truthful account of what was happening, Aizik makes it clear that he intends to keep on sending packages and he expects Kadya to do so as well. In this same card, he continues:

"Write me whether you sent out a package. It hurts me that all summer long I didn't send them any [packages]."

Much of the material in the postcards written in the years 1940 and 1941 deals with sending packages through HIAS or the Red Cross to Leibl's family. None of the postcards sent by Aizik to Kadya mention Leibl and his fate.
But the letters of this period most definitely do. In a letter dated April 7, 1940, (but postmarked April 8th, 1940), Aizik tells Kadya:

"There is here a letter from Leibl. It traveled nearly seven weeks getting here. The upshot of it is: 'For Leibl—' [Here Aizik was apparently quoting Leibl's Russian and in code it amounted to: As for Leibl, expect nothing. ZKN]. This is his private code. It is an indication that things are not (going) well for him. It's understandable that he misses his family [literally: his few souls- ZKN]."

This is Aizik's attempt to put a good spin on what his instinct tells him is not a good situation. He tries to comfort Kadya even as he tries to comfort himself.

Chapter Four: The US – (1935-1950)

More than a year later, in a letter dated September 9th, 1941, it is clear that Lola is permanently alone. Still Aizik does not (dare) speculate what might have happened to his son. In the letter to Kadya he speaks only of Lola. In this letter he tells Kadya he was thinking of not telling her about the card he got from Lola. But since she has already heard [of Leibl's probable "disappearance"] from others, he feels he can say something now:

"To tell the truth, I didn't want to send you Lola's [post]card. I didn't want to aggravate you when in any case you cannot help her. But because of the letter she sent you about her [own] family, I'm sending it to you. My heart calls out (literally: complains) in me for her fate. She [Lola] is lonely/alone. Before *shabes*, [on] Wednesday, I sent her a package for $16."

It seems that with all this, Aizik did not allow himself to imagine that his son had been murdered. Together with these two letters, dated 1940 and 1941, there is a third, undated letter, written not in Yiddish, but in Hebrew. Here it would seem that Aizik has no certain knowledge that his son has been murdered, but he does know that that is most probably what happened. What follows is a transcription of that letter:

Sunday, at the end of the Holiday, Philadelphia

My Dear Children Kadya and Simche,

To tell you the truth my head is empty. I have not a smidgen of anything to report. As for the envelope- the inside is empty and my time is a void. I have no work or anything of interest to torture myself with. The paper and my pencil are empty as well. I am filling up this immense void with an empty letter. If you think logically, it's hard to understand: how can a void be filled by a void? But if you look at the way the world continues to go on, you see amazing things everywhere. For example, when one goes out to pray in the synagogue in the morning, you see the sports field already filled with young boys wearing sports clothes and engaged in frantic running and throwing the ball from one to another. They turn and run as [swift as] deer from one part of the field to another; they call-out and yell, jump up at each other. Isn't this a case of the emptiness of the young boys filling the void of time in the empty field? Then one goes to the synagogue. Before the prayer begins, the few assembled [men there] are arguing loudly and vehemently: who among the two- Terah or Esau is important in the Other World. After all, Terah is the father of Abraham, he who discovered [the One] God, while Esau is the son of Isaac, he who was the pure [willing/sacrificial] lamb, so which is to be preferred? The debate was vociferous and reached upwards till [it came to] the two sinful kings of Judah- Ahaz and Menashe: which of these two did the righteous king Hezekiah defend- his father or his son? This issue was not decided definitively because in the meantime the beadle banged his gavel and called out: "Gentlemen, the time has come for the morning prayers."[69] And what do you say to that? Is that not a void in the empty space of the synagogue?

Peace, my children. Your father, Aizik. Don't forget to send my regards to those who live in your house.[70]

Much can be said about the reported/purported conversation that took place in the synagogue. Did it really take place? Perhaps it did. Both conversations are about Biblical fathers and sons, a subject that was paramount in Aizik's mind at the time. In both cases, there are issues of well known, indeed iconic, evil men: Terah, who, according to the rabbis, was an idol worshipper, and Esau, whom the rabbis view as the symbol of cruelty, in the first example, and Kings Ahaz and Menashe, well known idol worshippers, in the second example. Opposed to them are the righteous men, Abraham and his son, Isaac, in the first example, and King Hezekiah, in the second example. Is Aizik wondering whose behavior can be defended? He doesn't say. Is he choosing Isaac not only because of the coincidence with his own name, but because this son was "sacrificed"? Does he see this as a reflection of what has gone on in his own world? Most crucially, is he thinking of his own son, the one who might be sacrificed? About this, too, he says nothing outright; he speaks in riddles. But he does tell us that he finds no emotional comfort: all is a void.

There is no mention of death here. There could not be. At his stage, few Jews knew the horrific details of the murder of their loved ones. But some awareness had clearly filtered down. For those whose loved ones had been deported, there was only silence, an ache and a sense of futility. Aizik's cry says it all: there is a void that cannot be filled.

Although Kadya left most of the letters and documents pertaining to Leibl's attempted rescue in an Israeli archive, she chose one of those documents to take back with her to New York when she returned. It is a note from Leibl's wife, Lola, confirming the receipt of the family's cards, and saying "emigration is possible". It was dated July 24, 1940. Perhaps Kadya saved that note as a reminder to herself that she truly did what she could. r perhaps she saved that note because it spoke of a time when hope seemed possible. Along with the Red Cross note that officially documents the receipt of what the family sent, there is an official form that lists the recipients and their ages: Leibl was 47[71], Lola was 44 and their daughter Ilana was eight months.

The tense years of uncertainty over the fate of Leibl and his family had a paradoxical effect on Kadya. On the one hand, she was distraught and physically a wreck. She tore at her fingers and needed an operation.[72] This can understandably be seen as survivor's guilt.[73]

On the other hand, this was a time of frenzied creativity. She wrote the poems that later became the collection entitled *U*; Only King David Remained; she was writing the novella that would eventually be entitled *Fun Lublin Biz Nyu York: Der Togbukh fun Rivke Zylberg*, From Lublin to New York: The Diary of Rivke Zylberg. And yet, she told Ida, it did not seem like anyone would ever read her poetry. Nor would anyone produce her plays.[74] A sense of futility overtook her. As she put it: "Who needs these things now?"[75]

Aizik and Kadya

Most of what we know about Aizik's relationship to Kadya comes from the letters that the two exchanged during World War II, while Kadya was in New York and Aizik was living with Dora in Philadelphia. Indeed, only when we understand how deeply their lives inter-twined, can we understand Kadya's behavior after Aizik's death.

In the archival correspondence, Aizik proves himself not just a loving father, but also a keen observer of social norms, a confidante of and advisor to his daughter, a man sensitive to language nuances and possessed of a sense of humor, and a deeply religious man who was able to take the most severe of blows and not succumb to rancor or melancholy. Only when we see Aizik unburden himself in his letters to Kadya, do we see how very close the two were.

When Aizik lived in Philadelphia with his daughter, Dora, Dora's son, Ben, or as Aizik called him "Bune", served in the US army. During these years, Kadya and her husband Simche lived in three different places, all in New York.[76] Although all the postcards are formally addressed to Kadya, Simche, is (nearly) always included in the salutation.

In fact, the first postcard in this collection, although addressed to Kadya, begins with the opening: "Simche!", and goes on to ask where Kadya is. It is signed: *"dayn foter"*, your father. Clearly, for Aizik, Simche was a son. While it is true that there never can be a replacement for a lost child, it must have been some comfort to Aizik to imagine that in Simche he had found a son. Simche, for his part, lost his parents in the Holocaust. There is every reason to believe, then, that the relationship proved comforting for Simche as well.

Although Aizik lived with Dora, he seems to have had a "special relationship" with Kadya. Unlike her sisters, and like her father, Kadya was an intellectual: ideas excited her. And like her father, and unlike her sisters, Kadya was not an acculturated

Jew. Kadya spent more of her adulthood in Europe than her sisters did, and she received more of a Jewish education than they did.[77] As a result, she, like Aizik, felt she was an "outsider looking in" on the customs of the assimilated American Jews around them. That is exactly why Aizik felt only she would understand how he felt when the tumult and busy-ness of house-cleaning reminded him of life in Europe.

In a card postmarked January 12, 1942, Aizik describes a scene for Kadya:

"They're about to build a parlor...and all around there's washing and banging and cleaning, as it once was in our place before *Peysakh*/Passover."

There is another letter in this folder, one that has no year (and may well have been written after the war)[78] but is attributed to "*erev peysekh*, two hours before the holiday". It shares the same slightly mocking, outsider, tone of the card mentioned above. But this time it truly is *Peysekh* time. What bothers Aizik this time is not the hustle and bustle before the holiday; that is to be expected. What bothers him, he says, is that the household members are so pre-occupied with their industriousness that they have no time for each other:

"If I tell you one word: "busy", you'll already know everything. In the store, it's busy; in the kitchen it's busy. The black woman is *kashering* the sinks for *Peysekh*. Dora is everywhere– in the store, in the kitchen, in the market, at the butcher. She has to prepare the seder for the entire "camp". Edith..., Minka... For Ben, poor thing..., our Lina...So all are busy, each with his own thing, and somehow no one has time to see the others."

Kadya was born and grew up in (what the Jews called) "Berze"[79], the *shtetl* that Aizik lived for all of his life in Europe. That is the town that both of them knew as "home" in Europe. Aizik and Kadya knew this town as a slow-paced small town, barely touched by modernity, whose non-Jews were not especially industrious. As Max Weber noted in his book "The Protestant Ethic and the Spirit of Capitalism",[80] in the modernized, capitalistic West (and Philadelphia of the 1940s was most certainly a part of the capitalistic West), there was an energy and an industriousness unknown in the non-Protestant Russian Empire. How much of this industriousness can in fact be attributed to Protestantism is not at issue here. There is no question that in the above-mentioned letter Aizik pointed to something very real: the industriousness of the Jews in twentieth century Philadelphia is something that neither he nor Kadya ever saw "back home" in Europe.

Something else happened to American Jews: the communal emphasis and social cohesion that was so prevalent in Europe began to give way. In its place there was an emphasis on individualism unknown to Jews who were socialized in Europe. This was, as Emile Durkheim would have it, another consequence of modernity and the capitalistic world.[81] There is no knowing whether Aizik read either Weber or Durkheim, though given his intellectual appetite, it would not be surprising if he had. The point here is that, keen observer that he is, he is aware of these changes. He has known the Jews of Europe and he feels the difference between them and the Jews, his very own family, in the US. For his two Americanized daughters, Europe is a distant memory. They cannot be expected to see or feel this difference. But Kadya, a relatively new immigrant herself, very definitely understood what Aizik meant.

In a card post-marked May 1st 1940, Aizik responded to a suggestion that Kadya had made. Apparently, Kadya, who was then teaching, told him that she was thinking of finding new work. While Aizik did not dismiss her suggestion out of hand, he did caution her:

"In general, one should think cautiously about looking for new work."

Aizik points out two things. For one, if she stays in her present work:

"In time it can develop into a fine well-spring. One person tells another [person]."

Secondly, he goes on to suggest, ever so gently, that she needs to assert herself and work a bit more on her PR:

"And perhaps you have to [literally: one has to] work a bit more at broadcasting this." [herself and her work].

Then he makes his final suggestion:

"And so it may not be worthwhile to look for something new. Give it thought."

Kadya apparently heeded her father's advice; she did not give up the job she had. Six years later, when the war was over and Kadya was working on more than one project at a time, Aizik had the very opposite advice. This time he felt she was working too hard:

"You are tired, [and] have a cold. Wouldn't it then be a sensible thing to take more care, to lower your ambitions and live more leisurely?"

Here is a parent finely tuned to his daughter's needs. When she doesn't assert herself enough, he suggests that she put herself forward a bit more. But when, in his opinion, she is overworked, he watches and worries and suggests she cut back on her efforts and relax a bit more. Aizik also made a suggestion that changed his daughter's modus operandi. From the letters that Kadya sent Simche when he was still in Europe, it is clear that finding a printer/publisher for her work was a great burden. There were politicized publishers of Yiddish books like CYCO, associated with Communist/Socialist causes. Kadya wanted nothing to do with them.[82] Stein publishing company, located in Chicago, undertook to publish her work in the late 1930s, but they worked at a snail's pace. Punning on the name of the publisher's printing press – Stein (English, stone)–, she told Simche in one of her letters, her work lay in their place "like a stone" and did not move on to the printed page for far too long. In the early 1940s, Simche was in the US, working as a type-setter in a printing house. So Aizik suggested that Kadya take matters into her own hands and publish/print her work on her own. Clearly, this meant having Simche do the type-setting, almost certainly after his normal work hours.[83] Most probably, Kadya had to pay something for the electricity and the use of the machines, but when/if she went this route, the production of her work was in her own hands. Here is Aizik's suggestion:

"Perhaps it would be a good idea [literally: it would be a plan] to do this yourself, not have others do it. There's a printer who learns [Torah] with me. He'll tell me clearly how this is done."

Aizik's suggestion had a two-fold advantage: it put Kadya (along with Simche) in control of the final product, and it allowed her to set her own pace. Kadya eventually did as her father suggested, and she named "her own" printing press "*Papirene Brikn*", the Paper Bridges Press.[84] From other letters in the archive, it is clear that Kadya went as far as dreaming of setting up a printing press that was truly her own. But that proved too ambitious a project. Aizik's plan, on the other hand, was doable.

Aizik had a fine sense of humor and a "good ear" for language. He uses a brand of Yiddish intermixed with English when speaking of the Americanized family that surrounds him. This sort of "mixed language" arises naturally when an immigrant's native language is in contact with a more dominant, majority language. To Aizik this "mixed language" must have sounded strange indeed. Yet, he does not openly criticize the speakers or their language. Instead, he simply echoes what he hears. He knows full well that when Kadya reads what he writes, she may well cringe. But then, she may well smile. And that may have been his intention. In a card post-marked January 12, 1942, he tells Kadya:

"We returned from Florida on Tuesday *hepi* [a Yiddishized spelling of the English word "happy"] and happy [this time the word used is the usual Yiddish word "*freylekh*"]…the only-son [here he uses the Hebrew expression "*ben-yokhidl*"] had a good time [a Yiddishized spelling of the English expression].

Did Aizik's daughter, Dora, ever say "*hepi un freylekh*"? We'll never know. But if she didn't, she could have. And that is why Aizik, apparently a natural mimic, wrote this way.

As it happens, Dora's son was named "Ben", so the expression "*ben-yokhidl*" is a double play on words. "Ben" means both "son" and the person known as "Ben", and "*yokhidl*" means "only" and "unusual". And in the eyes of all parents, their son is always unusual.

Later on in the same postcard, Aizik makes a second bilingual pun. We should keep in mind that Aizik was a relatively older man when he immigrated to the US. This command of both languages is quite an achievement for an older man. Speaking of his daughter, Dora, he says:

"No matter what she does or says, one has always to answer with "*omnom keyn*": [Hebrew for "it is indeed so"] OK."

Here Aizik is suggesting that the English "O" of the expression "OK" stands for the Hebrew word "*omnom*", and the English "K" of the expression "OK" stands for the Hebrew word "*keyn*".

It was Aizik's habit to blend Hebrew into his Yiddish. He was equally comfortable with both languages, and skillful in weaving them together. In a card post-marked July 8, 1944, he tells Kadya:

"At our place [in Yiddish] all are properly where they should be and all are up to their usual activities [in Hebrew]."[85]

It is interesting to see how he describes these usual activities. About his son-in-law, Izzy, he says:

"Izzy often takes-in/grabs a **[game of]** pinochle."

In the expression Aizik uses, the words "game of" are missing. What's more, the word Aizik uses is "*khapt*", which means "grabs"/holds onto". izik has a good ear for language. If he says "*khapt a pinakl*, literally, "grabs a pinochle", that is probably the way American Jews of the 1940s spoke.

It is worth noting just when Aizik uses an English expression, and when he uses a Hebrew expression. His choice of one over the other is not random. When he wants to convey an issue that stems from the American part of his experience, he chooses English. This explains why, in a card post-marked April 3, 1946, he says about his relationship with his daughter, Dora:

"Dora and I have long forgotten our troubles."

Here instead of using the natural Yiddish word "*tsores*" for troubles, Aizik transliterates the English word, and writes "*trobls*" in Yiddish. Since the issue arose with his Americanized daughter, Aizik speaks of it in an Anglicized Yiddish.

Similarly, in this same card, when speaking of the post-war, revitalized pace of Dora's business, Aizik says:

"They are working at full strength and with '*entuziazm*' [a Yiddishized English word], as is the custom of the country." [In the original, *ke-minhag ha-medineh*, a Hebrew expression].

The (Yiddishized) English word "enthusiasm" is chosen because the driving force for this enthusiasm is that Protestant Ethic mentioned earlier. On the other hand, the expression "*ke-minhag ha-medine*", as is the custom of the state, is put into Hebrew. Here Aizik is the outsider looking in, and Hebrew is the outsider language in the US.

The letters mentioned above show that Aizik was free with advice when he felt it was called for. But in these letters, there is also a longing simply for Kadya's (and Simche's) company. In a card post-marked July 6th 1942, and addressed to "*mayne kinderlekh*", my dear-children, Aizk tells "his children" that he has forgotten what he wanted to say. But then he says "*efsher iz a plan...*", perhaps it's a good idea... By now we know that when he says this, he is suggesting something in earnest. His suggestion is that Kadya and Simche should come to him for a vacation. Although there is no way of knowing whether Kadya and Simche took him up on his suggestion, it is quite clear that this is the essence of his communication: he misses them and wants their company.

Two years later, in 1944, he invited them to visit him, this time, suggesting ever-so-gently, that they may have forgotten when *rosh ha-shana*, the Jewish New Year, is to be celebrated: "My Children! The first question is: do you know that this coming Sunday evening is the Jewish New Year- *Rosh Ha-shone*? The second question is: do you know that you can come to us even without an invitation? The third question:

I've forgotten it. But answer us immediately about the first two questions so we can know how much fish to buy."

It's quite clear from this correspondence that Aizik remained a religious Jew all his life. As for Kadya and Simche, there is no knowing how much of this traditional observance remained operative for them. They almost certainly celebrated the Jewish New Year; all of New York City knows when this holiday occurs. Having lived only in Philadelphia, Aizik did not know that. Not wanting to ask them outright about their observance, Aizik "jokes with them" and "reminds" them about the upcoming holiday.

There is another issue here. From what Aizik does say, it is apparent that Kadya and Simche have not been openly invited to spend the holiday in Philadelphia with the extended family. Rather than belabor that point and open wounds that are better left alone, Aizik simply tells them they do not need an invitation.

In this letter Aizik plays "dumb like a fox": he is (perhaps) losing his memory, so his veiled invitation (which is not an open invitation) takes on greater urgency. His children need not feel sorry for him. All they need do is help him put in the proper order of fish for the Holiday.

But Aizik does not always speak obliquely. At times, he simply speaks from the heart. This is what happens when he says:

"By now I long a great deal. I can't wait to see you."[86]

One cannot help noting that no cards were preserved from 1943. This is almost certainly not an accident. This was the year when Kadya co-edited *Svive* with Bashevis. It was also the year that Kadya's diary was transcribed for radio and serialized on the Yiddish radio station WEVD. She told Ida that it was going well.[87] This material underwent quite a few changes when it was adapted for the stage, so it is entirely plausible that changes were made for the radio medium as well. Unfortunately, virtually all of the recorded material connected to Yiddish radio has been lost. It would have been fascinating to see where the station breaks were made and how the chapters were divided live on radio.

That radio adaptation may have been going well, but it is quite clear that whatever it paid, was not enough to support Kadya and Simche. At the end of 1943, Kadya again told her friend Ida: "Simche is supporting me"[88].

It is possible that Kadya wrote only occasionally to Aizik that year, and taking his cue from her, he, too, was mostly silent. It has often been said that the battle of Stalingrad that ended in 1943 was the "turning point" of World War II.[89] This must have been a nerve-racking year for those Jews like Aizik and Kadya, whose loved ones were caught up in war-torn Europe. Till 1943, they could only watch helplessly as events in Europe unfolded and the world they knew was being wiped out. But in 1943, the Germans seemed vulnerable for the first time. While this year brought a glimmer of hope for the Allies, it did not bring any real relief for the Jews. It was not till mid-1944, with the successful Allied invasion of Normandy, that the Jews could finally bring themselves to imagine that some Jews might come out of Nazi-controlled Europe alive and well. Interestingly, all the postcards that pre-date 1944 say on their address side: "Buy US Savings Bonds, Ask Your Postmaster". But from 1944 onwards, we do not find this stamped onto the back-side of the postcards. And 1944 does seem a turning point in the correspondence between Kadya and Aizik.

By 1944 it was quite clear that there was no longer any possibility of helping out friends and/or family in Poland. Nevertheless, in a card postmarked July 8, 1944 we find Aizik mentioning, that Kadya's sister, Dora, was working (essentially, volunteering) for what he calls the "Russian Relief". The family knew that Leibl and his wife and daughter had escaped Warsaw and taken refuge in Bialystok,[90] a city that was then officially part of (Communist) Russia. This may well have been the trigger for Dora's volunteering at the Russian Relief. To be fair, though, even if Dora did not find her brother, by helping out at the Russian Relief, she was sending much-needed food and clothes to other starving and needy Russians/Jews.

Here is a description of "The Russian War Relief Fund" as it is presented by the (Internet site known as) The Virtual Jewish Library:

"In February 1943, the [Anti-Fascist] Committee met in plenary session, at which Mikhoels delivered a shocking report of the fate of Jews in areas liberated by the Red Army. He also gave details on the Jewish role in the struggle against the Nazis. Ehrenburg denounced the wave of Anti-Semitism then spreading through the country, whose slogan was that "one does not see Jews at the front," and urged that all circles of the Soviet public be supplied with information on the participation of Jews in the battles against the Germans. In the second half of 1943, Mikhoels and the poet Itzik Fefer were sent by the Committee on a propaganda tour to the U.S., Canada, Mexico, and Great Britain and were enthusiastically received by almost all sections of the Jewish public. This visit was regarded as the first step in renewing the contact between Soviet Jews and world Jewry that had been severed since October 1917... The third meeting of "representatives of the Jewish people" in the Soviet Union took place in April 1944, including for the first time a representative of religious Jewry, Rabbi Solomon Schliefer of Moscow."[91]

Essentially, the emissaries of the Russian Relief fund were sent to the Jews in Allied countries as fund-raisers. More than money, though, Soviet Russia was in need of blankets, shoes and sweaters: material that would see them through the biting cold of the war-front. Jewish communities around the US rallied to the cry to help their brethren in Soviet Russia.

The Wikipedia article on the history of the "Russian War Relief" paints an entirely different picture. According to them, the organization known as "Russian War Relief" (also known as the Russian War Relief Fund, and The American Committee for Russian War Relief) "was an alleged Communist front group, c. 1944". Furthermore, "According to a 1943 FBI report, the group was "infiltrated with known Communists, Communist leaders, fellow travelers, and front organizations"[92] There is a grain, but only a teeny grain, of truth to this. There is no doubt that the Soviet government used the Soviet Jews whom they sent abroad as a propaganda tool.[93] However, it is certainly not true that the American Jews who joined/volunteered for the

Russian War Relief effort were themselves Communists. It is certain that neither Dora, nor any other of the Molodowsky family members, were Communists, or even "fellow travelers."[94] It is true that Jews in the US felt compelled to do what they could to help fellow Jews in Russia, even Communist Russia. And if, by joining the organization known as the Russian War Relief and bringing succor to fellow Jews, they were, at the same time also supporting citizens of the Soviet Union, they saw nothing wrong with that.

With this in mind, we can see that any Jew who volunteered for the Russian Relief in 1944, was accomplishing what (s)he saw as at least three worthy goals: 1) bringing sorely needed aid to fellow Jews; 2) helping to fight Anti-Semitism in the Soviet Union; and 3) helping to re-establish contact between world Jewry and Soviet Jewry.

As far as Dora was concerned, the Russian Relief volunteering stint was a fine, altruistic effort. As it turned out however, years later Kadya suffered an unexpected invasion of her privacy brought on by this "harmless" altruistic act.

The wartime food shortages that Americans suffered in WWII do not come in for much attention in history books. Quite possibly this is because the situation in the US was far better than it was in Europe. But there most certainly were food shortages. We become acutely aware of this when we read, in four separate letters[95], that Ida sent Kadya and her sister Dora packages of sugar more than once. In fact, Kadya reports that her father Aizik told all comers with a shy smile, that the packages were sent to him by "a lady"[96]. And Ida was thoughtful as well as generous: the packages came to Dora and the family in Philadelphia in time for the Jewish holiday of *Rosh Ha-shono*; Kadya took two packages home for herself and left two packages in Philadelphia for Dora and their father.[97]

The war in Europe ended in May 1945, and four of the five postcards that Aizik sent Kadya in 1945 deal with the arrival in the US of Aizik's discharged grand-son,

Bune/Ben, Dora's soldier-son. Here the delight is almost palpable. In a card postmarked August 20th 1945, Aizik writes:

"Peace on the world. Bune is coming. When? That I don't know. I'm about to become completely healthy."

In the second of these anticipatory cards postmarked October 23rd, Aizik tells Kadya that Bune was supposed to have arrived, but he did not. In fact, at that point no one knew where he was. In the third card, post-marked October 28th, the family has finally heard from Bune. He'd disembarked in Virginia and would arrive in Philadelphia, but again, no one knew exactly when. As Aizik put it:

"But he is coming any day. I have no idea whether I will sleep tonight. In our house there's a wild excitement. Lina and her husband are sitting here in our house."

And finally, on October 29th, Aizik writes:

"Listen carefully, children, he's arriving tomorrow. Tomorrow, Tuesday, that is."

At this point Aizik gives Kadya and Simche a detailed account of where Bune and his wife will be each day after their arrival. Every day of the week a different family member is having them over, and in each place a modest celebration is planned. And when each individual member has had a chance to host the couple, then the entire family will be gathering for, as Aizik puts it: "*a groyse padi*", a big party.

Kadya's Next Book of Poems

If Aizik was "about to become completely healthy" when the war was over, Kadya was about ready for the catharsis that became her fifth book of poems: *Der Melekh Dovid Aleyn Iz Geblibn*: Only King David Remained. She had been writing these poems all through the war years. Once the war was over, the book was published (1946).

Interestingly, this is the first time that Kadya, using the publishing "firm" known as "Paper Bridges", admitted that the material was arranged and type-set by her husband, Simche, and actually printed in a printing press known as "Greenwich Press". Despite the use of the printing press machines of Greenwich Press, the firm that prints the book is nevertheless named as "Paper Bridges", the shadowy, pseudo-firm that is Kadya's (and Simche's) alone.

The first poem in this book is perhaps Kadya's best-known post-WWII poem. Entitled *"El Khanun"*, "Merciful God", it is Kadya's full-throated cry of anguish, an anger-filled reckoning with the God of Israel. Before I quote it and explicate what I believe are its crucial parts, I must stop short at the title. The translation given above, "Merciful God", is the one used by Katherine Hellerstein, the Yiddish scholar and literary critic who has put out a dual, English-Yiddish book of Kadya's poems. I would not have chosen that translation.

In Exodus, chapter 34 verse 6, God tells Moses how to appeal to Him when there is a need for Divine mercy. Essentially, He gives Moses the "winning" formula. Called in Jewish sources "the thirteen attributes [of God]", this prayer lists God's individual attributes, each of which petitioning mortals need to mention in order to have their prayers answered. This list begins with the name of God, recited twice; then it goes on to the phrase: *"el rakhum ve-khanun..."*: God [who is] merciful and grace-granting...There is no need for the verb to be: in Hebrew there simply is no verb "to be" in the present tense. There is no doubt that the word *"rakhum"* has to be translated as "merciful"; after all, Yiddish has a Hebrew-derived word *"rakhmones"*, which is properly translated into English as "mercy". If the English word "merciful" is the proper translation of the Hebrew word *"rakhum"*, what, then, to make of the attribute that follows: the adjective: *"khanun"*? In Hebrew, as well as in Yiddish, when a person is noticed by others, (s)he is said to have *"khen"*, something that might be translated into English as "grace" or "charm". And when God grants this attribute to others, he is said to be *"khanun"*. Unfortunately for translators into English, there already is a word "full-of-grace", but the English word "graceful" simply will not do the job here; it does not have the needed connotation. Nor will "gracious" be an appropriate translation here. Under these circumstances, we are stuck with the ungainly translation of "Grace-Granting". For all that this is not an especially apt or euphonic choice, it is probably the best that can be offered.

There is no question that the poet's tone here is ironic, or even one of mockery. Ordinarily, Jews are noticed; they stand out willy-nilly. They have a unique language; they have a unique culture; they have a unique set of sacred texts; and they have a unique connection to their ancestral land. Kadya will be the first to admit that they stand out by choice. But it is also a truth known to all Jews that they stand out because God Himself has noticed them and chosen them as His own people. And here Kadya has a gripe. If, when God Himself chooses this people as His own, they necessarily have to be murdered, then she, for one, is willing to do without such notice/grace. When it seemed, as it did after the Holocaust, that God's notice, or grace, entailed the cruelest of mass murders, then that "grace" is simply unwanted. And that is the essence of this poem.[98] Here is the first stanza of "*El Khanun*", Grace-granting God:

"Grace-granting God,
Choose another people,
In the meantime.
We're tired of dying and death
We have no more prayers,
Choose another people
In the meantime,
We have no more blood
To serve as sacrifices.
Our home has become a desert.
There's too little earth for our graves,
There are not enough laments for us,

Not enough keening poems

In the ancient holy-books..."

This poem is dated 1945. The war may have been over, but the Jewish people were just beginning to come to terms with the enormity of its destruction. Kadya was never one to deny the uniqueness of the Jewish people, but at this point the price seemed altogether too high. And she did not hesitate to say so.

When contemplating the curse that this blessing had become, Kadya had two suggestions. One was that God choose some other nation as His favorite:

"Grace-granting God

Lift up your fiery eye-brows,

And see the nations of the world–

Give them your prophecy and your High Holy Days..."[99]

The second suggestion is one that already hints at her impending Zionist bent. Here she suggests that the Jewish proclivity for study/intellectualism is part of the "Jewish problem". Accordingly, the solution is to de-intellectualize Jewish life. Substitute the life of the field-worker for the life of the book learner, return to the earth and to the simple life, and the "Jewish problem" will disappear:

"Grace-granting God,

Give us the plain clothes

Of shepherds tending sheep,

Of smithies wielding a hammer

Of launderers, of furriers,

And simpler tasks.

And do us one more favor:

Grace-granting God,

Take away from us the Divine Presence of genius."[100]

Chapter Four: The US – (1935-1950)

Some of the poems in this collection, composed when WWII was relatively young, record the poet's worries and doubts about the war's outcome. *A Lid fun Mayn Heym*, A Poem of My Home, dated 1941, is such a poem. The last lines of the poem say all that needs to be said:

"Shvayg mayn harts,
Dem shvertstn tsveyfl– tor men nit dermonen mit a vort,
Efsher tsitert nokh a tsveygl,
Un a foygl iz geblibn dort."[101]

silent, my heart/ One must not mention the gravest doubt with a word/ Perhaps a twig still quivers/ And a bird remains there.

A good deal of this book is devoted to the Jewish world that had disappeared forever. In a poem entitled "Echo" Kadya speaks of the world that "no longer exists". All that is left of it is an echo in her mind: "an echo of once– once was, once lived, once sang…"[102]

There is one poem in this collection that is especially telling. As I see it, the poet is thinking about Dovid Bergelson. Once again, Kadya enlists the Passover song *"khad-gadye"*, and once again it may have more than one meaning. On the one hand, it may bring to mind two characters, each of whom is doing just what the other one does. On the other hand, it may refer to the use of the term *khad gadye* as "a prison".

When the poem opens, Kadya confesses she has discarded a poem she wrote about "a tall, greying man" because its rhyme scheme was not good enough. Bergelson, we recall, was Kadya's tutor and early critic, and she would not want to disappoint him. In her mind's eye, Kadya observes his man, un-named, and says:

"Hob ikh gekukt afn troyerikn mentshn
Un batrakht im fun der nont
Un ikh hob dem roykh fun zayn lyulke

Un zayn groyem umet derkont."

So I looked at that sad man/ and I observed him up close/And I recognized the scent of his pipe/And his grey sadness.

Bergelson, as we recall, smoked a pipe. And we have every reason to believe that Kadya recognized its scent.

To be entirely fair, there is a line in the fifth stanza that throws some doubt on the identification of the greying man with Bergelson. It is the line in which the poet is accused by the greying man. He says to her:

"- *host farvorfn mikh tsulib a gram*"/- you discarded me for a rhyme."

Do we have any reason to believe that Kadya "discarded/threw off" Bergelson because of her poetry? No, we do not. But then, we have only hints of their last fleeting, apparent, meeting in Berlin in the early 1930s. Assuming they did meet, we have no idea of what was said between them.

Nevertheless, it seems to me that the seventh stanza contains a line that clinches the identification:

"Dos iz nit keyn roykh fun keyn lyulke
Nor a farviklter eybiker knoyl.
Dos iz nit keyn groye umet,
Nor a vort oyf farshvigenem moyl."[103]

This is not the smoke of a pipe/ But a complex eternal skein. /This is not grey sadness / But the speech of a silenced mouth.

While it is true that any number of Jewish writers were silenced by the Soviet authorities, the one who mattered most to Kadya was Dovid Bergelson. By this time Kadya had almost certainly been told by joint friends of Bergelson's misery.[104] In her imagination, both she and he, looking in the mirror, could do nothing but look down and away; there was no hope in sight.

Immediately after the seventh stanza, with its realization that the greying man has a "silenced mouth", comes the eighth stanza, in which the poet says that the situation in which the two find themselves, is a kind of prison:

"*Un ot hostu a khad gadye*"/ and here you have a prison.[105]

Bergelson was, in fact, in a kind of prison. He and Kadya would not see each other freely ever again, and he himself was unable to say what he truly felt.

It was during WWII, when European Jewish civilization was being destroyed, that Kadya began to voice remorse over her abandonment of traditional Judaism. While she did not then, or at any time afterward, become an Orthodox Jew, she did wonder whether the "waters of the well"[106] of Judaism "might be sweet".

To fully understand the following poem, we need to know some references. Because the Bible suggests that he never died[107], Elijah has taken on a number of roles in Jewish history. In Jewish folk tales he travels in time and appears anywhere and everywhere, working miracles and serving as a sort of "fairy Godmother."[108] It is in this role that Kadya mentioned him when she was "miraculously" saved from harm during the chaos of the WWI rush to escape the advancing armies, and again, when she escaped unharmed from a pogrom in Kiev.[109]

Just because he can be in many different places at one time, he is invited all over the world to join Jews at their Passover seder. Traditionally, a child opens the door to the outside at the appropriate time during the seder, and all rise and greet the prophet Elijah, who enters, joins the family and is given a cup of wine to drink.[110] It is this tradition that Kadya refers to when she speaks of "opening the door" for the prophet Elijah as a child.

In the later prophets, Elijah is named as the one who, in the End of Days, will bring his people word of their ultimate deliverance.[111] It is in this capacity that Kadya refers to him as the bearer of good tidings. Here then, are passages from the poem "*A Briv Tsu Eliyohu Ha-novi*", A Letter to Elijah the Prophet:

"Old tidings-bearer, Eliyohu/Elijah

I lost all addresses,
So I'm now writing a letter to you.
Surely you haven't forgotten an old friendship
When as a child I opened the door for you."[112]

When Kadya says she has lost "all addresses", she is in essence admitting she has lost the habit of prayer. After all, it is through prayer that one addresses God. But since Elijah always comes to the defense of unfortunate Jews, Kadya now appeals to him. She continues by confessing her problems:

"I have carelessly cut off all your traces…
And also the warmth of belief…

Between us such alien chasms have opened
It seems I have dug them in vain…"[113]

"I have fallen, and been trampled on,
And every dog that races by, lashes out,
But my heart races, taking up my last breath
To the eternal spring, which may still be sweet."[114]

Written in 1942, this poem still holds out some hope that Kadya's loved ones may yet live. She appeals to the prophet to let her know if in fact some have been saved, but then again, she admits she may not be able to handle the news:

"So many names stick in my throat…
I fear to ask you, so tell me nothing…
And if you've had no good tidings
Turn off my lamp
And close my eyes."

The elegiac tone of this collection continues in the well-known poem *"Toyter Shabes"*, Dead Sabbath. Here Kadya admits that when she was mired in the poverty of pre-WWII Warsaw, she thought herself unhappy, but she was wrong. Then, because of the vitality of argument and contention, she was truly happy; now that that entire world has been annihilated, she is truly unhappy:

"*Vi gliklekh kh'bin amol geveyn
Ven mayne fis hobn geshtroykhlt
In yidn-has, in dakhkes un in blote...*"[115]

How fortunate was I once/ When my feet bumped along/In Jew-hate, in want and in mire...
"*Itst iz ru/Di ru fun toytn shabes.*"
Now all is quiet./ [It's] the quiet of a dead *shabes* [Sabbath]."[116]
The Jewish Sabbath is a day of rest. When no more Jews live in Europe, and all are resting in their final resting places, then all are silent. But that Sabbath silence, the silence of the dead Jews, is a Dead Sabbath, horrible to contemplate.

The power of the title poem of this collection, "Only King David Remained" lies in its ability to home in on an essential metaphor long-held by the Jewish people: they are eternal just as the line of King David is eternal. A favorite Jewish folk song, known to all, has the following recurring line: "*Dovid, melekh Yisroel, khai, khai ve-kayom*", David, the King of Israel, is alive, is alive and he exists". Now clearly all know that the historic King David is no longer alive. But David, the historic figure, was the first to unite all the people. Accordingly, King David is a symbol of Jewish unity. And that unity, the folk say, (or would like to believe) is eternal. What's more, the prophets foretold that the Messiah will be a scion of the house of King David.[117] And when the Messiah, that longed-for scion of King David, will appear, the children of Israel will be redeemed, and peace will reign all over the world. King David, then, is the symbol and embodiment of the promise of redemption and a shining future. And the hope for this great future, for the Jewish people as well as for the world over, lives on.

This is how the story has traditionally been told. But suppose the people of Israel are not eternal? What then? This is the searing question that this poem asks, but does not need to answer. In this poem, King David has one son, but the people are no more.

> "*Der folk iz farshnitn–*
> *Vund un toyt.*
> *Di vegn dashotn,*
> *Di hayzer farbrent.*
> *Der melekh Dovid aleyn iz geblibn,*
> *Er, mit der kroyn in di hent.*"[118]

The folk is annihilated/Wound and death./ Paths in shadow,/Houses burned down./ Only King David remained,/ He, with his crown in his hands.

This poem has five stanzas. Stanzas two and three end with a repeat of "Only King David remained"…, but the lines that precede these two lines differ. Each presents the reader with a different picture of the destruction and its effects. Stanza two tells us:

| "*Es raysn kriye in himel* | In heaven they rend their clothes[119] |
| *Farsarfete, khoreve vent*". | Scorched, desolate walls. |

The third stanza contributes another layer to the picture of destruction:

| "*Di lonkes di grine fun kindheyt,* | The green meadows of childhood, |
| *Di tcherede shof– iz farlendt.*" | The flock of sheep– is ravaged. |

King David is/was a shepherd. If the flock of sheep is ravaged, that does not bode well for the king. But King David soldiers on. In stanzas four and five of this poem, he goes to his son, the Messiah, and gives him the kingly crown:

Der veg tsu zayn zun, der moshi'akh,	The path to his son, the Messiah
Vos dos folk hot fartroymt un tseshemt	Whom the folk dreamed up and celebrated
Ahiyn geyt der ovl, der melekh	That's where the mourner, the king goes
Er mit der kroyn in di hent.	He with his crown in his hands.
Ot iz dayn keyser, moshi'akh	Here is your crown, Messiah,
Ale perl geshoynt, nit farshvendt.	All the pearls intact, none missing.
Ot iz dayn keyser, moshi'akh	Here is your crown, Messiah,
Af di letste tsvey yidishe hent.	In the last two Jewish hands.

There is a son to take over the reign, but he has no people to rule over. They are all gone.

Like all good poems, this poem is multi-layered. If we move from the symbolic meaning of King David to the historic King David of the Bible, we get to a parallel between King David and Kadya herself. In the Bible, King David's son, Absalom, foments a revolt against his own father and attempts to usurp the throne. The revolt does not succeed; Absalom loses his life in the attempt, and King David is not overthrown. When the King hears of his beloved son's death he cries out: "If only I could have died instead of you, Absalom, my son, my son, Absalom."[120] Here we see the natural feeling of a parent who laments the death of his child (even a child who would have been a parricide). In the world as it should be, the child out-lives his parent. How awful it is, then, when the parent outlives his child.

Something similar, although by no means identical, holds for the survivors of the Holocaust in general, and Kadya in particular. Her friends and her family, her beloved younger brother and his family, did not escape death; she did. Why should she have lived while they died? There is no logical answer, of course. But feelings take no account of logic. Recall that Kadya tore at and injured her finger while she was agonizing over the news from Europe. Like many survivors of the Holocaust, she undoubtedly asked herself: Why them, and not me?

While many of the poems in this collection deal with the grief brought on by the Holocaust, this collection contains two, very surprising, personal poems. The first, entitled *Mayne Kinder*, My Children, is the only poem Kadya ever wrote about the children she never had. As the poem opens, the poet sees her four children ("two and two", as she puts it), through a mist of falling snow. The children circle her, tug at her dress, and beg her to play with them. But first they want to know why she has consigned them to the nether world and not allowed them into the world of the living. With a wink and a nod at the Jewish mother who plies her children with food, perhaps even to forestall conversation, the poem continues:

"*Kh'hob zey gegebn kikhelekh un yedern geheysen: es
Un kh'hob farentfert zikh, az kh'hob forlorn zeyer adres.*"[121]

I gave each one a cookie and told each one: Eat./ And I made up the excuse that I lost their address.

The elder son is full of complaints. He says:

"What good are your poems, the melodies and choirs?/ When under them swarm our faded souls?"[122]

He rants on, and ends his tirade with:

"Why did you prejudge me and have me put in limbo?"

This hits Kadya hard. She tells us her eyes filled up with tears. But her younger daughter, who had pity on her, nestled herself in her mother's lap and comforted her. Here is how the story resumes:

"I don't care – she [the daughter- ZKN] said./ And I recognized in her my own smile. –/ – I don't long for the world,/ And you can have the whole big deal./ I'd probably be a nuisance like you were/ Arguing with everyone, angry for years./ And what's this business of constant pen-scraping? / It's OK with me that I was never born."

Kadya is especially moved by this daughter's words. She continues:

"I wanted to give her a kiss, but in my hands/ I held only cold snow that had melted. / I wanted to take her round my knee/ But I could not find her wee little head."

The mist got thicker as the snow fell harder, and Kadya's children disappeared in the grey fog. Here is the last stanza of that poem:

"I heard only their wee footsteps/ Like little bells blown in the wind/ And I hear them now still in the quiet hours of night."[123]

The other personal poem, one of the oddest in the collection, is the seemingly confessional poem entitled "*A Lid Vegn Zikh*", A Poem about Myself. Its date, 1941, may well explain its splenetic tone. Until the Japanese attack on Pearl Harbor, on December 7, 1941, i.e., for most of 1941, Americans watched the rise of Nazism in Europe in the full belief that the US would not get involved in the war. For American Jews, this clearly meant heart-ache: their loved ones, trapped in Europe, were headed for almost-certain disaster, while they were simply helpless bystanders. Keeping this in mind, we hear Kadya say about herself:

"*Di gantse geografye ligt kapoyer,*
Un ale mayne libshaften – farsamte.
Di kro – der zinger iz, der treyster – a tkhoyer,
Un ale mayne libste zeyen oys vi umbakante."[124]

All geography is upside down,/ And all my loves poisoned./ The crow – is a singer, the comforter – a coward,/ And all my loved-ones seem unknown.

We should keep in mind that at this time, Simche, her husband, had been with her in the US for three years. Had she and Simche had a deeply loving relationship, it's hard to believe she would have said "**all** my loves poisoned". We can imagine that she was in a funk when she wrote this poem; that may well be. Nevertheless, the fact that Simche's presence does nothing to counteract the low point in her mood, speaks volumes. We may not know the details of their relationship all that well, but even if this relationship was advantageous to them both, and apparently it was, it was nevertheless a relationship that could not comfort her when she was down.

In this, rather depressed mood, Kadya recalls the days of old:

"*Ikh hob gehert amol dem gang fun hilkhedike marshn,*
 Ikh hob gezen amol dem flam fun fayerdike fonen…

Di velt iz yung geven,
Gevolt meshadekh zayn zikh mitn himel…"[125]

I once heard the step of resounding marches,/ I once saw the blaze of fiery flags…

The world was young/ I wanted to pair myself with heaven…

This sounds like the arrival of Communism. Kadya was indeed there when the Red Army marched into Odessa. In this poem, more than twenty years after that fact, she says "the world was young", but she means, of course, that she was young. Her explanation for her identification with the Communism of her twenty-something self is that she wanted then to pair herself with heaven. Put differently, for her this was idealistic striving to better the world.

Having put herself in a reminiscent frame of mind, she recalls the loves of those years and says:

"*Nor oyf keyn eyntsiker fun mayne libes hob ikh nit kharote*
Fun yedn friling blaybt in oyg a flam…"[126]
But I regret none of my loves./ Each spring leaves a flame in one's eye."

The love of her life in those early days of Communism was, as far as we can tell, Dovid Bergelson. If she had other lovers, and that is of course possible, there is no trace of them in her archives or in the letters that others of her generation left behind.

Two of the themes that recur in Kadya's poetry are the pleasant whiteness of snow[127] and a paper bridge. Recall that in the poem "My paper Bridge, published in 1930, the first three lines, later deleted, were "and who needs even me? …Unless it's the snow of my home."[128] She revisits these themes once again a decade and a half later.

In "*Der Melekh Dovid Aleyn iz Geblibn*", these themes crop up in a poem entitled "*A Lid Tsu Der Papirene Brik*", A Poem to the Paper Bridge. Whereas the poem written earlier was strictly personal, this poem mingles the communal with the personal:

Lead me, paper bridge, into you land

Which is white, and mild, and content.

I'm tired of the desert, where the manna pre-laid

Is made of milk and honey and bread."[129]

To properly appreciate this poem, we need to know the Biblical as well as the rabbinical exegesis on the story of the manna. The Bible tells us that in the desert, the children of Israel found the manna laid out and waiting for them, every day.[130] What's more, according to the rabbis, this manna had a magical property: it took on whatever flavor or taste, the eater desired.[131] So if the children of Israel wanted to eat milk, honey or bread, that's what the manna tasted like. This is the reality the poet does not want. It is unearned food.

According to the story in the poem, the simple folk built a paper bridge, and made it as strong as they could. This bridge was magical; it went all the way up to heaven:

> They built and they decorated it with many feathers
> Its steps hooked onto the heavens.
> I saw the bridge through a feather in the ceiling
> Through succah-roofs and through autumn apples.[132]

This is clearly the world of Jewish tradition: a world that attempts to reach spiritual heights. The word I have translated as "succah-roofs", "*skhakh*" in the original poem, is a Hebrew and Yiddish word used for the material that has grown in the ground and is placed on a "*succah*"/ tabernacle roof during the autumnal holiday known to Ashkenazic Jews as "*sukes/sikes*".

We can be certain that this is the bridge belonging to that old world when we proceed to the next stanza:

> I heard its flutter and its rustle
> In the velvet of the Torah mantles
> And I recognized its voice in the old school-teacher's
> Translation of a difficult word.[133]

But passage over that bridge was not for everyone. In fact, the poet tells us:

> Only he [the old school-teacher- ZKN] traversed that paper bridge
> And arrived whole and unharmed.

Next the poet speaks of the sorrow she has seen, rhyming the Hebrew word "*tehohm*", (an) abyss, with the word "Sodom", [pronounced [seh dome] in Hebrew and Yiddish], the city of iniquity:

> I've seen a lot under the sun:
> How a beaker of flowers– becomes an abyss
> I've seen a lot everywhere:

How shining cities– become Sodom.[134]

But the poet does not despair. Addressing the paper bridge, she asks that a new reality come into being. In this society nothing is gotten free; all is earned. But whatever is gotten, is rightly achieved. And no one is harmed:

Lead me, paper bridge, into your land

Which we built with honest hands,

In the light of need, and in pureness of hearts,

No person tortured, no child shamed.

There a tree still blooms

There a hen still crows

And at dawn announces

A shining morning.[135]

Is this poem an Anti-Soviet plea? That may well be. Although the poet is seemingly rejecting the magical, Biblical world of the desert, where food is free and not earned, there is every reason to see this poem as a cautionary tale against "unearned" bread of the workers' paradise. This interpretation becomes even more convincing when we consider the author's plea to make this new society one in which no person is tortured, as Jews were in the Soviet Union, and no child shamed, as were those children, who, willingly or not, turned against their own parents in the Soviet Union[136].

Rich as it has appeared till now, this collection of poems has yet more. It has a playful poem about fox cubs that bring the poet "shining rhymes/ a drop of wine, a streak of pure sun"[137]; it has a poem devoted to Dona Grazia Mendes, an important woman in Jewish history[138]; it has a poem, dripping with mordant satire, on life in general and the Sabbath in particular, in Brownsville[139]; it has a farcical poem about jealousy among intellectuals;[140] and its final, celebratory poem is located in the Land of Israel[141]. Probably the most wide-ranging of Kadya's poetry books, this nine-year accumulation of poems shows Kadya at the height of her powers.

On page ninety of this book, there are three lines that were printed upside-down, making these lines totally unintelligible– unless the reader turns the book upside-down. Now this is the one and only book put out by the pseudo-press "Paper Bridges", which explicitly tells us in its frontispiece that the type-setter was Simche Lev, Kadya's husband. Whatever Simche's flaws, he most certainly knew better than to place Hebrew letters upside down.

I imagine Simche bringing along an assistant and telling this assistant to continue with the type-setting while he went out to the bathroom. When Simche resumed the job, he never checked to see if the type-setting was done properly in his absence. That, in my understanding, is why the type-face stayed upside down, and the book was published with this egregious flaw.

Although Kadya left no evidence of how aggrieved she was with this faux pas, we can make a reasonable guess about the toll it took on her. Four years earlier, in 1942, when she published the "Diary of Rivke Zylberg", she told Ida Maze that the book was printed with so many mistakes, that she "was afraid to be alone with the book because the mistakes might devour her."[142] At least the writing in the "Diary" was legible. How much more aggravating it must've been to have poems published with their fonts upside down!

Had there been a market for this book, there would undoubtedly have been a second edition, and in this second edition, the three lines would have been printed right-side up. From the absence of a second edition, we can only surmise that there simply were not enough buyers to warrant another edition. The war may have been over in 1946, but many Jews were languishing in Displaced Persons Camps. The Jewish world was otherwise occupied, and didn't find the time for and/or didn't want to spend money on buying this book.

As was her wont, Dora congratulated Kadya on her new book, telling her, perhaps with more than a dose of wishful thinking, that the book would find its way into every Jewish home. Unlike her usual supportive gestures, she also added a bit of a sisterly jibe:

"You need not dress up; we're not coming [as planned ZKN].[143] We'll wait till the weather is better…"

There is a principle of Jewish law that says: "From the positive, one can deduce the negative".[144] The inverse seems to apply here. Using the negative to surmise the positive, we can suppose that ordinarily Kadya did "dress up" when she knew her sister intended to visit.

Dora and Leibl

The differences that first appeared when Kadya and Dora were young and single, remained throughout their lives. When the two young women spent a few weeks together in Biyalostok, Kadya was enthralled by the dream of Zion, and it was Dora who wore the stylish shoes. Decades later, Kadya was still a dreamer, and Dora was still the one who knew about fashion. Now that they were middle-aged, each of the sisters had gotten used to these differences. From what Dora says, it would appear that each did what she could to "try on" the other's life style. Dora began reading and writing Hebrew, while Kadya "spruced herself up" when she was expecting her sister to visit.

For all that the Molodowsky family knew the fate of most Polish Jews, they did not immediately know Leibel's fate. At some point, Leibl left his wife and daughter and ran eastward, looking for safety in Soviet-held territory. Many Jews did the same thing. And most met the same fate Leibl did: they were murdered. But there was no knowing for sure who would live and who would not. After the war, there was a concerted effort by all Jews who had family and loved ones in Europe. Local Yiddish newspapers had columns of relatives seeking loved ones. The Yiddish radio station had programs in which names of survivors, their native towns and their family-members names were solemnly read aloud in the hopes that someone listening would be able to offer a scrap of information. HIAS and the Red Cross had lists and these were pored over again and again. At *landsmanschaft*[145] meetings, stories of relatives last seen at junction spots were gleaned for crucial information. Knowing Kadya's deep sense of concern for Leibl, as well as her extended list of friends and acquaintances in Europe, one imagines she did most of the investigating of Leibl's whereabouts. It is not clear now how or when the Molodowsky family got the full story of Leibl's eventual death. But eventually they found out what had happened. Leibl died trying to escape from a Communist concentration camp, possibly in 1942 or 1943. His wife and daughter were murdered by the Nazis.[146]

Kadya Helps Rokhl Korn

Many of the Jews who had survived the war found themselves in Displaced Persons camps in Europe in the late 1940s. This was merely a temporary solution; each "refugee" as these survivors were then called, needed to find a permanent home. Kadya left no evidence anywhere that she was herself involved in finding friends and helping them to find a permanent place to live after the war. But she was involved. She did everything she could, and went everywhere she possible could go, desperately trying to help her friends. We know this because her friends preserved the relevant evidence.

Rokhl Korn was one such friend. The two women had been friends and co-editors in Warsaw. While Kadya waited out the war in New York, Rokhl Korn disappeared into the Russian hinterland, and was constantly on the run during WWII. She re-surfaced in a Displaced Persons Camp in Stockholm when the war was over. Kadya wrote to her there, but did not keep a copy of the letter she sent to Stockholm. Rokhl, on the other hand, most certainly did keep that letter.

Whereas Kadya was methodical, one could say almost obsessive, about preserving copies of her correspondence with her friend Rokhl, the reverse was not the case at all. Rokhl was rather indifferent about preserving her correspondence. While Kadya preserved 160 letters of correspondence between herself and her friend in an eleven-year period, Rokhl preserved only 23 letters sent to her by Kadya across a period of twenty-five years.[147] The earliest of these, the letter sent to her in a Displaced Persons camp in Stockholm, in March of 1947, clearly shows Kadya's delight in finding her friend. That letter begins with the salutation: "My Dear Rokhl,"*zolstu mir gezunt zayn*!, may you stay healthy [literally, for me]! And ends with: "*ikh kush dikh fil mol*", I kiss you many times. One can feel the excitement exuding through the paper. This was not a face-to-face meeting, but it was the best the two friends could do at the time.

Like all the rest of the Displaced Persons, Rokhl needed to figure out which place was the best next stop for her. Accordingly, in this first letter and in the following letters she sent to Rokhl, Kadya sent names and addresses of contacts that might be of help. She sent names and addresses of people in Los Angeles, and names of people she knew in Paris. She offered to go to HIAS to arrange the paper work for her friend's passport and immigration papers. In the end, Rokhl chose to go to Canada, where her daughter was living. There Ida Maze and the friends of Yiddish in Montreal came to her aid. But she must have been thrilled to get that letter from Kadya. We know this is so because she kept that letter with her as she traveled from Europe to the New World, and she deposited it in her archive in Montreal along with only a handful of other letters, thirty-five years later.

What Rokhl never knew and Kadya had no intention of revealing, was that all through the years of Rokhl's wandering, Kadya had encouraged Ida's superhuman efforts to sell Rokhl's books wherever and whenever they could be sold. The two women believed that Rokhl might someday come through alive and they wanted to be able to tell her she had earned money of her own.[148]

It would be wrong to suppose that Kadya was a self-deprecating, modest woman. She was not. She knew her worth, at least by the time she was in her forties, and had won many prizes for her work. It is a traditionally Jewish value to do good works/deeds "for their own sake", and not for the publicity or the public recognition that these efforts may bring. And in this Kadya was very traditionally Jewish. No one, and certainly not Rokhl, ever knew just how much time and effort Kadya devoted to aiding her friend, Rokhl. And that was how Kadya wanted it.

As soon as Kadya knew of Rokhl's whereabouts in Sweden, she sent Rokhl's address to Ida Maze. The two of them and Melekh Ravitch, by now Kadya's dear friend, sent letters back and forth trying to determine how they could all best help Rokhl. Much as she wanted to be of help, Kadya realized that Ida was better equipped, better networked and altogether more fit for the social work that was needed. She admitted this much to Ida and assured her that it was this work that guaranteed Ida "a fine portion in the world to come".[149]

A Prize Without an Audience

In 1947 Kadya received the Louis Lamed prize, a monetary award of $500, for the volume of poetry that she wrote in 1946, *Der Melekh Dovid Aleyn iz Geblibn*." As was her wont, she pretended it didn't much matter to her. First, she told Ida about it, and then she added "You've probably already seen this in the press."[150] Finally, she got to the quasi-disclaimer: "They give adults a toy to play with."[151] While we know from the detailed list she kept of all the critical reviews of her earlier work that she most definitely did care what the critics thought, by the time WWII had ended, there was a sense that for all the critical acclaim, the larger audience for this work had perished and would not return. It was that sense of near-futility that reared its head in this dismissive comment.

Kadya And The Zionist Dream

Nineteen forty-seven was also the year that the UN first discussed and then passed a resolution partitioning Mandate Palestine and offering the Jewish people a "national homeland" of their own. If we recall Kadya's anger with the God of the Jewish people, as it was expressed in *"El Khanun"*, we can better understand her only slightly controlled mixture of pleasure and relief at the thought that perhaps now the God of the Jewish people would allow them to have one place on earth where they could determine their own fate. Here is what she wrote to her friend Ida:

"What will become of our fate in the UN? If God will help and we'll own/have a small piece of land of our own, that'll ease our hearts somewhat. Even the lonely will have some place to put a foot down. Jews have prayed so very much, perhaps one time God will listen to us. It's about time."[152]

By the year's end, when the State of Israel had become a reality, Kadya began to muse that she might find the respite she needed so badly in Israel. She had been sick intermittently, and her doctor had recommended rest. She then told Ida:

"It seems to me that in the Land of Israel I will become a person again. With God's help."[153]

While she may have toyed with the idea of a visit to Israel in late 1947, it was not until nearly a year later in the summer of 1948, that she actually did something about it. Those years there were camps in the Jewish Diaspora, called *"hakhshara"*, training camps, that prepared Jews for "pioneer life" in Israel. Kadya told Ida that she spent one weekend in such a camp and enjoyed herself immensely.[154] Nevertheless, this was a gathering of youngsters, and by then Kadya was no youngster. Furthermore, these camps were meant for folks who intended to become members of a kibbutz, (a communal settlement whose main focus was agriculture) and, always the urbanite, Kadya had no intention whatsoever of joining an agricultural settlement. But this weekend re-kindled for her the long-dormant dream of life in Israel, a life she had dreamed about and had trained for even before the First World War. At this point she began seriously considering a move, or at the very least an exploratory trip, to Israel.

From the letters and postcards Kadya exchanged with Aizik, it's clear that Aizik himself would have loved to travel to Israel. But infirm and weak as he was, that was not possible. His excitement is obvious and genuine. When he tells Kadya "This I know: they are actually building themselves up."[155] This is clearly a reference to a Zionist song that was popular in the pre-state era: "*anu banu artsa livnot u-le-hibanot ba*'", we have arrived in the Land [of Israel] to build and to be built up". One can feel the delight and surprise in his voice. Knowing as we do how much he and Kadya were soul-mates, it is not surprising that Kadya herself uses very this same phrase in her letter to her friend Rokhl Korn: "they are building themselves and a country". This may sound trite, or even corny, to a twenty-first century reader, but to Jews who had just lived through the Holocaust, when every Jew who came into contact with the Germans was mocked as a "*musselmann*",[156] a weakling who could be easily bullied and could not possibly assume an active role in his own defense, the sort of assertiveness that the Jews of Palestine demonstrated seemed only a bit short of miraculous.

Recall that Kadya had many friends living in the new state of Israel. These were longstanding friends from her early years in the pre-World War I seminary for Hebrew teachers run by Yehiel Halperin. By now these former young adults were middle-aged. They were the young county's elite: the movers and shakers of the fledgling state. Some were members of the Knesset, Israel's Parliament.[157] Others were members of kibbutzim, the communal settlements that were seen as the pioneers of a new spirit of idealism mixed with land redemption. Yet others were the heads of national organizations, like the Pioneer Women.

It's easy to understand then, that when Kadya and Simche took their first trip to Israel in 1949, their old-time friends vied to host them. Although Kadya and Simche never said as much outright to any of their friends and correspondents, this trip was in fact an exploratory trip. Although they went as tourists, to see what life was like in

Israel, and not as immigrants, their clear intention was to see how they might fit into this new world.

By the time the two of them came to Israel, many of Kadya's Yiddish stories for children had been translated into Hebrew. These were now a part of the curriculum for all of Israel's publicly educated children. Whereas parents knew and were enchanted by Kadya's works in Yiddish, their natively educated children knew and were enchanted by Kadya's works in Hebrew. For both parents and children, then, Kadya was as close as one could come those days to a literary celebrity.

Kadya liked the hubbub and excitement of New York, but she left it for Israel after a 15-year stay. It does seem like she intended to make Israel her new home. After all, she went there to become the editor of a Yiddish language journal that she tellingly called *Heym*, home. And yet, she was not entirely at home there either. She left Israel and returned to New York after a mere three-year stay.

NOTES

[1] See http://jwa.org/encyclopedia/article/maze-ida
[2] We do not have a copy of this letter. But from Kadya's response, we can gather what was said in this letter.
[3] Once they met, Kadya endearingly called Ida "*Yaponitchka*", Japanese-lady. It was Ida's short stature and slany eyes that brought on this nick-name. That sort of humorous banter was common for Kadya.
[4] This, the first letter from Kadya in the Ida Maze archive in the Montreal Jewish Public library, is dated July 11, 1935.
[5] *Svive*, no. 37, September, 1972, p. 56.
[6] This, in a letter dated October 23, 1935.
[7] This, in a letter dated October 23, 1936.
[8] This, in a letter dated August 27, 1935.
[9] *Fun Lublin Biz Nyu York: Der Tog-Bukh fun Rivke Zylberg*, p.5. Henceforth, "The Diary..."
[10] This, in a letter dated November 23, 1935. The Yiddish says "*ikh ken shoyn a bisl English, gey ongeton in Amerikaner kleyder un zey oys a layt mit laytn glaykh*".
[11] See "The Diary...", p. 8.
[12] The word "*grine(r)*" is the Yiddish for a newly arrived immigrant.
[13] "The Diary...", p. 9.
[14] "The Diary..." p. 20.

[15] "The Diary..." pp. 21-22.
[16] "The Diary...", p. 42.
[17] "The Diary...", p. 55.
[18] "The Diary...", p. 59.
[19] "The Diary...", p. 76.
[20] "The Diary"., p. 91.
[21] "The Diary...", p. 136.
[22] "The Diary...", p. 175.
[23] "The Diary...", p. 192.
[24] "The Diary...", p. 195.
[25] "The Diary...", p. 245.
[26] "The Diary...", p. 246.
[27] "Red" is the nickname Larry is given because of the color of his hair. Rivke's fiancé is named "Leyzer" in Yiddish but he uses the name "Larry" in English.
[28] "The Diary...", p. 267.
[29] "The Diary...", p. 268.
[30] Although this photo is undated, it cannot have been taken after 1935. After that, Kadya left for the US, and the three man and Kadya were not toether again till the 1950s, when Kadya and Simche joined Sutzkever and Pinski in Israel.
[31] This, in the Makhon Lavon archive.
[32] *Svive,* no.37, September, 1972, p.60.
[33] This and the rest of what follows is from a letter dated November 14, 1937.
[34] This letter is dated March 11, 1939.
[35] There is no knowing if Kadya's hair worked its magic on Simche as well. Perhaps it did. We simply do not have enough information about their relationship to know whether this is so.
[36] This in a letter written in May of 1937.
[37] This is the title of one of Y. L. Peretz's short stories. See also : http://jwa.org/encyclopedia/article/bas-tovim-sarah, and http://www.yivoencyclopedia.org/article.aspx/Sore_bas_Toyvim
[38] Makhon Lavon archive, 104 IV, letters from 1937-38.
[39] Perhaps the man who ran Camp Mehia. If it is indeed the same person, then this is the man who invited Kadya to come to Detroit to teach.
[40] In the summer of 1937, Kadya did go to summer camp, but in the summer of 1938, she did not. Once Simche was with her, she did not go to camp.
[41] This, in an undated letter found in Makhon Lavon. From the fact that she mentions Kadya's working in camp, it would seem the letter was written in the summer of 1937, before Simche's arrival.
[42] She taught Yiddish in Camp Nayvelt just outside Brampton and bordering the Credit River in Canada in the summer of 1937. For more on Camp Nayvelt, see: http://www.winchevskycentre.org/institutions/naiveltHistory.html In addition, she was supposed to teach, or at least give lectures at Camp Mehia in Onstead, Michigan.

Chapter Four: The US – (1935-1950) 181

---

[43] This program took place at P.S. 149 at Sutton and Vermont Streets. Kadya received a certificate stating that she completed the program that lasted from January till July of 1941. (This document is in the YIVO archive.)
[44] "The Diary…" p. 277.
[45] We know this because in one of the little telephone books left in her Israeli archive, Kadya lists one "Rae Levit" and gives a phone number.
[46] This, in a letter dated February 28, 1936.
[47] This, in a letter dated May 20, 1937.
[48] Ibid.
[49] See Janet Hadda'sbook Issac Bashevis Singer: A Life, University of Wisconsin Press, 1997, p. 84.
[50] Apparently, there was a Jewish immigration lawyer who came up with this method. See Hadda, p. 89.
[51] In Land fun Mayn Gebeyn, pp. 24-25.
[52] For a sensitive literary analysis of the term *khad gadye* in Kadya's work see Kathryn Hellerstein's paper: "*Teguvat Meshoreret Yidish Be-Amerike- Kadye Molodovsky- El Nokhakh Ha-sho'a*". *Khulyot*,no. 3, 1996, pp.245-248. See also Chapter Four, p. 141.
[53] In Land fun Mayn Gebeyn, p. 13.
[54] http://en.wikipedia.org/wiki/State_Emblem_of_the_Soviet_Union
[55] Koestler published Darkness at Noon in German in 1940. The English version was published in 1941.
[56] This, in a letter she sent to Ida Maze in May of 1937.
[57] In Land fun Mayn Gebeyn, pp. 36-37.
[58] This, in a letter dated November 10, 1938, found in the Makhon Lavon archive.
[59] This, in a letter dated December 19, 1938, found in the Makhon Lavon archive.
[60] This, in a letter dated February 23, 1940, found in the Makhon Lavon archive.
[61] This, in a letter dated December 20, 1943, found in the Makhon Lavon archive.
[62] This, in a letter dated December 12, 1939, found in the Makhon Lavon archive.
[63] *Svive*, no. 38, January, 1973, pp. 58-59.
[64] Ibid.
[65] He discussed the topic many times in the letters he sent Kadya while he was in Europe and she in the US. It would seem that the book he published in 1941 is in fact this same work but with a different title.
[66] This, in a letter dated April 4, 1940, found in the Makhon Lavon archive.
[67] In this archive there are letters written in those years in Yiddish and in Hebrew from relatives of Simche as well as from other family members. A literary equivalent of these heart-rending, beseeching letters, can be seen in Y. Glatstein's semi-autobiographical memoir, *Ven Yash iz Gekumen*, translated into Hebrew as כשיאש הגיע Am Oved, Tel Aviv, 2006. In that Hebrew edition, sixteen pages are devoted to the entreaties of the local Polish Jews, begging the American hero returning to the US to get in touch with their relatives when he returns. See pp. 116-132.

[68] There is no way to know for certain what they are referring to, but it is my guess that they are speaking here of naturalization papers for Simche.

[69] Of course, both Kadya and Simche are aware that this quote is taken from a well-known section of the Passover haggadah.

[70] It's hard to know who Aizik was referring to. Kadya and Simche did not have children. It may well be that Aizik was referring to Genya, a family member (cousin?) who apparently lived in the same building.

[71] This could clearly not have been accurate. Kadya herself was only 46 in 1940, and Leibl was younger than she was. Quite possibly, the family upped his birthdate when they were trying to get him out of the Czar's army.

[72] She mentions this in a letter to Ida dated August 10, 1940 and once again in her memoir, *Svive*, no.38, January, 1973, p. 60.

[73] For Kathryn Hellerstein's view of this phenomenon from the viewpoint of a literary critic, see Hellerstein 1996, above, pp. 236-238.

[74] This, in a letter dated June 9, 1940, found in the Montreal archive,

[75] This, in a letter to Ida, dated June 25, 1940, found in the Montreal archive,

[76] In 1940 she lived on 231 Herzyl Street, in Brownsville, Brooklyn; in the years 1941-1942 she lived on 297 East 10th Street, a neighborhood now called the "East Village," and then called the "Lower East Side" of Manhattan, and from then till the end of this period, she lived in 602 East 170th St, in the Bronx.

[77] If we did not know this from Molodowsky's autobiography, we could guess this from the fact that Dora writes [arayt], when she means "all right", and she writes the Hebrew/Yiddish word "*efsher*" with an "*ayin*" and not an "*aleph*", as the Standard spelling would have it. In both cases we see the spelling of an autodidact, who writes "phonetically", i.e., as she hears what is said, instead of grammatically, as an educated person would.

[78] In this letter Aizik mentions Minkele and her child, and that would put the letter at a later date. I have mentioned this undated letter here because of what it says about Aizik and his need to share this "outsider" feeling with Kadya.

[79] The town was then called "Kartuz-Bereza" in Polish. Until the Russian Revolution it was part of Czarist Russia.

[80] The Protestant Ethic and the Spirit of Capitalism, written (in German) in 1904 and 1905, was translated into English in 1930.

[81] See Durkheim's Division of Labor in Society, written first as a dissertation in 1892, and then as a book (in French) in 1893. An English translation of the book was put put out by Free Press, in 1997.

[82] For more on her early leanings toward the Communist party, see Kahan Newman: "The Molodowsky-Korn Correspondence" in *Women in Judaism: A Multidisciplinary Journal*, volume 8, number 1, Jan. 2012, especially p. 5

[83] We find out that the two of them used to do the printing for "their" printing press in the evenings from the letters Molodowsky sent to Rokhl Korn. See Kahan Newman, 2011.
[84] For more on this, see the above-mentioned paper, pp. 17 ff, and end-note iii.
[85] This is reminiscent of a verse in Numbers 1/52. Quite clearly, Aizik knows his Biblical sources.
[86] This, in a letter written on October 22, 1941, found in the Makhon Lavon archive.
[87] This, in a letter dated March 23, 1943, found in the Makhon Lavon archive.
[88] This, in a letter dated December, 20, 1943, found in the Makhon Lavon archive.
[89] See: http://www.historynet.com/what-was-the-turning-point-of-world-war-ii.htm
[90] We know this not from any correspondence found in this folder, but from a post card in a different folder sent by one of Kadya's friends. Here there is a report of someone who heard from his own family that Leibl had fled with his family to Russian-occupied Bialystok. Much of the correspondence sent to Kadya during these years is taken up with information on the whereabouts of common friends and family in Europe.
[91] See: http://www.jewishvirtuallibrary.org/jsource/judaica/ejud_0002_0002_0_01147.html.
[92] The Jewish sources and the non-Jewish sources differ widely on how this effort is seen. The entry in the Encyclopedia Judaica, Ed. Michael Berenbaum and Fred Skolnik. Vol. 2. 2nd ed. Detroit: Macmillan Reference USA, 2007, p. 196, says: "On Aug. 24, 1941, a meeting of "representatives of the Jewish people was held in Moscow and it was addressed by Solomon *Mikhoels, Ilya *Ehrenburg, David *Bergelson, and others, who called on "our Jewish brethren throughout the world" to come to the aid of the Soviet Union. This appeal made a great impression on Jews in countries free of the Nazi yoke. In the U.S. the Jewish Council for Russian War Relief was established, headed by Albert Einstein…". However, an entirely different picture emerges from the Wikipedia Internet site. See: http://en.wikipedia.org/wiki/Russian_War_Relief
[93] That the Soviet Jews who formed this committee were simply exploited by their government can be seen by the fact that as soon as the war ended and they were no longer useful, they were arrested and/or murdered.
[94] It would seem that Kadya became somewhat disillusioned with Communism even before she left for the US. Later on, she was so opposed to the Communist (and even Socialist) ideology, that she did not want her books to be published by a "party" press.
[95] This sugar is referred to in letters dated May 30, 1945, June 27, 1945, August 30, 1945 and September, 11, 1945, all found in the Makhon Lvon archive.
[96] This, in the letter dated September 11th 1945, found in the Makhon Lavon archive.
[97] Ibid.

[98] David Roskies maintains that this tweaking/inversion of what is essentially a sacred text is a "parody of the sacred". See <u>Against the Apocalypse</u>, Harvard University Press, 1984, p.30.
[99] <u>Der Melekh Dovid Aleyz iz Geblibn</u>, p. 3.
[100] Op. Cit., p. 4.
[101] Op. Cit., p. 10.
[102] Op. Cit., p. 22.
[103] Op. Cit., p. 48.
[104] See Chapter Two, p.38.
[105] Harkavy's 1925 Yiddish-English dictionary gives "prison" as one of the meanings of the term *khad gadye*. He translates *"araynzetsn in khad gadye"* as "to put into prison. I am indebted to Kathryn Hellerstein for this realization. See her 1966 essay on this subject. The Harkavy reference can be found there on p. 253, note 3.
[106] This is a reference, as we will see to the words of the prophet Jeremiah, chapter 2, verse 33.
[107] See II Kings, chapter 2, verse 12. There Elijah simply ascends to heaven in a chariot.
[108] See <u>The Prophet Elijah in Modern Yiddish Folktales</u>, by Beatrice Weinreich, Columbia University Press, 1957.
[109] See Chapter Two, pp.31-32.
[110] Traditionally this cup is called "the cup of Elijah the Prophet". It assumes a position of honor at all Passover tables.
[111] See Malachi, chapter 3, verse 23.
[112] <u>Der Melekh Dovid Aleyn iz Geblibn</u>, p. 5.
[113] Ibid.
[114] This is page 6 of the same poem. Kadya is obviously referring here to the verse in Jeremiah in which the prophet castigates the children of Israel for digging wells that cannot hold water (looking to alien sources for support), when they have at their disposal a well-spring that will never disappoint them (their own God).
[115] <u>Der Melekh Dovid Aleyn iz Geblibn</u>, p. 69.
[116] Op. Cit., p. 70.
[117] See Isaiah, chapter 11, verse 1.
[118] <u>Der Melekh Dovid Aleyn iz Geblibn</u>, p. 74.
[119] Jewish custom has the mourner make a rip in her/his outer garment, and that garment is worn throughout the seven-day morning period. This outer rip is symbolic of the "torn heart" of the mourner.
[120] II Samuel, 19/1.
[121] <u>Der Melekh Dovid Aleyn iz Geblibn</u>, p. 86.
[122] Op. Cit., pp. 86-87.
[123] Op. Cit., p. 87.
[124] Op. Cit., p. 12.
[125] Op. Cit., p. 13.

[126] Ibid.
[127] So truly did Kadya identify with, and love, snow, that when Rivka Basman Ben-Haim wrote a poem dedicated to Kadya, she called that poem "A Whiteness". See: The Thirteenth Hour, Mayapple Pres, 2016, pp. 24-25.
[128] See Chapter 3, p. 12.
[129] *Der Melekh Dovid Aleyn iz Geblibn*, p. 84.
[130] Exodus, chapter 16, verse 4.
[131] Exodus Raba, 25/3.
[132] *Der Melekh Dovid Aleyn iz Geblibn*, p. 84.
[133] Ibid.
[134] Ibid.
[135] *Der Melekh Dovid Aleyn iz Geblibn*, p. 85.
[136] See Orland Figes, The Whisperers: Private Life in Stalin's Russia, Allen Lane, 2007, pp.123-126 and Timothy Snyder, Bloodlands, Europe Between Hitler and Stalin, Basic Books, 2010, who says that under Communism, children were supposed to be "the eyes and the ears of the party inside the family", p. 50.
[137] *Der Melekh Dovid Aleyn iz Geblibn*, p. 94.
[138] Op. Cit., pp. 96-97.
[139] This is a cycle of poems extending nearly 30 pages with incisive social satire. See pp. 99-129.
[140] *Der Melekh Dovid Aleyn iz Gebibn*, pp. 130-133.
[141] Op. Cit., pp. 154-155.
[142] This, in a letter dated March 9, 1942.
[143] This, in a letter dated November 8, 1947, found in the YIVO archive.
[144] The Rabbinic principle says: if one is given a positive, one can deduce the negative. In Hebrew "*Mi-klal hen, ata shome'a lav*"
[145] See end-note xxxv of chapter 3.
[146] See Hellerstein, 1999, footnote 74, p.58.
[147] Why she was so indifferent about her correspondence is a matter best left to her biographers. It is clear, though, that she felt her "work", her poetry and novels, were her true legacy. Her archive is in the Jewish Public Library of Montreal.
[148] See Kadya's letter to Ida from May 20, 1937, found in the Montreal archive.
[149] This, in a letter dated October 30, 1947, found in the Montreal archive.
[150] Ibid.
[151] Ibid.
[152] This, in a letter dated "end of rosh ha-shanah", [September 16] 1947, found in the Montreal archive.
[153] This, in a letter dated December 20, 1947, found in the Montreal archive.
[154] This in a letter dated September 3, 1948, found in the Montreal archive.
[155] This, in a postcard he wrote to her, dated October 13, 1946. For more on this song in the pre-state era, See: http://www.zemereshet.co.il/song.asp?id=717
[156] See http://en.wikipedia.org/wiki/Muselmann

[157] Two such women were Yehudit Simkhoni(t) and Sara Kafri. For more on the former, see: ttps://he.wikipedia.org/wiki/יהודית_שמחוני . For more on the latter, see: https://he.wikipedia.org/wiki/שרה_כפרי

CHAPTER FIVE: PARADISE LOST: THREE YEARS IN ISRAEL

Between the dream and the reality falls the shadow.

T. S. Eliot

There's a story told to all who would "make Aliyah", i.e., immigrate to Israel. Here's how it goes:

A man was once taken into the next world. There the receiving angel told him his good deeds and bad deeds were about equal. Accordingly, the new arrival could choose: either heaven or hell. Seeing that the new arrival was wavering, the angel suggested they tour each of the possible choices so the man could make an informed decision.

First, they peeked into heaven. There the man saw folks sitting and learning Torah. After that they peeked into hell. There the man saw folks at the beach, lolling around and having a grand time. He immediately decided on hell.

"No problem", the angel said, and threw the man into hell. But lo and behold! What the man saw was different from what he'd seen earlier: fiery sulfur, pitch and devils laughing.

The man tried banging on the closed door in an attempt to escape. He screamed out: "Hey, this isn't the place you showed me earlier!"

Through the closed door the receiving angel called back: "Then you were a tourist. Now you're a new immigrant".

It's in that spirit that we need to see Kadya's attempt to "make Aliyah", or actually live in Israel, not as a tourist, but as a new immigrant.

Austerity

The early 1950s were years of austerity in Israel. Most of the immigrants who arrived were penniless refugees from the Arab/Muslim world: Jews from technologically backward countries, like Yemen, Morocco, Tunisia and Algeria, the generally non-wealthy but idealistic Jews of Persia/Iran, and Iraq, and of course, refugees from the displaced persons camps that were emptying out in Europe. In the US, American citizens were enjoying a post-war boom. But in the new State of Israel, life was difficult.

The austerity plan, instituted in 1949 and formulated with the intention of establishing the new state on a firm economic footing, restricted the food and goods available to ordinary citizens. Each citizen was assigned to a given grocery shop at which (s)he could obtain the allotted amount of rationed goods, for example, meat or eggs, in exchange for "points" that were issued to each individual. The transactions were then registered in each person's account book.

The government's plan had a rationale. With the enormous influx of immigrants, the increased demand for food, it was felt, would far exceed the country's meager supply. Then, only the wealthy few would be able to purchase the necessities of life, while the overwhelming majority of the poor would be left to languish in hunger.

There is no question that the Socialist ideology of the state's elite played a role in formulating this solution. Socialist orthodoxy demanded equality between all the state's citizens. But it is also true that Great Britain herself had instituted such a policy in the Mandate era, and other European countries were dealing with the post-war threat of inflation in this same manner.

The daily allotment, determined by an American nutritionist, was: unlimited access to standard bread, 60 grams of corn, 58 grams of sugar, 60 grams of flour, 17 grams of rice, 8 grams of pasta, 200 grams of low-fat cheese, 600 grams of onion and 5 grams of biscuit. Each citizen was allowed 75 grams of meat a month, and eggs, soap, chocolate, salted fish and milk powder were allotted in variable amounts, depending on supply. This allotment was not assigned whole cloth; allowances were made for the

Chapter Five: Paradise Lost-Three Yeasr in Israel 189

age and the situation of each citizen: pregnant women were allowed a greater portion of meat and cheese, and babies were allowed a larger portion of sugar and cornstarch.[1]

Loyal patriot that she was, Kadya never complained about this arrangement to anyone. But the archive that she left in Israel tells the story.

In the *Makhon Lavon* archive in Israel, along with the once-crucial documents, like Simche's Polish passport, the 1938 New Year's card addressed to Simche and sent from Aizik, and the note in French from what can only be considered Simche's one-time paramour, is a card for "food supplement for the ill", and the name of the ill person: Kadya Molodowsky. This chit was issued in 1951, a year after Kadya arrived in Israel, and its cost is announced openly: 50 "*prutot*", or cents. It is clear, then, that the usual food allotment did not suffice; Kadya needed, and paid for, "extra" food.

Apparently, Dora, always Kadya's guardian angel, knew of Kadya's need. It must have been she who wanted to send Kadya a "food package". In September 8, 1950, a year before Kadya paid for this extra food allotment given out by the government, a letter written in Yiddish was sent to Kadya from the Max Rosenthal Travel Bureau. Here it is translated into English:

"Due to the strict regulations of the Israeli government, the sending of food packages is regulated under licenses, so that we have permission to send package certificates according to their content, of which there is a copy below.

In the meantime, we're sending you a certificate for the Standard B package, which can be picked up from our representative on 87 Allenby Street, Tel Aviv.

It is also possible for you to get a food package via the post, and this usually takes up to 8 weeks for you to receive. Then you will have to see that the [government ZKN] regulations are met."

What follows were prices for overseas shipping of used clothing and food parcels. A note was appended saying that prices included merchandise, shipping, insurance and duty [levied] in Israel. The Standard B food package, apparently the one Dora wanted to send Kadya, included meat, butter, coffee, tea, dried fruit, cheese, a can of [powdered] milk, [a can of] sardines and cacao. It cost $16.25, Israeli duty prepaid.

The picture that emerges from these documents is clear. At first Kadya asked for help from abroad. But she could not and did not want to lean on her sister alone. Always proud, and especially sensitive to her presumed poverty, she was determined to make a go of things on her own. By the time she had been in the country for a year, she realized that she could not manage without asking for a special privilege. She made her peace with the new reality: she caved in and asked for the allotment given to the sick. When she asked for this allotment, she was informed that she had gotten a food allotment in 1949, when she came as a tourist. Now that she was a citizen, that allotment would be deducted from what she was presently eligible for. The extra food allotment she was given was valid for one month only.

Kadya knew when she decided to return to Israel in 1950, that food would be a problem. When she was in Israel on her exploratory trip in 1949, she wrote to her friend Rokhl:

"Life [in Israel] is hard. I lost another seven pounds of my meager weight, but I feel stronger in spirit".[2]

And in the time in between that exploratory trip and her formal immigration, she admitted, if offhandedly, that she was not all that strong:

"Now I am preparing for the long trip to the Land of Israel. I travel there with a peculiar kind of happiness– to the land of miracle and destiny, as you say. Now I have to recite Psalms so that my strength should last."

The months of 1949 that Kadya spent in Israel may have given her a foretaste of the difficulties awaiting her were she to immigrate, but the full weight of the reality did not hit her then. For one thing, part of the time, she, like most tourists, stayed in a guest house. As is the case today in Third World countries, tourists who lodged in guest houses at the time were fed a menu that in no way represented the daily fare of an average citizen. In addition, many of Kadya's friends lived on communal farms, called *kibbutzim* or *moshavim* in Hebrew. In these settlements, food rationing was meaningless. Resident members were not buying food at assigned grocery stores, and the rations, chits and stamps in a personal notebook that plagued the city folks were unknown at these places. If the farm raised chickens, and many did, one only needed to wait till the home-grown food showed up at the communal dining room. Eggs, rationed in cities, were available on the farms; as long as the member requests were reasonable, an egg or two could be had for the asking.

From the information that can be gleaned at this distance in time, it appears that Kadya never appealed to her farm-friends for "donations" of food. Had she asked, they would most certainly have shared. But once again, her pride kicked in; she could not bring herself to ask. Had they shared, she would not have had to pay for the extra ration allotted to the sick.

A slang word in Hebrew, known to all residents of Israel, is the word "*protektsiya*". One who has *protektsiya*, has "pull" or influence in the "right" places. There is no question that Kadya, friend to nearly all the country's elite, definitely had *protektsiya*. Despite this, she soldiered on, poorly nourished and losing weight, preferring to do things "by the books" and not by dint of personal favor. This unwillingness to call on personal favors plagued her throughout her stay in Israel. As we will see later, when she was desperate, she did indeed resort to her networked friends. But that action was reserved for dire situations, not daily accommodations.

Finding Housing

The housing that Kadya and Simche got was itself a product of *protektsiya*, although it is doubtful that Kadya thought of it this way at the time. The Pioneer Women (called *Mo'etset Ha-Po'alot*, or The Council of Women-Workers in Hebrew), the women's branch of the Israeli Labor party, was run by Kadya's women-friends.

Before we explain the role that this organization played in Kadya's stay in Israel, it is worth stopping at the mere name of this group: *Mo'etset Ha-Po'alot*.

Each word of this 2-part term is fraught with historical overtones. At the time, Soviet Russia was called "*Brit Ha-Mo'etsot*", or the "Alliance of Councils", to give the precise meaning of the Hebrew term. ***Mo'ets**[et/ot]*, the part of the term shared by the Hebrew name for the Russian political entity of the time, and the women's labor part of Israel, is a give-away for those who look closely. It is the Hebrew equivalent of the Russian word "*soviet*", a council, a body that takes [and gives] advice. Whose advice? The workers' advice, of course. The Soviet system was supposed to be of the workers, by the workers, and for the workers. And in fact, the second part of that two-part name is "*Ha-Po'alot*", [the] women workers. The women's organization in Israel that Kadya belonged to was a "workers' party". The name of the organization that came to Kadya's aid, then, was a clear echo of the ideology that reigned in Israeli politics of the time: a sort of Jewish Socialism.

Moetset Ha-Po'alot, whose name in Israel, as we have seen, had definite overtones of Socialism, went by an entirely different name in the US. There it was called "Pioneer Women". It is ironic that so communalist and Socialist a party should have had such an individualistic name in the US. But the name change was a stroke of brilliance. In the US, pioneers were admirable; their very name suggested hardships overcome personally in a rugged landscape. What's more, the glow attached to pioneers was useful for fund-raising. Although nominally affiliated with Israel's Labor Party, the women's branch of this party did its own fund-raising and used the monies it raised as it saw fit.

Bebe Idelsohn, whom Kadya apparently knew from Europe, was in charge of this party's funds when Kadya arrived in Israel. It is not altogether clear how the women managed to procure an apartment for Kadya, if in fact they did so. In a letter Bebe wrote to Kadya in 1949, she admitted that finding an apartment was "not an easy problem [to solve ZKN] now."[3] But she managed it. Even before she and Simche

Chapter Five: Paradise Lost-Three Yeasr in Israel

landed in Israel, Kadya knew that an apartment was waiting for them in Tel Aviv. Admittedly the apartment was then on the northern fringes of the Israel's major city, but it was theirs.

Or so they thought. Among the papers left in the Israeli archive is a court decision ruling that the apartment did in fact rightfully belong to Kadya and Simche. It is not altogether clear now why anyone would have contested this ownership. Nevertheless, it is a fact that someone did. Even this simple roof over their heads, was not theirs without a battle. Like so many other things that characterized life in Israel, the simplest things could, and did, become issues needing urgent attention and the intervention of friends.

To this day it is not entirely clear whether *Mo'etset Ha-Po'alot* only found the apartment for Kadya and Simche, or actually laid out some of the funds for this apartment. What is clear, though, is that Kadya and Simche bought that apartment, and the loans the couple took out in Israel were repaid in full before the couple left Israel for good.[4] In her memoir, written twenty years after she returned to New York Kadya said:

"We bought an apartment in a communally-owned house, a house of ten families. It was a meeting place of Jews from all over the world. One family was from Iraq. They spoke Arabic...Their daughter became the translator between her parents and their neighbors."[5]

Simche's Issues

The austerity difficulties and the legal problems over their apartment in Israel were not Kadya's and Simche's sole cause of aggravation in their new country. As often happens in ports, the shipping company that brought their goods into the country was not above reproach; the couple was charged twice for the same shipment. Simche protested and managed to get recompense for his complaints. On June 8th, 1950, The

Max Rosenthal Travel Bureau sent the couple a check of $64 "for baggage payment that was collected from them twice by mistake." Nor was that Simche's only complaint. Once again, he complained, and once again he was compensated. Two months after that first check came. On August 4th of 1950, the very same shipping company sent Simche a check for $74.98 "representing reimbursement for costs of repair and expenses on damage done to Mr. Symche [sic] Lew's shipments."

A Linguistic Home

It would be wrong to suppose that life in Israel was without its comforts. The mark of a writer thriving in a new language is her ability to play with the new material at her disposal. Modern, Israeli Hebrew was not Kadya's native medium, and yet, after living in Israel for a short while, she was pleased at her ability to show off a neologism, one that melded her native Yiddish with her newly acquired Hebrew. In a letter she wrote to Rokhl Korn, she suggested that Rokhl do as "we do in Tel Aviv" and write her a "*mikhtavl*", a little letter. In this word, *mikhtavl*, the Hebrew word "*mikhtav*", letter, forms the base, and the suffix [l], is a diminutive (meaning little or dear) taken from the Yiddish. This little neologism is the strongest possible evidence of cultural acclimation. Whereas Kadya's first year in the US was linguistically disorienting and frustrating, her first year in Israel brought her a comforting alignment of the personal and the public. For the first time in her life, her native Jewish culture corresponded with the culture of the land in which she lived. And she was not only culturally at home, she was linguistically at home.

In the Israel of 1950, Hebrew was the language of the land, but Yiddish was still spoken by a great many of Israel's Ashkenazic/European-descendant citizens. And Kadya was known as a Yiddish writer. The plan hatched by Kadya's friends in Israel was to start a Yiddish language literary journal which would be edited by Kadya. The details of this venture were apparently discussed in person in 1949, when Kadya was on her preparatory trip.[6] When she arrived as a new immigrant in Israel, in January of 1950, an office was waiting for her. So, too, were printing presses and staff. Even the name of the journal, *Heym* (home) had been already chosen.

Kadya had not felt at home anywhere for years. She called her new journal *Heym*, or home, and doing so, announced that in Israel she (believed she) had finally found a home.

The time has come to re-visit the language debate in Israel. By 1950, it was impossible to speak of a language war. There had been a war, but it was a war against the Jewish people. The great majority of the world's Yiddish speakers had been murdered in World War II. In Israel, no one seriously questioned the need to use Hebrew to unite the disparate Jewish communities that were pouring into the country in the early years of the state's existence. Almost alone among the Yiddish writers of her generation, Kadya was comfortable in both languages.

As Kadya saw it, establishing a Yiddish journal in Israel, where the common language was Hebrew, was itself an indication that the formerly warring camps had made peace. There was room for Yiddish and Yiddish literature, she believed, in a country whose Jewish language was Hebrew, the language of the Bible, and not Yiddish, the language of the Ashkenazic Jewish diaspora. But not all her colleagues saw it that way.

The accusations against her began while she was on her preparatory trip of 1949, even before she had settled in Israel as a new immigrant. In a letter she sent Rokhl while she was in Israel on that trip, she confided:

"In New York…they've already accused me of having sold out Yiddish here. Where they get that, I don't know, but they are a bit like the Culture-Congress, as long as they make noise."[7] Kadya may well have been referring to Leyvik's attack on her. H. Leyvik, then the one of the most esteemed, if not **the** most esteemed of the older generation of Yiddish writers attacked her in a letter she preserved in her Israeli archive. What follows is a translation of that letter:

"That you should have openly agreed that Yiddish needs to be brought as a sacrifice in Israel– then let it be brought! I wrote about that to [Avrom] Sutzkever, [then the youngest and probably the greatest of the younger generation of Yiddish writers. ZKN] even before I got your letter…I did not at all believe and even now I cannot believe that you could say such a thing. Now, why even begin to imagine such a thing, that Yiddish must [underlining in the original] be brought as a sacrifice? Haven't we brought enough sacrifices? And how could such a thing come out of your mouth?[8]

Pinski wrote me…[that] since he's been in Israel he hasn't heard Yiddish spoken, only Hebrew everywhere. How can one understand that?"[9]

Apparently, Kadya had indeed used the word "sacrifice" when speaking about veering away from Yiddish in Israel, and it was the unfortunate choice of the word "sacrifice" that brought down upon her the wrath of Leyvik. Nevertheless, had Leyvik looked at the substance of what Kadya had said, and not gotten hung up on this one word, he would have seen that Kadya's position was the only tenable one under the circumstances.

Leyvik may also have been annoyed with Kadya because when she spoke to the general public, she spoke in Hebrew. Knowing Israel as she did, her position was a no-brainer. Had she insisted on speaking only Yiddish at all times, she would not have been understood by the new generation that had grown up in Israel hearing mostly Hebrew and speaking Hebrew.

That trickle of criticism against Kadya for her position on the two Jewish languages became a torrent of vitriol after she became a new immigrant. For many Yiddish writers living in the Jewish Diaspora, the new Jewish state was seen as the potential savior of Yiddish. Considering the small slice of the Jewish world they knew, that made some sense. Their Jewish world did not include the communities of the Muslim world, proud Jewish communities on their own right. The Jewish communities of Egypt, Syria and Iraq/Iran-Babylonia, Morocco, Algeria, Tunisia and Yemen had known centuries of communal Jewish activity, but European Jews knew nothing of that. As far as they were concerned, their world, the world of Jewish creativity that had been circumscribed by Yiddish, was all there was. Now that a Jewish state had been established, they wanted all communication in the new state to be in Yiddish.

In a letter written in 1950, Kadya's friend Melekh Ravitch made it quite clear that he, too, was upset with her:

"I am angry at your unfriendly treatment of the Yiddish writers in Israel...Your st anding with your back to Yiddish literature in Israel and even more so to the Yiddish writers there is not an acceptable way. Listen to the word of an old friend and repent..."[10]

It is hard to figure out just what upset Kadya's detractors. After all, in her journal, she featured Yiddish writers, and she made sure to pay them on time.

Living in Israel as she did, Kadya got to see firsthand the multitude of other Jewish communities. She knew full well that it would be foolhardy in the extreme, (not to mention unwise and unworkable), to insist that all the people in the country speak what was essentially the native language of only a part of the people.

Long after Kadya left the country, Kathryn Hellerstein interviewed M. Tsanin, one of the activists fighting for Yiddish in the early years of the state, in an attempt to uncover the truth about the language issues of Kadya's time in Israel. This is what he had to say:

"Molodowsky chose to ingratiate herself with the Zionists by speaking in Yiddish against the Yiddish language and in support of Hebrew, arguing that Yiddish was not necessary in Israel."[11] Neither Leyvik nor Tsanin were fair in their accusations. Kadya did not say that Yiddish ought never to be spoken, as Levik implied, only that it could and should not be forced on all speakers. Nor did she ever imagine that Yiddish was not necessary at all in Israel, as Tsanin implied. Had she believed that, she would not have toiled over establishing and nurturing a Yiddish-language literary journal in Israel. But she did realize (as they did not) that it would have been cultural imperialism for the European, Ashkenazic leaders of Israel to impose their language on the

Sephardic, non-European Jews of Israel. What's more, she did not need to "ingratiate herself with the Zionists"; she herself was a Zionist.

It is fascinating to see how this issue morphed over the years. In real time, Kadya responded to the attacks from abroad on Yiddish writers in Israel with an offensive of her own:

"One can do nothing for Yiddish in Israel if such cold winds come from America...After all, one cannot heal one limb when a second limb shows signs of crippling paralysis. And from there [the US- ZKN] the healing has to begin..."[12]

Essentially, Kadya's defense was an offence: the position of Yiddish in the US was what needed attention. Quite apart from hurling responsibility to those across the ocean, Kadya insisted, once again, in real time, in an interview with a foreign correspondent that:

"There is no antagonism to Yiddish in Israel..."[13]

That same article pointed out that "The *Histadruth*, which had invited Kadya to Israel, was now issuing a monthly periodical in Yiddish entitled *Di Goldene Keyt*."[14]

And yet, years later, when interviewed in Hebrew, she claimed that she left the country (in 1952) because of the antagonism that prevailed against Yiddish.

"In the years that I lived in Israel, there was a great antagonism to the Yiddish language, and I was not interested in fighting for it. I am not a fighter, and so I returned to my readers in America."[15]

Virtually every part of the above statement is patently untrue. For one thing, while she was living in Israel, Kadya herself claimed (in the interview quoted above as well as in her letters to her friend Rokhl Korn) that there was no antagonism to Yiddish in Israel.

Furthermore, she most definitely was a fighter. And when she fought, she fought long and hard. The fighting spirit characterized her years in Warsaw and then later, her years in New York. She herself confessed this was so in a poem about herself. Indeed, the Yiddish journal she edited, and did her best to foster, was part of her fight for a rightful place for Yiddish in a country whose Jews came from all corners of the globe. The immigrants came speaking a wide range of diverse languages, but all were forced to communicate in the shared, ancestral language: Hebrew. What's more, it is doubtful that she had more readers in the US than she had in Israel.

Why, then, this dissimulation? It is my contention that Kadya wanted to cover the tracks of her "defeat" in Israel. She and Simche had believed he would be able to support them in Israel, as he had while they lived in the US. But that did not happen. More of this later on.

The Ruling Socialist Party

For all that she seemed a loyal party member of the ruling Socialist party, Kadya was by no means a blind follower of all party dictates. The Labor movement in Israel was bound up with the communal settlement of the Land of Israel. While Kadya had friends who lived in communal settlements, she herself never showed any inclination to be anything other than an urban dweller. In this she was unlike her Socialist friends and at one with the great majority of the Sephardic immigrants. Most of the latter had not grown up with Socialist sentiment, and most had no hankering for communal life.

In the YIVO archive in New York City, there is an unpublished (and apparently never-staged) play entitled *"Oyf Eygene Erd"*, On Our-Own Land. It is sub-titled: "a drama about the new immigrants in Israel during the years of the great wave of immigration, after the establishment of the State of Israel." While the piece itself is more a play of ideas than a drama, it is fascinating for its spot-on observations, observations that can only have come from first-hand, intimate experience.

In this play, the rift between the immigrants who have arrived from the Orient and the "welcoming", native-born Israelis, who care for them in the makeshift immigrant camps, is stark and unvarnished. Alexandra, a Moroccan-born young girl who is learning a trade in the tent city of immigrants, hears the "natives" mock her and her kind, calling them "raw human material". Their mockery brings on her own comment on the situation. Here Kadya inserted by hand the following passage:

(She becomes upset and excited): "I am more intelligent than they, but they are full of themselves."

This is by no means the only rift in this camp. There is also tension between the native, Israeli-born Jews of European descent and the European-born Holocaust survivors, who have come from displaced persons camps in Europe. Kadya has one of the survivors say about the man who runs the immigrant camp:

"He's a Jew and I'm a Jew. He lives in Israel, and I live in Israel. But the two of us come together like my cap and God's forehead."

The new immigrants hear over and over again how hard it was for the original settlers to get the country up to its present standard. All knew that many of Europe's Jews did not immigrate to Israel before WWII because the early Zionists were anti-religious. Consequently, Kadya has one of the Holocaust survivors cry out:

"You built the land, but we guarded the Torah. We paid dearly for that guardianship."

Finally, there is a rift between the parents' generation of early settlers who were Socialist farmers, and the younger generation, who are fed-up with an enforced communalism. Here Kadya puts the protest in the mouth of a son at odds with his mother:

"I can't stand the constant "we" and "us". For once I want to say 'I'".

It is not clear when Kadya wrote this play, but it must have been after she left Israel and returned to New York. None of the rifts on display in that piece would have surprised Israelis at the time. But the American Jewish public was for the most part unaware of these problems. If Kadya made no effort to have this play performed, that is almost certainly due to her reluctance to "air dirty laundry in public". She saw these problems first-hand, and she was moved enough to write about them, but the end-product was not for public consumption.

She did write a novel about life in Israel, one which was published after she left Israel. The germ of that novel can be found in this play, but the social rifts are softened in the novel. A comparison of the archived, unpublished play, and the published novel await the efforts of a promising graduate student.

Mo'etset Ha-Po'alot, the organization that supported Kadya's literary journal, was, during those years, a social service organization. The party's funds were used to support education and vocational training for the immigrant women and children who had arrived in Israel with no resources. Kadya traveled the country, examining and reporting on these activities in the journal that she edited. But the journal articles, intended as Public Relations material for the organization that sponsored it, did not dwell on the tensions that made their way into her un-staged drama.

One can't help wondering how the Yemenite women in the immigrant camps, women who had been married off at 12 or 13, and had become mothers at 14, saw this middle-aged European-born woman. Coming as these women did from a Patriarchal society in which women had no independent say on how their lives were run, it must have been strange indeed to hear this "alien"/Ashkenazic woman urging them to acquire a skill and some education and claim their rights as working women. Some did just that, of course, as the young, fictional Moroccan-born "Alexandra" of Kadya's play (and novel) demonstrates. But most were in no position to question the social norms they had grown up with. It would be a generation, sometimes two, before the feminist message of women's education and women's work took root in this population.

The working woman was, in theory, the heroine of *Mo'etset Ha-Po'alot*. But the fact remains that the working life of women was hard indeed. Unlike Kadya, who was childless, most working mothers had to juggle childcare and their jobs. In communal settlements, this was a lesser problem. Some of these settlements had communal arrangements for child-rearing. Here children slept not with their parents, but in a children's room, along with their age-mates. They ate together and spent their day together, and saw their parents only for a small fraction of the day. Whatever else can be said for this arrangement, it did free the women up for attending to their communal jobs without the distraction of child-care.

This "solution" was not available to urban dwellers. For them *Mo'estset Ha-Po'alot* offered day-care centers and crèches. This, too, was a limited solution; it worked only for the mothers of the very young. Because children in elementary school in Israel were dismissed from class at one PM, a mother who had a full-time job was simply unable to attend to her "older" children once they had gotten out of class. It is doubtful if Kadya ever realized the extent of this problem. By the time she arrived in Israel, most of her friends were middle-aged, and this sort of question did not arise in their lives.

Dora's Invaluable Help

There were drawbacks to life in Israel that Kadya divulged to no one but her sister. One of these was the tendency of Israelis to insinuate themselves into each other's affairs. For fifteen years, from 1935 to 1950, Kadya had lived in New York. There she had learned, as all New Yorkers do, that the key to well-being in the city is the ability to mind one's business. This principle, which can probably be traced to the early colonial period of the US, when the first flag of the navy had the inscription: "Don't Tread On Me",[16] and the first minted coin by the US said "Mind Your Business",[17] was especially sacrosanct in a densely populated city like New York. By the time she arrived in Israel, Kadya had internalized this notion. But life in Israel ran on completely different principles.

In a letter to her sister Dora, Kadya apparently reported that a neighbor of hers, a woman she had never formally met, knocked on her door one day and complained that Kadya was profligate in her use of electricity. The light in Kadya's apartment was on until all hours of the night, it seemed. And that, the neighbor announced, was irresponsible!

It is not as though there was a declared national blackout or a national emergency at the time. At the time, every citizen was free to use electricity as (s)he saw fit. And Kadya was paying for the electricity that she used. Nevertheless, this neighbor had, on her own initiative, decided to point out the "wastefulness" inherent in Kadya's behavior.

Wanting to be a good neighbor and wanting to "fit in" socially in her new environment, Kadya took this tongue lashing passively, and did not admonish her nosy neighbor. But she did relate the story to her sister.

Dora, a loyal sister and feisty in her own way, told Kadya: "I would have answered her".[18] In this she reinforced Kadya's sense that she need not accept all the mores of her "newly adopted" country.

Dora did more than just urge Kadya to assert herself when attacked. She kept Kadya's finances intact. Kadya sold books abroad and these funds went to Dora and Kadya's father Aizik, her two book-keepers in the US. Dora managed Kadya's US bank transactions. She also collected the rent for Kadya's New York apartment, and made sure that Kadya's US taxes were paid.[19]

One of Kadya's casual correspondents commented in a letter to her that it must have been hard for her to adapt to the scrappy life of an Israeli citizen after having lived in the "flesh-pot" [in Hebrew *sir ha-basar* ZKN] of the US. There was some truth to this, but it was not the truth the correspondent undoubtedly meant. The writer apparently thought Kadya would miss the abundant portions of food she was used to eating in the US. This was simply not the case. While the lack of adequate nutrition was something that needed to be addressed, the food issue does not seem to have been a deal-breaker for Kadya. Never an esthete, or what modern folks might call a "foodie", she did what she needed to do to get herself the food she needed. And then she proceeded to what she felt was truly important.

Pioneer Women Renege on a Contract

There were issues that Kadya encountered that she apparently never told anyone about. Or if she did, the information was never made public. One of them was her run-in with the Pioneer Women, known in Israel as *Mo'etset Ha-Po'alot*. At some point during her stay in Israel, she was asked to author a book about the contributions to this organization from women-donors the world over. Because so many different women from so many different countries had taken part in the philanthropic activities that this organization undertook, and because Kadya wanted to give each of them her due, she sent out a flurry of letters to the far-flung corners of the world, asking for the relevant information. As she was gathering it all and forming a coherent narrative, she received word that the project had been canceled. She had been given an advance, and she was allowed to keep that. But she was asked to forego the rest of the agreed-upon sum. And this, despite the fact that she already spent many hours on this work. It's not as though she had much choice in the matter; she agreed to forego the rest of the sum. But there is no question that this soured her relationship with an organization that she had seen as her natural home.[20]

Drawbacks of the Socialist System

The fifteen years she spent in the US, from 1935 to 1950, had changed Kadya's attitude somewhat to the platitudes of her youth. In her days in Kiev, and later in Warsaw, she subscribed to the Socialist belief that the only guarantor of the good life for ordinary citizens was a centralized government. The capitalist system, she and her Socialist friends then believed, was necessarily exploitive and detrimental to the social good. But Kadya's sisters Dora, and Lina, like so many poor Jewish immigrants to the US between the Word Wars, were not exploiters by any means. Lina may have married a man of means, but Dora did not. She and her husband worked very hard at the Litman Kiddie shop. Like all small business people, they had some good years, and some not-so-good years. They changed their supplies to meet the changing demand; they made improvements to their store when they could, and they moved up and on with the changing American economy. In the post WWII era, when times were booming, their business prospered along with so many others. They moved their shop; they first renovated their house, and then moved into a bigger one; they bought a television and a car. As these improvements came into their family life, Kadya received reports from Aizik, (who had his own take on these things) if not from Dora (who may well not have wanted her sister to feel left out). Other relatives in the family, also former impoverished immigrants prospered as well, some more, and some less. Clearly, the capitalist system worked pretty well.

Kadya was not a systematic thinker or a theorist; she was a writer and a poet. What gripped her attention was not the construction of potential social or economic systems, but human lives as they are lived. Great observer of the minutia of human lives that she was, she could not help noticing that life for ordinary folk had improved immeasurably under capitalism in the US. She noticed this and portrayed these improvements in the short stories she wrote.

It was with this background that she experienced the restrictions on the movement of capital and the price control and price fixing of the early years of the State of Israel. For many years after the establishment of the State of Israel, Israeli citizens were not allowed to have bank accounts in dollars. All foreign monies had to be changed into Israeli currency and only then deposited in Israeli banks. Young and insecure as the country was in the early 1950s, its currency was an iffy proposition, and no one in their right mind changed solid dollars into Israeli lira. Most immigrants to Israel of those years came with nothing at all in the way of savings. Accordingly, this issue did not apply to them. But Kadya and Simche did have some savings in dollars. And they took some of this with them. Naturally, the bank of Israel was happy to change their dollars into Israeli lira at an exorbitant exchange rate. It also charged them a deposit surcharge and was unwilling to let these funds out of the country. Loyal citizens that they were, the couple did not complain. They even bought Israeli government bonds, as they had bought US government bonds during World War II.

In the post WWII US and Canada, Jews were buying Kadya's books. This was not the Warsaw-like crush to read Kadya's latest Yiddish book, but it was a trickle. Ida was Kadya's go-to-person for this in Canada, while Dora was Kadya's go-to person for this in the US. These two women collected Kadya's earnings for her and were responsible for getting the monies to her. But neither woman wanted to see Kadya suffer, as these hard-earned funds were gobbled up by the Israeli currency-control system. Even Lipa Lehrer, the publisher of the *Matones* publishing press, told her that he was aware he owed her money, but uncertain of the best way to get it to her.[21] Apparently Ida and Dora consulted with each other on this. Their solution was to find trusted friends and relatives who were traveling to Israel as tourists or were going to Israel on missions to whom they could entrust the cash they had collected. They complained to Kadya when they could not find appropriate candidates and they lamented the unfairness of the Israeli system to her in their letters. For her part, Kadya gave paid lectures whenever she could, in person and on the radio, in Yiddish and in Hebrew. She, who had not had to support herself after Simche found himself a job as a type-setter in New York, was once again trying to earn a living for herself in Israel.

Dora, who was both proud of Kadya, and concerned that her sister was not getting all that she needed, never failed to offer help. As Passover approached in 1952, she wrote to Kadya:

"Write to us. Perhaps you need something for Passover. We hear that the situation is difficult [in Israel ZKN].[22]"

Dora was not the only one who worried that Kadya did not have all she needed in Israel. Just as Dora offered to send Kadya things, so Sarah offered to help. In fact, she didn't wait for an answer. In March of 1952, she informed Kadya that she had already sent out a package for her. What bothered Sarah, she said, was that packages took so long to arrive.[23]

Quite apart from the issue of currency control was the issue of price controls. In her Israeli archive, Kadya left behind her a small flyer that citizens were given in 1951. There is no way one can know for sure why she preserved this flyer. I will venture a guess from what I know of her biography.

Addressed to "All the citizens of Israel" this was a memorandum from Israel's Prime Minister David Ben-Gurion concerning the government's policy on price controls. In an exhortation to the citizens not to attempt to enrich themselves at the expense of the public and the state, it demanded that the public; - return all surplus to store owners, - sell all goods exclusively at the legal price determined by the government, - not sell any regulated items for anything but government-issued chits, - cooperate fully in this public fight. Furthermore, all citizens were given a list of "thou shalt-nots": all citizens were told not to- sell items on the black market, - agree to pay over-valued prices, consume more than the government allotted each individual. Women's organizations were told they could play a crucial role in rooting out the evils (and presumably) evil-doers. Finally, this flyer tells all: "And your camp must be pure/holy"! [exclamation point in the original ZKN]

Can folks be ordered not to consume more than the government tells them to? Will consumers never pay inflated prices for much-valued, but hard-to-find items? Will folks refrain from enriching themselves when they are in possession of hard-to attain items? Can family and friends of store keepers truly not expect "special treatment" from the purveyors of goods and services? What are friends for, then? Finally, did the prime minister truly believe that mothers and fathers would not give special treatment to their own children? What sort of man would expect such abnormal/inhuman behavior?

Kadya had seen rationing of goods during WWII and she and her family had known exactly how to behave. When Ida visited Kadya in New York, she brought along sugar, an item that was being rationed in the US, but not in Canada. Kadya had siphoned off some for herself and Simche, and then taken some to her sister Dora and her father Aizik in Philadelphia. Friends and family do just that in times of need, and they are proud of this. What was Ben-Gurion thinking?

The ultimate half-comical punch-line of that flyer was almost too absurd. Those words are a quote from the Hebrew Bible, but oh, what a quote! In order to get the full comic effect of this quote one has to know the relevant passage from the Bible. Here are verses 13-15 from Deuteronomy chapter 23:

Verse 13: "Thou shalt have a place also without the camp, whither thou shalt go forth abroad. Verse 14: And thou shalt have a paddle among thy weapons; and it shall be, when thou sittest down abroad, thou shalt dig therewith, and shalt turn back and cover that which cometh from thee. Verse 15: For the LORD thy God walketh in the midst of thy camp, to deliver thee, and to give up thine enemies before thee; therefore **shall thy camp be pure/holy**…"

This passage, then, is a Biblical injunction about simple hygienic practice. Put bluntly, it urges, or rather, commands, the children of Israel to designate a spot outside their camp for defecation, and urges each person to clean up properly after (s)/he defecates. Now it is true that the word "pure/holy" is used here. But it is used for a most mundane, most basic, human need. The Hebrew Bible does indeed treat basic human physical needs with great seriousness, and it does endow human needs with holiness, but Ben-Gurion did not believe in the concept of the sacred, as opposed to the profane. He and his Socialist friends were outright atheists, mockers of traditional religion.

Can Ben-Gurion have been suggesting with this quote that his flyer was "no more than shit"?! One doubts this strongly. The early Socialist leaders of Israel took themselves and their orders very seriously. They were not given to self-mockery.

But Kadya had studied the Hebrew Bible. And unlike the all-too-serious leaders of the party, she knew how to indulge in self-mockery. It is quite likely that she knew the origin of this quote and got a well-deserved smile from this unintended self-mockery. In fact, this may well be why she saved this yellowing bit of social engineering.

We saw earlier that the government of Israel regulated all shipments of personal goods into Israel, and taxed everything exorbitantly. Surprisingly, it stuck to this policy even when the incoming goods were used goods intended for the *Mo'etset Ha-Po'alot* volunteers, women who were themselves trying to help an overstressed government handle the flood of new, impoverished immigrants. Among the papers Kadya left in her Israeli archive is the evidence for this rather self-destructive behavior of government and quasi-governmental agencies in Israel.

One such document is a torn letter, written in English by Bebe Idelsohn, addressed to the general secretary of the Labor party. It is clear that the men of the Labor party were trying to stymie the efforts of the women's branch of the Labor party. Were they worried that the women would acquire too much political power? It is impossible to know now why they behaved as they did. But it is evident that they had some sort of gripe. Equally evident is Bebe's refusal to allow her group to become irrelevant. Here is how her letter went:

"Upon my return to Israel, I was told by… that in your letter of October 25 and December 28, 1950, you wrote that no help should be accepted by the *Batei Halutsot* (Pioneer Women's Houses) from *Mo'etset Ha-Po'alot*. We here are very much surprised to hear that you think you can decide this matter by yourselves."

On the back of this torn letter was a different hand-written note, this time written in Hebrew and addressed directly to the relevant government office. It is a note protesting the fact that the government insists on preventing packages from coming directly to the offices of *Mo'etset Ha-Po'alot*. Instead, the office of Commerce and Industry insists that the women volunteers obtain an import permit for each of the packages, a procedure that unnecessarily delays the delivery of these much-needed goods into the hands of the immigrants. She reminds the ministry that the Welfare office recommended these goods be customs free; they are, after all, good-hearted donations of used clothing and equipment that were sent by Jews from abroad, and they were meant to reach their needy recipients with all due haste. Finally, Bebe suggests she can provide the ministry with a detailed list of all the institutions and addresses her organization has worked with and helped in the past. Well-meaning women from all over the world trusted her organization with its goods, and Bebe was truly dedicated to seeing that she did not betray their trust.

Lack of Telephones

In those days, governmental regulation covered every aspect of life in the country, telephone lines included. Although Kadya had had a telephone in New York since the 1940s, a decade later she was unable to obtain one in Israel. This had nothing to do with her status as a new immigrant; telephones were rare in all of Israel.

Melekh Ravitch, Kadya's friend from her salad days in Warsaw, saw fit to tweak her about this one time when he tried, but was unable to find her, on his visit to Israel. In a letter dated October 23, 1950, Ravitch tells Kadya he left the country without saying goodbye to her not because he was angry, but because there are still no telephones in Israel.

What Kadya apparently never told him was that in August of that year she had paid out 120 Israeli lira, not so small a sum (roughly $50) in those days, for the privilege

Chapter Five: Paradise Lost-Three Yeasr in Israel 211

of getting a phone, whenever one would be available. But the receipt came with a caveat: "One can hope that the phone might be delivered no later than six months after payment is received." Jews always hope; daily they pray and hope that the Messiah will deliver the entire world from its hatreds and peace will reign everywhere. But hope is one thing, and reality is another. In the Israel of the 1950s, the reality was that most citizens simply did not get phones, whether or not they had ordered and paid for one.

Elite Status

Despite the fact that Kadya did not have the creature comforts in Israel that she had had in New York, the fact is she was admired by those who knew her work, and she was a welcomed guest in the parties of the influential elite. In her Israeli archive she kept the personal invitation that she and Simche got from the then-Prime Minister of Israel, David Ben Gurion to a personal reception he and his wife were giving on Israel's Independence Day in 1950. If she went, she probably reported the event to her sister and to Rokhl Korn with her usual skeptical eye. But Dora saved none of her letters and Rokhl saved only a handful. We will never know, then, how she liked (or disliked) mingling with the politically powerful.

Helping the Unfortunate

While she was a young woman, barely 20 years old, Kadya empathized with the plight of the unfortunates she encountered. Her attraction to Socialism was founded on just this empathy: for a while at least, she truly believed that only under a Socialist form of government would the lot of the poor be ameliorated. This preoccupation with actively helping the poor was part of what brought her to the volunteers of the Women's

Labor party. But she also got involved in trying to help ordinary folks whom she happened to meet.

In the archive she left behind a curious correspondence she had with one of the higher-ups in the *Histadrut*, the Labor Party's workers' union. Kadya had apparently gotten to know the owner of a street-stand/kiosk who had fallen on hard times. It is not clear whether he lost the permit for his stand or got sick and was unable to work. What is clear is that he was suffering, and Kadya felt moved to help him.

In an amazing display of naiveté, Kadya demanded that the workers' union help this small businessman, the self-employed owner of this kiosk. But the union was powerless to help: it was a meant to help "workers" who were union members. This kiosk owner was a "businessman", not a worker. What's more, he had never paid union dues. Because she was so respected, Kadya got the attention of the higher-ups in the union, but they too were unable to help. Here is their response:

"In answer to your letter of 17.01.1951 about the plight of Mr.___:

This man is not a member of the *Histadrut* [the workers' union] and he was never registered [as a worker ZKN] in the labor office. <u>Till now he was the owner of a kiosk and he needed neither the *Histadrut* nor the Labor office.</u> [underlining in the original ZKN] There is, therefore, no cause to speak of an injustice that was done to him."

Appended to this is a note from the higher-up Labor official, a personal friend of Kadya's, who informs her that he has tried registering this man as a union member, and that should he succeed in getting this man registered in the labor office, help might be forthcoming.

This must have called forth Kadya's ire, because on the side of this note, in a different color ink, is the comment of Kadya's friend:

"I tried; I explained, and there is a small chance something can be done…But the fault does not lie with us, and this time it is not our public that was guilty…"

The entire correspondence had been conducted till here in Hebrew. Suddenly the correspondent added a sentence in Yiddish:

"Unfortunately, this was dealt with ex post facto– too late."

One wonders what lesson Kadya learned from this incident. For her, one suffering man was just like another suffering man. But for the Party, there was "us"/the workers/employees, otherwise known as "our public", and everyone else/the employers. Even worse, the small businessman in question elicited no one's empathy simply because he was not "a worker", and had not paid union dues. It may well be that the characters in her unpublished play draw on this experience of hers. If that is the case, her lesson remained for the drawer only; no one among her public readers had any inkling that this issue upset her.

Feminist Issues

From her very first appearance on the public scene, Kadya was known for her strong interest in women's issues. While it is true that she wrote no "feminist" poetry in the three years that she edited *Heym* in Israel, her journal did provide a platform for her feminist friends. In the third issue of *Heym*, her friend Yehudit Simkhonit, then a member of parliament, outlined her program for legal reform on women's issues. It was extraordinarily ambitious. Given the difficulties then facing women in Israel, it was, in fact, almost utopian.

The first issue it wanted to reform was the inferior position of women matters pertaining to marriage and divorce.[24] These issues, then, as now, are settled in Israeli rabbinical courts, where the active agents in both marriage and divorce are men, not women.[25] Exactly how this change would come about, Simkhonit did not say. But before change could happen, there needed to be an awareness of the problem. And that was part of Simkhonit's platform.

In addition, a call went out to end discrimination against women in the workplace.[26] Once again, the devil was in the details. How one could guarantee equal pay for equal work was not clear. But the goal was clear.

Other suggestions were giving new mothers a stipend, and allowing mothers to take paid leave after childbirth.[27] These suggestions did in fact become law.

Simkhonit was clear-sighted enough to realize that just because the workers' union had made gains, there was no guarantee that these gains would not be rescinded. She pointed out that in addition to making demands and getting concessions from the *Histadrut*, it would behoove women to have these gains established as the law of the land.

A glance at the issues of *Heym* reveals a journal that served party interests. Unlike *Di Goldene Keyt*, a purely literary journal which maintained high standards, *Heym* devoted much of its space to the doings of the workers' party. If Kadya agreed to a lesser literary standard for this journal, that can only be because her feminist concerns were paramount. Here she had an opportunity to help shape the future of the working woman in the new Jewish state. If Kadya herself did not work towards the feminist goals that Simkhonit envisioned, and she did not, she did at least provide a platform for these concerns in her journal.

Aizik and the Family Back Home

While she was in Israel working on her journal, Aizik reported on events "back home". When Dora became a grandmother, Aizik sent off a letter that very day, informing Kadya of the news and even informing her of the baby's birth weight[28].

Not long afterwards, in describing the hustle-bustle of the family and Dora's attempts to be everywhere at once: in the store (selling baby clothes), shopping and buying food, in the kitchen preparing food, he includes a description of the mother and her new-born:

"Minkele spends her time with her new-born "genius"" [Yiddish: *khokhem*].²⁹

Aizik could have spoken that way with no one but Kadya. It's not as though he was unhappy with the arrival of the baby; that was by no means the case. But removed from the child-rearing at the distance of four generations, he was able to watch the mother's overvaluing of her child's achievements with some detachment. Kadya, who truly loved children, and had an uncanny way of channeling a child's mind, nevertheless, was also detached in this case. The Yiddish word Aizik used, "*khokhem*", is often used in just this way: derogatorily. Still, the intended tone was not biting or nasty; it was simply a tone of detached irony. That is certainly what Aizik intended, and it was almost certainly the way Kadya understood it. The two of them were equal onlookers in this case.

In this same vein Aizik spoke of his great-grandchildren's photos. When he knew that his grandchildren were about to send photos of their children to Kadya, he wrote:

"Listen to me, Kadya: Prepare in your house a respectful place: one of these days Edith will send you a photo of her handsome son Leibele; choose an honored spot for it. I'm of the opinion that Minkele will be jealous and will send you a photo of her Dovidl. This way you will have in your house the 'two heavenly bodies.'"³⁰

The expression Aizik used for the "two heavenly bodies": "*shney ha-me'oros* is an expression derived from the Hebrew Bible's story of the creation of the world. In Genesis, the sun and the moon, the crucial sources of light by day and by night, are referred to in just this phrase. Of course, for parents, their young children are so crucial a part of their world, that the children might be said to be "their day and their night". Was Aizik being ever so ironic here? It would seem so. But he could depend on Kadya to understand him.

The sense of being an outsider looking in extended to other things as well. Neither Aizik nor Kadya was ever fully at home in the US. Along with the birth of

Dora's grandsons came Aizik's news of the arrival of TV in Dora's home. This is Aizik's description of it in his letter to Kadya:

"Secondly I can inform you that in our house things are always joyful because of the television which was brought into the dining room. Every evening the family gathers around it and dissolves in laughter. What they are laughing at and what they see there: may I never know from evil as I don't know what is so amazing there that their livers shake from laughter."[31]

Early television programs relied heavily on comedy, and comedy is notoriously culture-dependent. It is likely that Aizik was missing the social cues that were the linchpin of the TV comedy programs his family watched and enjoyed. Did this outsider nature of his existence in his adopted country disturb him? It would seem it didn't. But he was not so out of touch with this new world as to be unaware of his outsider status. He reported it to Kadya because he knew that she, too, felt very much the same way in the US.

A second new acquisition "back home" was the new car that Dora's family bought. Here is Aizik's description of that:

"Moreover, you most probably know by now that they bought a new car for $2300– so they now drive home. When they arrive home, they tell such wonder stories about this car- that to me it often seems the car is a living object. "[32]

In that same letter, Aizik, always the gentle admonisher, points out to Kadya that when she left for Israel, she didn't properly take leave of one of her friends. This friend is, perhaps, hurt and disappointed, Aizik suggests. "Perhaps a good plan would be", Aizik suggests, for Kadya to write to this friend from Israel. Kadya was a middle-aged woman and could certainly be relied onto see to her own business. But neither she nor Aizik felt it was unseemly for Aizik to gently reproach her when he thought a reproach was called for.

In 1950 Aizik started writing to Kadya in Hebrew. It's impossible to know if he chose Hebrew because he wanted "to get practice" writing to someone who was

Chapter Five: Paradise Lost-Three Yeasr in Israel   217

now using Hebrew daily, or because he felt it was better to say what he wanted to say in Hebrew. Dora was far less likely to read a letter written in Hebrew before she sent it off. In these letters, he tells Kadya about Dora's new grandchildren:

In October he informed Kadya that Dora's spirits were exalted because of her grandchildren, who were handsomer, smarter and cleverer than any other children in the world, and all day she "dwells/thinks constantly" on them. Here Aizik uses the same word that the Bible uses in Joshua 1/8 for the commandment that the children of Israel "think constantly of [the Torah] day and night". Dora sings to her grandchildren in Russian, Polish and Yiddish, and now that she has joined the Pioneer Women, she even sings to them in Hebrew.[33]

A month later, in November of that year he wrote:

"This is to inform you how wonderful our situation and Dora's is, now that she has beautiful grandchildren, the geniuses of their generation. They would be worthy of royalty, were kingship granted these days to those who are handsome and brilliant.

Mrs. Dora Litman, a member of the Pioneer Women's committee in our city, is now otherwise preoccupied with her work in the store, so she delegated her responsibilities to me."[34] And here Aizik sends Kadya a list of subscribers to her journal. Some of the subscribers on the list were recruited by Dora, while others were recruited by Aizik himself.

In April of 1951, we get a sense of Aizik's discomfort with the way in which his great-grandchildren were being brought up. Naturally, this is something he speaks of only tangentially, and even then, in a most-ironic tone. Nevertheless, there is no question that there is more than a hint of disapproval in his tone:

"My dear ones, if a long span of time will elapse and you will not get a letter from me, you will know that even my new pencil has been stolen from me. Not, God forbid, that we have any robbers in this house. They simply take from me, and forget to return…

What can I tell you about these little rascals who together manage to break and destroy whatever they find and run away on their little feet to all corners of the house…When the family sits down together to eat, these little rascals force the family to see to their possessions, that they not be torn or destroyed. And those of the household, instead of getting angry with them or scolding them or punishing them for their deeds, applaud them for their feats and delight in their behavior. And the little ones, who have no [critical] sense, do not feel there is anything wrong with their behavior. And since that is the case, how will they ever behave differently?"[35]

There is no question that American parents were far more likely to be tolerant of the sort of behavior Aizik describes than any European-born parent would have been. In the US, even children (or perhaps, especially children) have rights, whereas such "rights" were unheard of in the Old Country. Clearly, Aizik looked on and did not approve. But clever man that he was, he voiced no disapproval to his daughter or his grandchildren. Instead, he confided in Kadya, who, he was sure, would understand him completely. We have no idea whether or how Kadya responded. But there is little doubt that with her background, she understood what Aizik meant, and she empathized.

By the summer of 1950, Aizik's handwriting became nearly illegible. A cataract problem prevented him from seeing well. He did try to write to Kadya, but there was no deciphering what he was saying. To deal with this handicap, Dora reported, she read to Aizik, and he listened. In his squiggly hand-writing, Aizik confirmed what Dora reported. He reported that he had made his peace with the new situation ("It didn't break me", he announces), but it is clear that he is not pleased.

Dora and Lina came to the rescue. By the late 1940s, it became possible to rehabilitate patients after cataract surgery.[36] Aizik was nearly 90 by then, but that did not deter him. Because he was willing to risk the surgery and attempt to regain his sight with prescription glasses, his daughters went ahead with the surgery. It was, in fact, one of the first cases of a cataract operation on so elderly a patient.[37] And it succeeded.

Chapter Five: Paradise Lost-Three Yeasr in Israel

By September, Dora was able to report that Aizik had put on the corrective lenses he'd been given after his operation. And he did in fact see well.[38]

A bit more than a month later, Aizik wrote a moving letter to Kadya and Simche making them his witness to his thankfulness to God for his recovery:

"This is the day I've hoped for; I can see with my eyes. Thank God for it is good, for His grace is eternal."[39] As Kadya and Simche surely knew, this is a quote from Psalms 136/1. It is a prayer that is often sung in the synagogue and it is part of the regular holiday and New Moon service. For Aizik, this was a personal holiday.

At the end of that letter, Dora writes a postscript, in Hebrew this time, perhaps to show Kadya she had in fact improved her skills, as befit a newly elected member of the local Pioneer women's committee. She told Kadya and Simche:

"I was truly so happy that I felt like dancing in the streets... We are privileged to see him sitting and writing...He is more like himself from day to day and it is a joy to see him come and go on his own..."[40]

For all this improvement, Aizik remained an older man, and his health dribbled away slowly. By April of 1951, Aizk confessed that he felt a lassitude come over him that he could not explain. He found himself unable to exert himself. He knew it was an expected correlation of old age and he was powerless against it. Here is how he explained himself to Kadya and Simche:

"You should know, my children, that Sloth, that despicable witch, has caught me in her net. I have married her, and she follows me wherever I go. Sleep and torpor surround me and pull me...And see what a surprise: card-playing has distanced itself both from me and from torpor. Why? How come? Who knows?"

We see here that same lightly mocking, ironic tone that we saw when Aizik spoke of his grandchildren and their obsession with their children. But this time the mockery is turned inward. Aizik is fully aware of what is happening to him, but through it all, he maintains a sense of humor.

It was Aizik's declining health that prompted Lina to write to Kadya.[41] It is possible, of course, that she wrote other letters to Kadya, letters that Kadya did not save. But from the archival remains, it seems that there was very little correspondence between them. From what we can tell, whatever Kadya and Lina knew of each other, came to them through the intermediary of Dora's correspondence.

Kadya's Need to See Aizik

In one of the few letters from Lina that Kadya kept in her archive is a letter in which Lina disclaims any negligence in caring for her father. Of course, it was Dora who housed their father and cared for him in an on-going way. But Lina wanted Kadya to be aware that she, too, did what she could:

"Believe me, my dear, I am doing the best that I can for our father. As soon as he is uncomfortable, we call the doctor immediately…The medicine makes him feel better.

If I hadn't gotten him [Aizik] to the doctors this summer, who knows what would have become of him! Kadya, I hear you are thinking of coming here this summer. How wonderful that would be for us all. We would all be delighted to see you."[42]

This suggestion was reinforced by Dora in subsequent letters. It was clear to both sisters that Aizik's health was declining. It was also clear to them that Kadya had a job and a life in Israel. Although they respected her professionalism, they also realized that she would be heartbroken if Aizik died in her absence. While they didn't say this outright, they certainly hinted as much. In May of 1951, Dora wrote:

"It would be very good if you hop on over here to see us. The entire family would love it and it would be a great joy."[43]

Chapter Five: Paradise Lost-Three Yeasr in Israel

In her letter to Kadya, Dora suggested that Aizik had gone upstairs to play a game of pinochle. But when that same letter was given to Aizik so he could add his own contribution before the letter was sent off, he said:

"What Dorale said earlier in this letter that I went upstairs to play cards is not correct. I went upstairs to learn *mishnayes* [the Hebrew part of the Talmud, typically recited and "learned" in memory of loved ones on the Jewish calendar date of their death] for the soul of one of my friends whose *yortsayt* [anniversary of their death] is today."[44]

That letter was Aizik as Kadya had always known him: determined, of an independent mind, and unafraid of saying exactly what was on his mind. Taking that into account, Kadya had no reason to believe there was any reason for her to drop her work right away and plan a trip to the US. Because the broad hints of the two sisters went unheeded, Dora finally spoke out loud and clear:

"We've made no plans for this summer because we hope you will be with us. Our father has insisted he would like to see you this summer and the whole family believes you need to be here. Father wants you to know he will cover all your expenses and we all wish you a good trip. Let us know whether you want to travel by boat or by plane so we can arrange everything for you..."[45]

The rest of this letter is devoted to Aizik's contribution. As he did once before, he tries her to convey to Kadya and Simche what it feels like to have one's strength drain away unwittingly:

"I have already told you that two women have attached themselves to me with great love: their names are "Sloth" and "Torpor". They are always with me. And despite the fact that they are each other's rivals, as it says [in the Bible: I Samuel, 1/6- ZKN] "and her rival was sorely vexed", in me they live in great harmony.

It is such peace and friendship, that whatever one rival says, the other agrees to. When Torpor hints that she wants to hug me, Sloth smiles and says [to me ZKN]: go ahead, embrace her in your arms, it will be good and pleasant. And when Sloth insists on my staying up and not falling asleep? Her rival shakes her head and says: yes, yes, I'm all for that. And so I am not myself. I have neither mind nor strength to fight them. Even now I hear the voice of my lovers call me: Enough! Enough! And I have no strength to resist them. So I say to them: Let it be as you say: enough!"[46]

For all that this letter shows a man who is very self-aware, a man resigned to his dwindling powers, there is still a sly humor here. The metaphor of the two witches, Sloth and Torpor, who embrace this charming, elderly man, is chilling even as it is touching. Kadya must have cried when she read it.

Earlier we saw Dora's suggestion that Kadya "hop on over" for a visit. What Dora did not know was that getting out of Israel was no easy feat in those years. From the documents that she left behind, we know that Kadya had difficulty getting out. It would appear that she did not tell Dora about it, for in July as Dora began applying pressure, she appears unaware of Kadya's difficulties:

"We're waiting to hear about the plans for your visit…This is not an easy time for our father. He is weak and old so it's hard for him…He sits in the soft chair and sleeps; he seems content to sleep, but he doesn't eat much. It seems the sleep preserves his little bit of strength."[47]

By now the message was clear: it was imperative that Kadya get to her father. What Kadya's sisters did not know was that in those years any Israeli citizen who wanted to leave the country needed not just a passport, but also an exit permit.[48] Kadya did write to the regional office of immigration asking for this permit. She did not leave a copy of this original letter in her archive, but she did leave a copy of the response. Ordinarily, a government office will acknowledge the date the original letter was received. From the fact that this is not the case in the response letter, there is reason to believe that the response was not given too soon after the original request made its way to the desk of the authorities. Moreover, the date of the response letter has been tampered with: the original typed date, which was clearly July (the numeral 7) in the original, has been changed to August (the numeral 8). At some point, then, some

Chapter Five: Paradise Lost-Three Yeasr in Israel

official was embarrassed enough with the handling of this case to want to tamper with the document. The response, in essence, was not a response. Instead it was a request that Kadya provide the Regional Office of Immigration (*Misrad Ha-aliyah Ha-mekhozi*) with a letter of recommendation from the Ministry of Education and Culture. Naturally, this required the drafting of another letter, the wait till this letter reached the proper authorities, and then the wait for a response from these authorities. Kadya did as she was asked. This is how her letter was phrased:

"I hereby request a recommendation from you to the Immigration Office that I get an exit permit to travel to the United States.

Till now I have written ten books: poetry, prose and children's verse, some of which were translated [into Hebrew- ZKN] in the book "*Pitkhu et Ha-sha'ar*", [an extraordinarily popular children's book in Israel ZKN]. [I'd like to go] to the United States to publish a book of poems that I have recently written. Some of these poems have been translated into Hebrew and have appeared in "*Davar*", "Weekly *Davar*", and other publications. Besides that, I want to publish a children's book of poems.

The publishing company in the US has already prepared pictures for this book and when I get there we will complete that project.

I will be very grateful to you if you give me this recommendation with all due haste, because my time is limited, and as the winter begins I'd like to return to continue my work as editor of *Heym* that is put out here in Israel by *Moetset Ha-po'alot*."

Respectfully,

Kadya Molodowsky

It is clear that this is a rough, first-draft of the letter that was eventually sent. There are elisions and typos in this letter, something that so punctilious an editor as Kadya would never have sent off. There is every reason to believe that the final letter she sent off suffered from none of these flaws. We will, therefore, ignore these issues.

The critical question here is not one of style; it is one of content. Kadya wanted to leave because her elderly father's health was failing. Why didn't she say this in her letter? She left no answer, so I will do my best to supply the answer that makes sense to me.

As I understand it, Kadya was so deeply attached to her father, that she simply could not speak about him to strangers. To do so would have been to trespass on very private, emotional territory. As I see it, that same explanation covers Kadya's absence from her father's funeral. Just as Kadya could not bring herself to speak to the Israeli authorities about wanting to go to the US to see her father on his death-bed, so she could not bear to face a crowd of onlookers and publicly bare her grief over his death.

In a letter found in Ida Maze's archive, Simche tells Ida that the couple had arrived in the US in time to visit a moribund Aizik. He also explained that he was writing because Kadya was in the hospital at her father's bed-side. Later in the same letter, Kadya explained what it was like to see her father on his death-bed:

"He asked me a few hours before his death not to cry, so I try to listen to him. But my heart grieves deeply."[49]

It was not the public display of grief that mattered to Kadya. She grieved deeply, but she did not feel that her grief was a public affair. She wanted to be left to grieve in private.

Kadya left no record of the response she got from the Ministry of Education. But she did leave another letter, one that says everything about the way things were done in Israel those days. It is a hand-written copy of a note that was probably sent, written in English on the General Council of Women Workers' (*Mo'etset Ha-Po'alot*) stationary, addressed to "*Chaver* Kaplan", from "Bert". "*Chaver*", which literally means "friend", was the term of address used by all Socialists when they addressed each other. The addressee, the Mr. Kaplan in question, was the then-finance minister of Israel.[50] And the "Bert" in question was Bert Goldstein, the president of the American branch of Pioneer Women, or as she was called, the female Labor Zionist leader. Here is what her note said:

Chapter Five: Paradise Lost-Three Yeasr in Israel

"Pursuant to my conversation on the phone with you, I am enclosing the cable which Kadya Molodowsky received. Beyond any question of a doubt this is genuine, and I would appreciate it as much as if you were doing a favor for me if you would help Kadya and her husband with an exit visa."

It would appear, then, that the Ministry of Education took its time answering Kadya's request. Apparently, they took so long, and as a result Kadya dawdled so long, that the sisters resorted to sending a telegram. There was precious little time left. Having tried all the usual avenues open to an average citizen, Kadya finally called upon her "*protektsiya*": she resorted to her networked connections. Bert Goldstein was a superb fund-raiser, and the young State of Israel was badly in need of her services. The Ministry of Finance, then, was a perfect pressure point. Bert first called (on a then-hard-to-find telephone!!) and finally sent off a personal plea to the Finance Minister of Israel. Finally, Kadya got her exit permit.

Kadya did get to Philadelphia, and as we have seen, she did speak to her father on his death-bed. But this merry-go-round of bureaucratic demands, the protracted wait, and the worry over perhaps arriving too late, must have taken their toll on Kadya. Loyal patriot that she was, she did not speak of these things in public. If she told her friends Rokhl and/or Ida or Sarah Dubow about her travails, she almost certainly asked them not to spread slander about the country in public. The fact is that none of her friends preserved letters from Kadya complaining about this morass. Nor did they ever speak of it publicly. And Kadya herself never spoke of it publicly. Nevertheless, she did leave the relevant documents in her archive. They speak eloquently of the unnecessary aggravation that a fiercely loyal daughter suffered for wanting to leave Israel so she could be with her beloved, dying father on his death-bed.

In addition to doing everything it could to prevent its citizens from leaving the country, the Israeli government of those years also made life very hard for those whom it did allow to leave. In a letter to her friend Ida, written right before Aizik's death,

Kadya tells Ida how fortunate she [Ida] is to be living alongside her mother in Montreal, while Kadya herself has:

"always [lived] apart [literally "torn from" ZKN] my father, and this has grieved me greatly."[51]

Of course, Kadya could have chosen to live alongside her father in Philadelphia; she chose not to do so. In the way we have of imagining we can have all our druthers simultaneously, Kadya fantasized that she might have been able to live in the midst of the exciting hubbub of the Yiddish literary world that was New York, and at the same time live near her father. Naturally, that was impossible: she needed to choose between the two. And when forced to make a decision, she preferred living in New York, and occasionally visiting Aizik, calling him and writing to him, while Dora, in whose house he lived, did the drudge work of seeing to his daily needs.

In this same letter, Kadya tells Ida the truth about the restrictions the Israeli government placed on her and Simche:

"One cannot take out more than $14 per person from Israel. As a result, we arrived (one should say descended) [in Philadelphia- ZKN] without a cent."[52]

Ever resourceful, Kadya wrote to Ida, who was responsible for the literary events at the Montreal Jewish Public library, and suggested the library might help bring her there to speak. That would help fill her coffers.

It is quite clear that Kadya did not want to slander "her" country "on the record", but she hinted she had much more to say:

"It is impossible to write you about all of this in a letter. When we'll see each other, we'll discuss this."[53]

While she does not say much outright, she does hint rather broadly that something is amiss:

"One needs a lot of strength to overcome things."[54]

Kadya Gives Lecture Tours

She did speak in Montreal, as she had suggested. Her two lectures were entitled: "The Small Trains of the Large Building– The State of Israel", and "Poetry in the Time of Mass-production". To the best of my knowledge, there is no record of these talks in the Montreal library. One can't help wondering how much of the nitty-gritty reality she let seep into her descriptions of real life in the new State of Israel.

Kadya stayed in the US for a while, some of the time with her sister in Philadelphia and some of the time with other family in New York. She also did a bit of traveling to friends and apparently lectured (and was remunerated for that) wherever she went. While she was away, she complained that without her, the work on *Heym* did not proceed at the pace it should have.[55] The fact is she was unique in her boundless energy; she was *Heym*'s moving force. In her absence, the pace of work slowed down.

Despite the aggravation she suffered getting an exit visa, and despite the barreling post-war prosperity that she witnessed in the US when she was there in 1951, Kadya returned to Israel, apparently still hoping she could rely on Simche to support them. She had told the authorities she wanted to continue editing *Heym*, and she did just that.

Return to Israel: The Last Year

She returned to Israel at the end of 1951 and left Israel for good on the Nassau Shipping Line at the end of October, 1952.[56] If she wrote Ida any letters in the intervening year, none have been kept. Similarly, although Rokhl Korn kept some of the letters Kadya wrote her, she saved none that were written in that crucial year.

While still in Israel, Kadya wrote a batch of poems that eventually made their way into a book dedicated to her father and entitled *In Yerusholayim Kumen Malokhim*, Angels Come to Jerusalem.[57] This book was published in New York in 1952.

We know that Kadya and Simche together saw to the publication of this book because the name of the publishing company is *Papirene Brik*, Paper Bridges, located in New York. Now as we know, there was no such publishing company. "Paper Bridges" was the name that Kadya and Simche gave to their mutual undertaking when the two of them used machinery belonging to others while Simche did the type-setting.

The very title of the collection announces Kadya's spiritual high: for her, Jerusalem was a city of spiritual epiphanies. She herself felt an uplift of spirit there.

Tucked away in that collection is a poem that clearly referred to the Soviet poets, who had sold their souls to the Communist regime. Very likely, Kadya was referring not just to any poet, but to Dovid Bergelson, the Soviet poet with whom she had felt such a sense of closeness:

Here an angel brings a poet from Hell to the top of a high mountain, and the reason for his punishment is spelled out:

"Vayl er hot fargesn zayn tatn un mamen/ Er hot gezungn fun mentch un hot mentshn farakht/ Un gots shefa tsebitn oyf gramen"[58]

Because he forgot his father and mother/ He sang about Man and scorned men / And traded God's abundance for verse.

The poem that lent the collection its name, *"In Yerusholayim Kumen Malokhim"*, Angels Come to Jerusalem, says just what it seems to be saying: for Kadya the city of Jerusalem was sacred. In the following lines of that poem Kadya says that the angels come:

Un efenen tirn fun yidishe heyzer/ Zey lernen di kinder tsu lib hobn toyre... And open [the] doors of Jewish houses / They teach children to love Torah...

For a person who had once joined forces with atheistic Socialists, this does seem like an about-face. It both is and it isn't. Kadya may have spoken respectfully of "loving Torah", but it would be wrong to say she became religious. For "observant" Jews, to be religious is to commit one's self to the observance of positive commandments. Kadya may have respected those who kept the positive commandments of Sabbath observance, but she herself never became a traditional Sabbath observer. However, she was impressed with what she saw as the redemption of the Jewish people, and to some extent she did make her peace with the Jewish God. In an aerogram she sent Ida, she said:

"Here in Tel Aviv they are nearly ready to murder me because I live well with the Creator of the world."[59]

Not only in Tel Aviv were there people who could not understand Kadya's near-mystical acceptance of God and His workings in the new State of Israel. Even Kadya's long-term friend, Melekh Ravitch, found her pronouncements difficult to process.

For him, as for many of the secular Yiddishists, religion was an outdated hold-out, unnecessary in the Modern Era. Talk of angels was, as they saw it, patent nonsense. Melekh Ravitch, who had known Kadya in her early years when she had joined him in rejecting religion, did not hesitate to remind her of those years. He wrote with more than a little pointed irony: "My dear Kadya, to actually speak of "kneeling before God"...It seems you have become truly pious lately."[60]

Ida Maze, Kadya's Canadian friend, also found Kadya's emphasis on the other-worldly events not to her taste. In response to a poem of Kadya's entitled: "Magic Sounds"[61], she wrote:

"In front of me is your poem "Magic Sounds"....Kadyele cut it out! I don't do magic like that." [in Yiddish: "*Kadyele lozt op! Kh'kishuft nit azoy.*"][62]

What Ida did not understand was that it was precisely Kadya's willingness to drop rationalism and let her imagination fly, that brought her to write stories about shoes that wander off to the end of the world and wash-basins that go from house to house turning around without the help of human beings. Besides, both Melekh Ravitch and Ida Maze did not truly understand Kadya. She had never been ideologically committed to secularism. She had always had respect for observant Jews, even though she herself was never traditionally religious. She had always had excellent relations with the editors of the religious newspapers (*Der Tog* and *Di Morgn Jurnal*). Indeed, she published her stories and poems in all kinds of Yiddish publications: religious as well as non-religious.

Kadya's friends Rokhl Korn and Ida Maze had their misgivings about Kadya's potential adjustment in Israel from the very beginning. A month after Kadya arrived in Israel, Rokhl wrote: "You celebrated the Diaspora in America. [Here she is speaking sarcastically. ZKN] But we can never escape ourselves no matter where we go. We carry our sadness with us everywhere…"[63]

Similarly, Ida Maze wrote to Kadya later that year:

"It seems to me that even when you are in the Land of Israel, you will still be in the Diaspora."[64]

She went on to say she truly hoped that all would be well for Kadya in her new home. But she (and Rokhl Korn as well) were onto something. Once she left Europe, Kadya was not truly at home anywhere.

It may be that Kadya would have had a problem everywhere she went. That fact is, though, that it was Simche's difficulties that tipped the scale.

What exactly happened between 1951, when Kadya and Simche returned to Israel from abroad, and the end of 1952, when they left Israel for good? More to the point, what happened that made Kadya decide to leave? In French, whenever one wants to solve the mystery surrounding a man, one is told: "cherchez la femme": seek out the woman/the wife. In a parallel way, we need to say in this case: to solve the mystery surrounding the woman, seek out the man/the husband. The solution to the mystery of Kadya's abandonment of Israel, it seems to me, lies with her husband, Simche.

Simche As Wage-Earner

While they were living in Europe as a young couple, both Kadya and Simche worked, and the couple had a joint income. While the two of them lived apart, from 1935 to 1938, Kadya supported herself. By 1950, when the two of them moved, as they thought, permanently, to Israel, they had been married for just about 30 years, and Kadya had been their sole supporter for only three of those years. They probably realized that Kadya's income from the editorship of *Heym* would not allow them to live comfortably. But they assumed her income would only be supplemental. It was Simche, they supposed, who would be the main supporter of the two of them, as he had been for most of the years the two of them had lived in New York.

From the Makhon Lavon archive we learn that Simche imported four Linotype machines to Israel, one intended for printing Polish, (apparently for the four Polish-language newspapers that were printed in Israel at the time[65]), at an estimated cost of 3,420 Lira or $13, 680 at the time. That was a very large sum for those years. It speaks of printing ambitions and a desire to settle in Israel.

In the words of the cognoscenti, for the world of printing in those years, "to embark on Linotype was to embark on greatness."[66] When they lived in New York, Simche set type, but others owned the machines he worked on. In Israel, he owned these gold-standard machines, and he intended to run a printing press on his own, or at least in a partnership with others.

Long before they moved to Israel, Kadya had this dream of running her own printing press. She must have told Ezra Korman about this, for a letter dated January 7, 1941, found in the Makhon Lavon archive, gives his response. There Korman tries to disabuse Kadya from taking on so ambitious a project. There is more to running a business of this sort than meets the eye, he tells her. One needs not only machines. One needs good type-setters, good agents and reliable distributors. These are a few different skills, he tells her, and when amateurs try to do it all, they usually end up with disastrous results. Echoing what she had heard from Korman, Kadya wrote to a friend of hers:

"May God send us a publishing company".

And further on in the same letter:

"The most difficult thing [for a book] is distribution".[67]

Keeping this lesson in mind, Kadya and Simche wanted to find adequate partners for their publishing company-to-be when they arrived in Israel.

Once again, the documents in Makhon Lavon tell the rest of the story. Among the other papers that the couple left there, is a torn-up contract for a partnership in a printing press. Simche was to have been one of the partners; that is clear. Where there should have been the name(s) of the other partner(s), there is only a blank space.

In his identity card, Simche listed his profession as writer, historian and printer. The first two were more like hobbies; in the US he found he could not earn a living from either of these. The third, printing, is what he expected to do for a living in Israel.

In the same folder that held Simche's Polish passport, with that note in French from a long-ago paramour, are a batch of unused, personalized printed New Year's greeting/calling cards, dated September, 1951. They were printed for Simche and they name him as the manager (in Hebrew, *menahel*) of the printing press called: *Bet Ha-defus Ha-klali B"M* (In English "The General Printing House, Inc."). Its address was *Rekhov Ha-shuk*, 26, or in English, The Market Street, 26, Tel Aviv [68]

This, it would seem, was jumping the gun. Simche may have wanted to be the manager of this press; he may have been promised the position of manager, had the partnership gone through. But the fact remains that he did not assume the managership of this press. A year after Simche arrived in Israel, he still did not have that coveted job. Natan Blanc, the man who later became Simche's representative in the publishing house where the Linotype machines were used, wrote to Simche in January of 1951:

"As I understand it, nothing has become of all those permits. And that's a pity."[69]

It is not clear which permits Natan Blanc was referring to. In those days, one needed a permit to ride a bicycle[70]; it is no surprise, then, that permits were needed to establish a business that had the latest printing presses. Whatever these permits were, Simche didn't get them. And that effectively prevented him from assuming the managership he so sorely wanted.

Chapter Five: Paradise Lost-Three Yeasr in Israel

When he did not get the position of manager in the printing press, Simche resorted to his other marketable skill: writing. Over the three years they were in Israel, Kadya put out twelve issues of *Heym*; Simche wrote articles in ten of these.[71] Simche's articles entailed journalistic reporting and traveling, something he would not have had time for had he held down a full-time job at the printing house. It is my understanding that Kadya "assigned" him these tasks, both to make him feel he was doing something worthwhile, and to shore up the family income.[72]

In the years they lived in New York, Simche put out one volume of his ambitious multi-volume history of the Jews of Europe (from a Socialist standpoint). He brought with him to Israel old newspaper clippings about the rise of Socialism in Poland and Russia, intending to work on the second volume of this magnum opus. And in fact, in a letter to Ida, dated April 2, 1951, Kadya reported that Simche was working on his second book, entitled: "Chapters of Jewish History".[73] But it is abundantly clear that this dream was abandoned when the couple left Israel at the end of 1952, a little more than a year later. The yellowing articles about the Jewish involvement in the Socialist uprisings of Eastern Europe were deposited in Makhon Lavon. They are a silent testimony to Simche's realization that the second volume of his magnum opus would not come into being.

Letters to Kadya dated 1951-1952 ask about Simche and wonder aloud why he is silent and does not write.[74] Israelis who knew the couple that year have told me that they knew Simche to be a silent man. These observations contrast sharply with the comments of Rokhl Korn, who interacted with Simche once the couple had returned to New York. Back in New York, Simche was his former self, voluble and charming. The reason for this difference is obvious: in Israel, Simche was unemployed, and constantly on tenterhooks, wondering if he would ever get that hoped-for partnership in a printing press. In New York, once he found employment again, he was supporting himself and Kadya. Once that happened, his self-confidence was restored, and he reverted to his former sociability.

Kadya's Depression

When she explained to her friends why she was leaving, Kadya told them she was physically exhausted, and she was. But she was not only exhausted, she was depressed. The material she left in private notebooks in the Makhon Lavon archive speak volumes. They show a far darker picture than any she allowed her friends to see. In a small notebook that fits easily into a woman's pocketbook Kadya wrote down odd, fleeting thoughts, fragments of poems and projects begun, but not completed.

Among the unpublished and apparently incomplete poems is one entitled "*Dem Mentsh Baym Fenster*", The Person at the Window. This poem, re-written at least five times, begins with the lines: "Such sadness/ Such pain and evil/ And there is no wind/ And there is no laughter." The poem's message of pain and suffering, dread and anticipated danger, rolls along on a lilting rhythm and has a delightful rhyme scheme.

This very same jarring juxtaposition of a dark message accompanied by a pleasant rhyme scheme and a wonderful rhythm also characterizes two Mother Goose rhymed stories that Kadya translated into Yiddish. She did not leave one version of the longer poem; she left a few versions. It would seem that none of them pleased her entirely. In any case, she never published these poems or revised them.

Here, too, among her travel notes is a fragment she allowed herself to write: "*un vi es benkt a froy nokh kint oyf knien*", and how a woman longs for a child on her lap...Kadya never spoke directly of her childlessness to her family; that, at least is what her niece and nephew reported. Nor did she ever say anything about this in her autobiographical memoir. Even here, in the notebook meant for her eyes alone, she could not, or did not, develop the thought. Apparently, the thought remained just that; words failed her.

But the outside world saw none of this. Outwardly, Kadya continued to edit her journal even as she sought other gainful employment. In addition to her editorial work,

Kadya ran around the country, giving paid talks wherever she could. Traveling on the country's bumpy roads in hot buses (those days air-conditioned buses were unheard of in Israel) in sweltering weather would have enervated even a young person.

In her memoir Kadya discloses only a fistful of what was bothering her at the time. Speaking in an understatement, she says that:

"Editing the journal *Heym* was by no means an easy job...Even obtaining paper for the journal was not an easy thing. Sometimes I had to travel to Jerusalem where I would get permission for paper.[75]

By then Kadya was 55, undernourished, and steadily losing weight. The hectic pace of travel and lecturing was a serious drain on her health.

Opened by the Censor

In October of 1952, at a time when Kadya and Simche had apparently realized they could no longer stay in Israel, Kadya got what can only be considered the coup de grace, the final blow. Once again, we know about this only from a document Kadya left in Makhon Lavon.

In this case, Kadya saved both the letter and the letter's envelope sent to her by her sister, Dora. The letter itself was entirely mundane and innocent. In it, Dora told Kadya that she and Lina were preparing a head-stone for Aizik's grave, now that the 11-month period of mourning had ended. It asked about her health and well-being, and assured her the whole family would be delighted to see her and Simche once more. It's not the letter that begs for an explanation; it is the envelope.

On the side of the letter is a government-issued stamp that says in Hebrew: "*niftakh al yedei ha-tsenzur*", opened by the censor.[76] It is obvious that this shocked Kadya: she would not have saved the envelope had she not believed it was important for later researchers. Of all the citizens of Israel, Kadya was probably the very last person open to suspicion. She made no public mention of the harrowing, gratuitously cruel, run-around she got when she asked for an exit visa to visit her moribund father. She never went public with the aggravation she had over the legal right to her apartment. If she had any doubts about the government policy of rationing and price controls, she never said so publicly. Despite the outrage heaped on her by her Yiddishist friends, she defended the favoring of Hebrew over Yiddish to her colleagues overseas, and she was an ardent Zionist, one who trumpeted the advances of the new State of Israel at every opportunity. Why, then, was she suddenly suspect, and why was her personal mail opened by the censor?

To the best of my knowledge, Kadya never found out. However, I believe I have the answer.

The early 1950s were the years of Joseph McCarthy's ascendency. And J. Edgar Hoover, then head of the FBI, fully cooperated with McCarthy is his attempt to root out "fellow travelers" of Communism. Among the Americans who were suspect, were those who, approximately ten years earlier, had been active in the Russian War Relief effort.[77] The FBI documents that were de-classified only in 2012, seventy years after the censor's opening of Dora's letter, do not allow readers to identify who was being followed: all names in the original documents were blackened out when the papers were made public. But Dora had been active in the Philadelphia branch of the Russian War Relief. Indeed, like so many other loyal American Jews, she was proud of the fact that in helping an important American ally, she may also have been helping fellow Jews. Even better, she may have been helping her beloved brother and his family, trapped in the Soviet Union.

If anyone was under suspicion, then, it was Dora, not Kadya. And if any government was to blame for this intrusion into the private lives of sisters dealing with their father's gravesite, it was the US government, not the Israeli government. But Kadya could not have known this.

There was no way the Israeli government of 1952 could have refused a request from the FBI to open Dora's letter; that would have been a case of the proverbial fly

Chapter Five: Paradise Lost-Three Yeasr in Israel   237

stepping on the elephant's toe; Israel was a teeny, impoverished, embattled country, while the US was the world's greatest power. Accordingly, the Israeli censor opened up Dora's letter to Kadya. Only after establishing the innocence of the writer and the letter's recipient, did they send the letter on to Kadya.

Caught up in events she knew nothing about, baffled by the suspicions lodged against her, and almost certainly deeply hurt, Kadya said nothing publicly. She simply left that letter in her Israeli archive and left it to future generations to explain what had happened.

Kadya wrote a poem entitled "Prayer", which, if read carefully, hints at the difficulties she had during her three-year stay in Israel. What follows are the last few lines of each of the three stanzas:

"Let the spark of my eye not die out
From resenting a Jew.

Let my heart not contract with sorrow
At the injustice of Jews.

May God help me...
So my tablecloth white from joyous effort
Should not darken
From anger at Jews."[78]

Return to the U.S.

Kadya received that censored letter on October 10th of 1952. At that point, she had already withdrawn what she had in the bank,[79] and Simche had already re-paid the loan he took when they arrived.[80] This time, their exit permit was issued without a problem. It arrived on October 16th, and on October 22 the couple gave power of attorney over their apartment to friends that they trusted.

Kadya's tension can be sensed in the last issue of *Heym* that she put out. Her usual fastidiousness in proof-reading failed her this time. Two out of three poems authored by Avrohom Sutzkever were not given their correct titles,[81] and the original poems, written in his own hand-writing, were not returned to him.[82] They were left in her archive, where they can still be read.

Kadya left Israel for good on the Nassau Shipping Line at the end of October, 1952.[83] If she wrote Ida any letters in 1952, none have been kept. Similarly, although Rokhl Korn kept some of the letters Kadya wrote her, she saved none that were written in that crucial, last year of Kadya's three-year stay.

I suspected that Kadya left Israel mostly because of her husband's inability to support them, but my suspicion was based the circumstantial evidence found in the Makhon Lavon archive only. As it turned out, Amir Shomroni, an Israeli scholar who visited the YIVO archive in New York, found hard evidence to back up my suspicion.[84]

In a seemingly innocent folder, Shomroni found a hand-written, never-published confession. Here Kadya gave voice to her heartbreak and told the whole truth.

She lists reasons of her own for wanting to leave: the events at Yehiel Halperins' memorial service and her difficulties with Bebe Idelshohn. The first incident, as she relates it in this unpublished "confession" says more about her contrarian nature than it does about anything else.

Yehiel Halperin, we will recall, was the visionary who started a Hebrew teachers' language seminary in Europe even before WWI. Kadya was among the students of his first class. As such, she seemed a perfect candidate to deliver a eulogy at his funeral. She did prepare a eulogy, but when she began to speak, it was clear to those assembled that she was going to speak in Yiddish! Given that Halperin had devoted his entire life to the revival of Hebrew, Kadya's choice of language was strange indeed. Halperin's widow, very much annoyed (or perhaps perplexed), stopped Kadya as she was speaking and asked her to speak in Hebrew. Kadya did not budge. She reminded the audience that she edited a Yiddish journal that was read world over (She may have overblown the facts here), and that Jewish readers abroad had no problem with Yiddish. Finally, she made it clear that she intended to speak in Yiddish. Halperin's widow stood her ground and insisted on Hebrew only. At that point, Kadya fell silent.

As for her difficulties with Bebe Idelsohn, it is clear that their clashes were the sort that regularly happen in a work place. Idelsohn was apparently quick to anger and she had a temper. While this made for less than ideal work conditions, it is hard to believe that this alone could have pushed Kadya and Simche into deciding to leave had there been no other difficulties.

After mentioning these two reasons for her departure from Israel, Kadya finally got to the essence of their difficulties. In a laconic, much-crossed out passage, Kadya related the story of the printing presses that Simche imported, and the fact that the partnership that was to be, never materialized. She says in the crossed-out passage that the owners of the press did not pay Simche the sum that was due him. She did not need to add that Simche was therefore unemployed. The readers, had there been any, would have figured that out themselves. But Kadya never published that confession. It languished, unread in her New York archive.

The company that reneged on a partnership with Simche agreed finally to rent the printing presses that Simche himself had imported. But they were not the only ones that dealt unscrupulously with the couple. Kadya, too, was unfairly treated.

The Israeli publishing company that printed and sold the most popular of Kadya's translated Hebrew books for children, *(Pitkhu et Ha-sha'ar*, Open the Gate) dealt unethically with her. While Kadya left no account of how much she received from them for the publishing of her book, she did leave a copy of the letter she sent to Netta Blanc, the woman-friend in Israel who was dealing with the *Kibbutz Ha-me'uchad* publishing firm on her behalf.

In the letter dated May 24, 1968, she wrote:

"May God help, and then perhaps the *Kibbutz Ha-Me-uchad* will become decent and stop bargaining so much.

The account is very simple: I got paid from them for the first edition. [underlining in the original. At this point twenty-three years have gone by since the original payment was made. ZKN]. I no longer remember how much they paid me [for that edition ZKN]. I never received anything from them after that. This means that they owe me for all the following editions. (So it was stated in our original written agreement.)"[85]

It would seem that Kadya simply gave up trying to get them to pay her. She was never compensated for the later editions despite the written agreement that she had. As we have seen, at this point she did not expect to live from her earnings. Simche supported the two of them and both had made their peace with that arrangement.

Kadya and Simche returned to New York at the end of 1952. It is telling that Kadya returned to New York with the receipts for work she had done in Israel. Those three years were the second three-year stretch in which she had supported herself and Simche.

Once they returned to the US, Simche took over. At that time, "typesetters' wages were 'relatively prosperous'".[86] As soon as Simche got work as a type-setter, the couple resumed the arrangement that characterized most of their lives from the time that Kadya saved Simche from almost-certain death in Nazi-controlled Europe: Simche supported the two of them, while Kadya wrote and edited Yiddish stories, plays, poems and essays for an ever-dwindling reading public.

NOTES

[1] See http://humanities.tau.ac.il/zionism/templates/ol_similu/files/israel I/Israel I_Rozin.pdf
[2] Kahan Newman, "The Correspondence Between Kadya Molodowsky and Rokhl Korn", p.22
[3] This, in a letter dated January 10, 1949, found in the Makhon Lavon archive.

[4] The evidence for the ownership of the apartment as well as the repayment of loans can be found in the Makhon Lavon archive.
[5] *Svive*, no. 39, May, 1973, p. 57.
[6] Amir Shomroni points out that on her 1949 trip, Kadya was present at the very first conference of the Workers' party. Ben Gurion and Golda Meyerson were there as well, and Kadya recited some of her poems in Yiddish. See *Ha-Aretz Musaf,* March 9, 2018, p. 44
[7] This, in a letter dated May 19, 1949, found in the Makhon Lavon archive
[8] This, in a letter dated April 30th, 1949, found in the Makhon Lavon archive.
[9] This, in a letter dated April 30, 1949, found in the Makhon Lavon archive.
[10] This, in a letter dated October 23, 1950, found in the Makhon Lavon archive.
[11] Kathryn Hellerstein, Paper Bridges, 1999, p. 46.
[12] This, in an undated, first draft of a letter (that was apparently sent) found in Makhon Lavon.
[13] *Zionist Review*, Friday July 8, 1949, p. 13. The facts are more complex. The question was one of media choice. Yiddish authors did not encounter discrimination. This is what Kadya meant, and she was right. These was a Yiddish-language newspaper, a Yiddish language publishing house, and there were two Yiddish language literary journals. But the situation for other media was different. In the early years of the state, there were attempts to prevent the establishment of Yiddish theater, and there were no attempts at Yiddish film-making. Even when the government did not actively forbid expression in these media, social pressure was brought to bear against it. Kadya's account of the tiff at Yehiel Halperin's funeral is an indication of the public resentment against Yiddish at that time. For more on this, see the article by Dan Miron, p. 10, in: https://forum.otzar.org/download/file.php?id=42467 and the book written by Diego Roytman: *Ha-bama Ke-vayit Ara'i*, Magnes Press, 2017.
[14] Ibid.
[15] This interview, conducted in Hebrew some time during the 1960s, can be found at the following link
http://www.dafdaf.co.il/Details.asp?MenuID=2&SubMenuID=144&PageID=1257&Ot=%EE&SubTextID=1259
[16] See: https://en.wikipedia.org/wiki/Gadsden_flag
[17] https://en.wikipedia.org/wiki/Fugio_Cent
[18] This, in a letter dated March 31st, 1950, found in the Makhon Lavon archive.
[19] This, in a letter from Dora dated March 31, 1950. And on May 5, 1952 Dora spoke of getting power of attorney so she could handle Kadya's finances. Both letters are found in the Makhon Lavon archive.
[20] The relevant letters to and from Kadya, found in the Makhon Lavon archive, are dated May 25, 1951, and June 3, 1951.
[21] This, in a letter sent by Lipa Lehrer, dated March 3, 1951, found in the Makhon Lavon archive. Then, later that year, in a letter dated May 21, 1951, he again asks her how he should go about paying her.

[22] This, in a letter dated March 8, 1952 found in the Makhon Lavon archive.
[23] This, in a letter dated March 17, 1952 found in the Makhon Lavon archive.
[24] *Heym*, no. 3, Ocotober, 1950, p. 8.
[25] These days there are family courts where property settlements can be arranged. But if a husband and wife been married by an officially recognized rabbi, they must go to a rabbinical court to obtain a divorce.
[26] See fn. xxiv.
[27] Ibid.
[28] This, in an undated letter, apparently written in 1951, found in the Makhon Lavon archive.
[29] This, in the same undated letter mentioned above.
[30] This, in a letter dated May 11, 1950, found in the Makhon Lavon archive.
[31] This in an undated letter, found in the Makhon Lavon archive. It was obviously written in the early 1950s.
[32] See the letter mentioned in end-note vi.
[33] This, in a letter dated October 15, 1950, found in the Makhon Lavon archive.
[34] This, in a letter dated November 30, 1950, found in the Makhon Lavon archive.
[35] This, in a letter dated February 21, 1951, found in the Makhon Lavon archive.
[36] See http://www.aaofoundation.org/what/heritage/exhibits/online/cataract/21st_century.cfm
[37] Ben, Kadya's nephew, told me his family kept the newspaper clippings and the congratulations the family got for risking the operation and for the operation's success.
[38] This, in a letter dated September 9, 1950, found in the Makhon Lavon archive.
[39] This letter is dated October 10, 1950, found in the Makhon Lavon archive.
[40] Ibid.
[41] The only letters in the archive written by Lina are one dated April 6, 1951, and one dated April 10, 1952. Both of these can be found in the Makhon Lavon archive.
[42] This letter, dated April 6, 1951, was found in the Makhon Lavon archive.
[43] This letter, dated May 16, 1951, was found in the Makhon Lavon archive.
[44] Ibid.
[45] The exact date of this letter is unclear. It is either June 23, or June 25, 1951. It was found in the Makhon Lavon archive.
[46] Ibid.
[47] This letter, dated July, 16, 1951, was found in the Makhon Lavon archive.
[48] For more on this see, Orit Rozin's article in the Journal of Israeli History 03/2011; 30: 1-21
http://www.researchgate.net/publication/233037749_Negotiating_the_right_to_exit_the_country_in_1950s_Israel_Voice_loyalty_and_citizenship

Chapter Five: Paradise Lost-Three Yeasr in Israel

[49] This letter was started the 10th of September, but finished later. It is clear from this that the couple arrived in the US at the beginning of September, and that Kadya did in fact get to her father's bed-side for a final farewell.

[50] See http://www.knesset.gov.il/govt/heb/membyparameter.asp?par=4&min=3

[51] This, in a letter dated September 27, 1951, found in the Montreal archive.

[52] Ibid. Kadya suggests the use of the word "descended" because a trip to Israel is, in Jewish tradition and in the Hebrew language, an "ascension", while a trip out of Israel is a "descension".

[53] ibid

[54] ibid

[55] This, in a letter sent from Chicago, dated November 18, 1951, found in the Makhon Lavon archive.

[56] A letter dated October 29, 1952, was written while Kadya and Simche were on the boat going back to the US.

[57] This is the more idiomatic rendering of the Yiddish title. The (less native-sounding) name Kadya and Simche gave the book when they published it in New York was: "Angels Come to Jerusalem."

[58] *In Yerusholayim*,,,, p. 21. The poem is entitled: "*Oyf Der Ander Zayt Fun Mayn Kholem Un Lid*", On the Other Side of My Dream and Poem.

[59] This aerogram, found in the Ida Maze's Montreal archive, seems to have its date intentionally ripped out. Intention or not, there is no way to know when this letter was written.

[60] This, in a letter sent on April 14, 1950, found in the Makhon Lavon archive. While this is dated before the publication of Kadya's book, the poems themselves had appeared individually in *Heym* before they were collected and published in book form.

[61] I have not been able to locate this poem.

[62] This, in a letter date October 5, 1951, found in the Makhon Lavon archive.

[63] This, in a letter dated February 11, 1950, found in the Makhon Lavon archive.

[64] This, in a letter written on June 28th, 1950, found in the Makhon Lavon archive.

[65] Nowiny Poranne, Chwila, Nowiny Izraelskie and Nowośći Codzienny. Thanks to Amir Shomroni for this information.

[66] http://www.theatlantic.com/technology/archive/2011/05/celebrating-linotype-125-years-since-its-debut/238968/

[67] This, in a letter dated May 11, 1942, found in the Makhon Lavon archive, in which Kadya wrote to one Sh. Bukhovitch.

[68] Amir Shomroni reports that at least one person, Ita Givonit, from Bet Alfa, did in fact receive this greeting card. If in fact she received Simche's business card, that would indicate that Simche was very sure this deal would go through, and the job would be his.

[69] This, in a letter dated January, 30, 1951, found in the Makhon Lavon archive.

[70] Personal communication.

[71] His articles appeared in numbers 2, 3, twice in issue 4, 5, 6, 8, 9, 10 and 11. Thanks to Amir Shomroni for doing the math.

[72] Kadya paid contributors to her journal. There was no reason for her not to pay Simche, just as she paid the others. It is quite probable that only "insiders" realized that Simche Lev was Kadya Molodowsky's husband.

[73] This, in a letter found in the Ida Maze's Montreal archive.

[74] Hava and Meir Drost, friends and supporters of Kadya asked about Simche in a letter dated March 29, 1950; Lipa Lehrer asks about Simche in a letter dated August, 8, 1950, and Ida Maze, in a letter dated July 21, 1950, asks why Simche has not written. All these are found in the Makhon Lavon archive.

[75] Svive, no. 41, April, 1974, p. 50.

[76] This envelope was postmarked October 10, 1952.

[77] See: http://en.wikipedia.org/wiki/Russian_War_Relief and for the FBI's suspicions that Edward Clark Carter, the head of the Russian War Relief effort, was a "fellow traveler", see: http://en.wikipedia.org/wiki/Edward_Clark_Carter

[78] Originally printed n *Hey*m, this was reprinted in Angels Come in Jerusalem, p. 15.

[79] She did this on September 14th, 1952.

[80] He did this on October 1st, 1952.

[81] The heading for the poems is "Two Miniatures", and the poems that are in the Molodowsky archive were in fact printed. However, each of the two poems has the title intended for the other poem.

[82] The poems are: 1) "In Dorf Uriel", and 2) *"Der Kval fun Nevu'e"*

[83] A letter dated October 29, 1952, was written while Kadya and Simche were on the boat going back to the US.

[84] See Shomroni's doctoral dissertation

קדיה מולודובסקי: אמריקה וישראל בחייה וביצירתה בשנים 1935-1953

p.133,ff.

[85] This, in a letter found in the YIVO archive.

[86] See http://www.theatlantic.com/technology/archive/2011/05/celebrating-linotype-125-years-since-its-debut/238968/

CHAPTER SIX: RETURN TO THE US: THE FIRST DECADE 1952-1962

"One must sometimes renew old paths"

Rivka Basman Ben-Haim

Back in the US

Kadya left Israel almost in stealth. Only her family, and the Drosts, friends who lived outside of Israel, knew for certain when she was leaving. Because Israel is a small country, and the elite (of whom Kadya was a member) were a tightly-knit group that knew each other's affairs, word of her departure got out somehow. Most, if not all, of this elite knew Kadya by name, if not in person. They had celebrated her arrival a mere three years earlier, and they were confused and hurt that she was "deserting" them.

Zalman Shazar (whose last name was an acronym for "Shneyur Zalman Rubashov"), then president of Israel, was so upset with Kadya's decision, that he composed a poem in Yiddish addressing her decision and hinting that with forbearance and determination she could yet find her place in the young state. Kadya left this handwritten poem in her Israeli archive.

She left no trace of a response, if indeed she did respond. It was not as though she had abandoned her belief that Israel was the rightful homeland for the Jews of the world; that belief was as firm as ever. It was simply a personal issue. Simche had not found the job he wanted. He was unhappy and unemployed. And without his income, Kadya was exhausting herself trying to support them both.

Kadya had no trouble getting out of Israel this time. By December, she and Simche were back in New York.

In those years, Israeli law forbade its citizens to (send or) take money out of the country. Each person was allotted $10 when (s)he exited the country.[1] It was with this pittance in their pockets that Kadya and Simche found themselves back in New York. They knew that Simche would eventually find a job, although they had no idea that their stay in Israel would complicate even that. Simche was skilled and his skill was in demand. But they needed funds to tide them over for the interim.

It is not as though they were penniless. But their Israeli funds were tied up. Simche had invested a small fortune in Linotype machines which he had personally imported into Israel. These were left behind when the couple emigrated. Simche was paid for their use by the publishing/printing company *Ha-defus Ha'klali*, which used them, but this rental money could not be taken out of Israel. The couple also had an apartment on *Yehuda Ha-Makkabi* Street in Tel Aviv. Whether the couple did anything with the rent money from that apartment, is also not clear. In any case, they could not take that money out of Israel either.

One of the first things Kadya and Simche did when they returned was to print Kadya's last book of poems, "Angels Come in Jerusalem". As was their wont, Kadya gave Simche the proof-read copy, and Simche did the type-setting and the printing. This copy has the imprint of *Papirene Brik* and Futuro Press, the company where Simche worked before he and Kadya left for Israel. They must have printed the book right away: they did not return till the end of 1952, and the book has a 1952 imprint.

One wonders why Kadya did not print that book while she was still in Israel. Some of the poems had already appeared in *Heym* and some in *Di Goldene Keyt*; they did not need proof-reading. Quite possibly Israeli printing was not done on quality paper. Like most things, paper was in short supply in Israel at that time, and quality paper was certainly not found easily or cheaply. It is also possible that the Israeli printing was done in limited numbers and Kadya wanted to be able to hand out copies to her friends and relatives in the United States. She dedicated this book to her (recently deceased) father, and that undoubtedly made it special for her. This was the last time the couple used their pseudo-press, *Papirene Brik*.

Kadya owned an apartment in the Bronx. In 1942, Genia Morowitz, Kadya's relative, sold a 3-family apartment house in the Bronx[2] to Kadya for the grand sum of $1: essentially, she gifted her place to Kadya. When the couple returned to New York, then, they were able to use the rent they received from this apartment to rent another apartment.

Kadya always had a keen sense for living "where the action" was. When the couple lived in Europe, she insisted they move to Warsaw from Brisk so they could be in the thick of literary ferment. When she arrived in the US, Kadya left Philadelphia for New York for the very same reason. And even when she was in New York, she always gravitated to the seat of Yiddishist activity. After Simche joined her in New York, they lived in Brownsville, where the "*amkha*", the common folk, who spoke Yiddish, lived. Kadya undoubtedly saw herself as one of these people and wanted to live among them. And, in fact, Simche was pleased with life there. But Kadya was not. We know this from the scathing portrait she drew of Brownsville in her poem of that title[3]. In fact, "Brownsville" was not one poem, but a cycle of poems in which Kadya depicted Jewish life as she saw it. Hellerstein calls that cycle of poems a "story of cultural decline".[4]

Before WWII, the Yiddish-speaking elite lived in the Bronx. There one could find an active Sholem Aleichem House, where Yiddish writers were invited to speak regularly. The Bronx had a built-in audience of educated Yiddish readers as well. The Amalgamated housing,[5] built not all that far from the Sholem Aleichem House, boasted a large union membership of communally active, Yiddish-speakers and readers. The Mlotek family, well-known Yiddish musicologists, lived there and so did Dr. Mordkhe Shechter, and Prof. Joshua Fishman, Yiddish linguists and researchers. Beila Schecter-Gottesman, the Yiddish poet, also lived in the Bronx at the time. That explains why, from 1942 till she left for Israel in 1950, Kadya lived in the Bronx.[6]

When she moved back to the US, in the early 1950s, Kadya did not move back to the Bronx[7] nor to Brooklyn, but to the Lower East Side. Times were changing, and she wanted to change with them.

While Kadya and Simche were able to pay the rent for an apartment in Manhattan, being able to pay the rent, and having funds for ongoing expenses, are not the same thing. Kadya and Simche still needed a regular source of income.

Before they left for Israel, Simche had been a member of the union of typesetters. That had not come easy. For reasons unknown to him, the union hesitated to grant him membership when he first applied for it. Quite possibly, word of his membership in the Communist Party in Warsaw had followed him to the US. Whatever the reason for the union's hesitation, Simche did eventually earn membership in the union. In those days, union membership was no meager thing. It guaranteed members health care, a pension, and life insurance, rights that Simche and his fellow agitators could only have dreamt of in Warsaw. Now that he was back in the US and asking for membership, it was denied him. As it turned out, the union suspended his membership because he had not paid his dues for the three years he had lived in Israel.

In a moving letter that exudes agitation and concern, Simche wrote the union asking to be reinstated. "Israel's laws prohibit any money from being sent out of the country"[8], he explained. It was not as though he did not want to pay his dues; he simply **could not** pay them.

That was in April of 1953. During the first few months of their lives back in New York, Kadya resorted to the strategy that had worked for her nearly twenty years earlier, when she had first arrived in the US: a lecture tour. Kadya had name recognition; her name drew crowds. She wrote to her friends, Sarah Dubow in Chicago, Hava Drost in Los Angeles, and Ida Maze in Montreal and she mapped out a tour schedule.

These were her friends and she was glad to see them. But her trips were not pleasure trips taken to renew old times. They were a stop-gap measure intended to provide the family with income while Simche looked for and found appropriate work and was reinstated into the type-setters' union.

Chapter Six: Return to the US: The first Decade 1952-1962   249

The Second Iteration of Rivke Zylberg: The Play

While still in Israel, Kadya re-wrote the novella, "The Diary of Rivke Zylberg" as a play. She must have circulated it among her friends in attempt to elicit feedback; the copy she left behind in her Israeli archive has Hebrew comments in the margins, apparently made by Asher Barash. Shortly after she returned to the US, the play based on the novella was ready to be produced.

"A House On Grand Street", which was performed in the now defunct President Theater, is the only drama performed wholly in Yiddish ever to be presented on Broadway. The fact that Kadya found backers for this venture is evidence of her sterling reputation. A Broadway drama is always a risk; a drama performed solely in Yiddish was extraordinarily risky. But Kadya's name made the venture seem worthwhile.

The play merits careful attention for more than one reason. For one thing, the play was never printed; it remains in the YIVO archive in a hand-written copy full of deletions and revisions. As such, it is a window into Kadya's thinking. For another, the time gap between the novella and the play is important. In the approximately thirteen years that passed between the writing of the novella and the production of the play, Kadya had had time to introspect and re-assess the immigrant experience in general, and the behavior of her heroine, in particular. Although Rivke Zylberg of the play still attracts men simply by displaying her hair, she is a somewhat changed young woman. Finally, the play has altered background details and an altered time frame.

First, to that window into Kadya's thinking. Already in the first scene of the play, Kadya intended to mention Rivke's hair. She considered inserting the following line but then crossed it out and noted on the side of the page that it would be best inserted later: As was the case in the novella, the admirer of Rivke's hair is the neighbor, Mrs. Shor:

"Rivke doesn't need to go to the beauty parlor. Although her hair is not fancily arranged, the boys like her anyway."

Instead of having a neighbor comment on Rivke's hair in this first scene, Eddy, the cousin's steady boyfriend, comments on Rivke's hair in the first scene. When Selma, the cousin, is not in the room, Eddy goes over to Rivke and says:

"Rivke, your hair is so beautiful, quiet [in the original: "*dayne hor zenen azelekhe shyene, shtile.*"] You don't need any beauty parlor."

While it is hard to know just what "still/quiet" hair would be like, it is clear that Eddy is attracted to Rivke's hair. What's more, he realizes that unlike his fiancé, Selma, Rivke is blessed with a natural (and non-costly) beauty.

As was the case in the novella, Rivke's neighbor, Mrs. Shor, harps on the ticking biological clock that Rivke needs to take into account. She recites the story of her sister, Golde, who was so intent on studying that she dismissed the suitors who came her way. Golde ended up unmarried, and presumably miserable. Speaking of this sister, Mrs. Shor says: "She had long braids, just like yours." As was true of the novella heroine, the play heroine has long braids; they are her feminine gift. The implication here is clear: even with such a winning card as her long, beautiful braids, Rivke can, if she is not careful, forfeit marriage and end up unhappy.

Once again, as was the case in the novella, for all that Eddy is attracted to Rivke, the true suitor in the picture is Eddy's friend. In the novella this friend was called "Red" most of the time. But this was a nickname his friends gave him; his English name was "Larry". In the play, the nickname "Red" is dropped[9], and the character is called "Larry" throughout.

The first time we see Rivke and Larry interacting and discussing her braids, we arrive at a critical junction in the development of Kadya's persona. Once again, because this is a hand-written manuscript, we can see Kadya's rejected thoughts on the page, both of which are legible even though they have been crossed out. Then comes the final, and most revealing, passage.

Chapter Six: Return to the US: The first Decade 1952-1962

The scene begins when Larry offers to help Rivke comb her hair. One of Kadya's crossed-out passage has Rivke responding with:

"What are you doing? I can do this myself".

This would be the reaction of a restrained woman whose personal space is invaded when a man offers to help her with her grooming.

The second crossed-out passage is yet more extreme. It has Rivke showing a bit more annoyance and using sharper language. Here she responds with:

"Leave me alone! Are you crazy?"

But this passage, too, was nixed. Kadya obviously had a complete change of heart. Instead of portraying a woman who feels offended at having a man take over her grooming, she presents a woman who is open to, and even accepting of intimacy. In this corrected version, Rivke responds with:

"*Vi zogt men oyf English* (How do they say it in English): Help Yourself".

Now this is a sea-change. Nothing of this sort took place in the novella. This is a woman far more at home with the intimacy that her suitor has offered.

When the novella was written, Sarah was still offering to groom Kadya's hair. Can that explain why Rivke of the novella did not have a suitor offer to groom her hair? Perhaps. By the time Rivke of the play appears, Kadya had been living far away from Sarah for over a decade. Is this change in Kadya's life responsible for the change in the hair-grooming scene? That seems possible.

In the novella it was clear that Selma did not like Rivke. It was obvious that her problem lay with Eddy's attraction to, and maybe even preference for, Rivke. Nevertheless, she did not openly voice her grievances. While that attraction (and possible preference) remains in the play, we get to hear more from Selma in the play. Here she has an outburst of jealousy that gives voice to her grievance. After Eddy "accidentally" calls Selma "Rivke", Selma tells her parents:

> "I cannot stand it. I can't tolerate her quiet, her demeaning me, her smile, her braids, her braids! I'm suffocating."

We have here an emotional outburst that lays bare a grab-bag of issues. Apart from Rivke's character traits, the one element that nearly sends Selma off the deep end is Rivke's braids! The exclamation point is no figment of my imagination; it is there in the text. Presumably, the actress who played Selma onstage was expected to shout or otherwise inflect her voice when she got to this passage. Rivke's braids hit Selma in the jugular. They rob her of breath and they are the true cause of her unhappiness.

We saw in the novella how Rivke's braids worked their magic on her future in-laws. The play includes this story as well. The only difference here is that instead of hearing about this magic from Rivke herself, we hear how Mrs. Kramer imagines the scene. After Mr. Kramer asks Rivke what she said to her in-laws at this meeting, Mrs. Kramer jumps in and says:

> "Rivke didn't need to say anything. All she had to do is show her braids."

In the play, as in the novella, it is the braids that bring on love and marriage.

Now for the differences between the novella and the play. In the novella, Rivke nearly steals her cousin's beau, Eddy. It is true that she does not actively encourage Eddy, but she is less than forceful about keeping him away from her and true to his commitment to Selma. In the play, on the other hand, she makes it quite clear from the very beginning that she has no interest in Eddy as long as he and her cousin Selma consider themselves a couple.

One can't help wondering if this has something to do with Kadya's personal reckoning. We know that Zeitlin reports on Kadya's flirtations when she was officially married to Simche. In a letter dated November 3, 1933, he told Opotashu that "when no one was looking she snuggled up to the first fellow she could find".[10] Was she then flirting with someone else's beau, as Rivke does in the novella? There is no knowing now. We do know that the later, altered, version of Rivke does not flirt with a man who is "taken".

One of the most contested issues in feminist theory is the question of luring or avoiding the stares of men. Can women avoid the male gaze that comes their way? Ought they try to do so? Or is this perhaps to be welcomed as a sign of one's desirability and/or femininity?

Kadya, a writer, and not a feminist theoretician, did not speak directly to this issue. However, there is a fascinating line in the play that gives us a glimpse of Kadya's opinion.

Mrs. Shor is one of the characters in this story who feels she truly understands Rivke. Since her judgments are generally reliable, the audience is likely to trust them. When the neighborhood women gather together to gossip about Rivke, Mrs. Shor says:

"Don't worry. The boys appreciate her. She forces them to think of her."

How, exactly, does Rivke do this? Mrs. Shor doesn't say. But the spectators at this play get her point. Rivke uses whatever feminine wiles she has, to draw attention to herself. Is it the way she walks? Perhaps. Modern readers might think pheromones. Whatever it is, Rivke somehow intentionally broadcasts feminine attractiveness and availability. If we accept the view that Rivke is representative of Kadya's feminine self, then perhaps the line we just quoted can be seen as Kadya's way of saying that as a young woman she projected feminine availability.

The novella, written as a diary, is told in the first person. Rivke, the new immigrant (or *grine* as she is called in Yiddish), "tells" her diary about her travails, as young ladies are wont to do. Accordingly, the reader of the novella gets to see only Rivke's point of view. The play, by its very nature, gives a far wider scope for alternative points of view. Because each of the characters gets to speak to others as well as to mutter to him/herself, the listener/audience sees Rivke as others see her.

Already in the beginning of the play, before we even get to see or hear much of Rivke, we are told by Selma, Rivke's cousin, that Rivke thinks too much of herself. "*Aza Yakhsnte*", What a stuck-up woman! Selma says, referring to Rivke. To make sure the audience gets the point, Kadya underlined the word "*yakhsnte*" in her manuscript.

Here Kadya is sharing with us an important insight. Over the years that separated the two works that featured Rivke Zylberg, Kadya realized that in the eyes of her new-found American family, she was stuck up. Perhaps she was rightfully so. She was better educated, more in touch with Jewish tradition and altogether more accomplished than her American family members. But that didn't make her any more likeable. In fact, this awareness of her own worth probably made her difficult, if not almost unbearable, to live with.

Already in the first scene of the first act of this play we get five different views of how Rivke struck the people around her. We will deal with them one at a time.

The first estimation of her, given rather begrudgingly by her own cousin Selma, is that Rivke is "*nish*t *keyn mi'ese*", not ugly. Coming as this does from the mouth of a single woman who senses from the very beginning that Rivke will compete with her for the attentions of the available young bachelors, this is something of a compliment, even if it is a begrudging one.

Since we are making the comparison between Rivke and Kadya, we are forced to say that when estimating her own womanly qualities, Kadya did not honestly believe she could claim to be beautiful. But then again, she did not believe she was ugly either.

In the manuscript of the play that Kadya left in the YIVO archive, this cousin Selma also claims that Rivke is not an interesting person. But that judgment never made its way into the play: the line is crossed out in the manuscript. Substituting Kadya for Rivke, we could say that the author considered the possibility that others found her uninteresting, but then dismissed that possibility. Whatever else others thought of her, they didn't find her uninteresting.

The next two judgments of Rivke are essentially an "unpacking" of the word we encountered before: *yakhsnte*. Continuing with her description of her newly arrived cousin, Selma says that Rivke is "proud" and "believes she is smarter than we are". In all likelihood, this is a fair account of Kadya when she first met her American family.

When considering in retrospect the impression she made on her family, Kadya realized she did not make a secret of her superiority.

The next judgment we get of Rivke is that she is *an ernste*, a level-headed, serious person. While it is true that Kadya loved a good joke and certainly knew how to laugh, this period of her life, (when she herself had found safety while her husband, her brother and her friends in Europe were clearly in danger), was a very trying time for her. Preying on her mind at the time was the awful possibility that her loved ones back home might not make it out of Europe alive. And that brought on a pall she could not shake. Under those circumstances, it was certainly reasonable to call Rivke/Kadya "serious", or not fun-loving.

The fifth judgment that Selma passes on Rivke is a more complex one. She says that Rivke is a "*tsnu'e*", a modest woman. But what does this mean? There are a few innuendos that cling to the Yiddish use of the word "*tsnu'e*". One is a lack of open sexuality. A woman who does not dress provokingly, or flaunt her body in public, is said to be a "*tsnu'e*". Another understanding of the term concerns behavior. A woman who is reticent publicly, and does not thrust herself into the public eye, is also said to be a "*tsnu'e*". Finally, there is the issue of self-image. A woman who makes do with who she is, and does not invest much time and effort in make-up or attempt to beautify herself, might also be considered a "*tsnu'e*". It's fair to say that each of these traits characterizes Rivke.

But do these traits characterize Kadya? More particularly, did they ever characterize Kadya? The situation is complicated and answers are not easy to come by.

When she was a younger woman in Warsaw, Kadya had tongues wagging at her immodest behavior. But what we know of this supposedly immodest behavior comes from the observations of A(ha)ron Zeitlin, Kadya's non-friend and sometime nemesis.

Even supposing that Zeitlin knew whereof he spoke, all that had happened in Europe, where Kadya was "at home" in the warm environment of Yiddish-speaking, inter-war Warsaw. In the US, amidst her Americanized, assimilationist family, she felt alien, and none of that behavior ever surfaced.

Of course, even when the novella was written, Kadya (unlike her protagonist Rivke) was a middle-aged, married woman and not a single woman in her twenties. Did this older Kadya wish now to see her younger self as a "*tsnu'e*"? That is certainly a possibility. We all remake our own images of the past as we age.

From her memoir, we know that Kadya was not inclined to spend time on make-up. Although Rivke is much younger, and perhaps not in need of the artificial interventions that come with make-up, she, too, shows no interest in make-up. From her memoir and from letters she wrote, we know that Kadya agreed, rather unwillingly, to put on some make-up from time to time. But she was never one to spend lots of time or lots of money on this. In creating a character that was averse to make-up, was Kadya then, foisting her own inclinations onto this protagonist? That does seem likely.

Not much further into the play, Selma once again comments on Rivke. Her judgment of the facts is correct, but her explanation of them is entirely off. Speaking of Rivke, Selma says:

"*Zi iz a rebitsen. Zi darf nisht keyn kleyder*" "She is a *rebitsen*/rabbi's wife. She needs no dresses."

What was Selma noticing? That her new-immigrant cousin did not have many dresses. This was most definitely true of Kadya when she arrived in the US; she tells us this much in her memoir. But why was it the case? Once again, Kadya tells us the answer in her memoir. She was so impoverished in Warsaw, that she simply could not afford what an American woman considered a decent wardrobe. In the US, even lower-middle class Jewish women simply could not imagine the degree of poverty that Warsaw Jews like Kadya had lived with.

Not realizing just how impoverished her cousin was, Selma came up with what seemed to her a reasonable explanation for her cousin's lack of dresses: her cousin was apparently too absorbed in "spiritual matters" to care about clothing. For Selma this

Chapter Six: Return to the US: The first Decade 1952-1962

seemed a reasonable explanation. But the reader of the novella and the observer of the play know this is not the case.

The fact is Kadya would not have objected then to having more dresses. Indeed, as she became "Americanized", she learned to accept a larger wardrobe as a natural part of a woman's possessions. And this change happened rather rapidly. In her memoir, Kadya tells us that when she got ready to take her first trip across the US, she packed into her suitcase "all the three dresses"[11] that her sister had bought her.

When Selma claimed Rivke was a *rebitsin*, a religious woman, she was wrong; Rivke was not at all religious. Why, then, did Selma think Rivke religious? Quite probably because Rivke could read and write "Jewish".

Since Hebrew and Yiddish are both written in the Hebrew alphabet, a Yiddish-speaking Jewish family in Europe, one that had given its children a secular Yiddish-speaking education, was assured that its children could read and write both Jewish languages, Hebrew as well as Yiddish.[12] The situation was entirely different in the US. A secular, English-speaking Jewish family, one whose children had had only a public-school education, could not produce Jewishly literate children. In order to have Jewishly literate children, (youngsters who could at least read the words of the Hebrew Bible and/or Sholem Aleichem, the great Yiddish novelist) Jewish families had to invest in Jewish education. This was generally costly, and only very committed secular families stretched themselves financially to provide their children with this education.

As a result, native-born American Jews like Selma did not usually know the difference between a Yiddish book and a Hebrew book. Nor could they tell the difference between a secular Jewish book and a religious Jewish book. For them, the two were one and the same: both were written in that "other, Jewish alphabet" that was closed to them. If Rivke could open such books and find her way in them, she was, in Selma's understanding, necessarily religious.

The heroine's attitude towards the Jewish homeland also changes in the move from novella to play. Rivke of the novella toys with the idea of joining her former beau in Palestine. She does not join him because circumstances intervene: after Italy joins the war in Europe, the path to Palestine is blocked. Rivke of the play, on the other hand, has an opportunity to immigrate to Israel, but she chooses not to do so. Instead, she decides to marry her American suitor and remain in the US. Like her creator, Kadya, Rivke's high opinion of life in Israel increased as her inclination to live in Israel decreased. In this, Rivke, and her creator, Kadya, accurately reflected the position of American "Zionists". They were eager to heap fulsome praise on the Jewish homeland, and just as eager to let others settle in and suffer for the Jewish state.

Whereas Rivke's preference for Larry, her American boyfriend, over Leyzer, (her European boyfriend living in the Jewish homeland), has no emotional justification in the novella, in the play, there is one heart-to-heart conversation, a dialog between Rivke and Larry, that shows a true meeting of spirits. In it, Rivke reveals what is truly troubling her. And Larry does his best to comfort her.

Larry, sensing that something is troubling Rivke, begs her not "to be sad". But what Rivke feels is not exactly sadness. She does her best to explain to Larry what her problem is:

"I have a strange feeling, Larry. It's as though I were living in a borrowed/uncertain world."

When asked what she means, she says:

"The chair I'm sitting on is lent to me for a short time, the bed I sleep in is lent to me for a few nights, and even the steps I walk on are lent to me and will not be there again on my way back. Where can I find a reliable world?"

In response Larry says:

"Rivke, the world belongs to all of us, to you, to me, to everyone. No one borrows a piece of it from someone else. Everyone takes whatever piece of the world that he can. And you can take a lot."

We have here Kadya's distilled sense of loss and indebtedness that made her early immigrant life so miserable. The world she knew was gone. The world she was now a part of was not really hers. She owned very little, and what she did have had been foisted on her. (Recall her borrowed shoes and the three dresses, bought for her by her sisters, which replaced her own "rags".) In this play, in her memoir, and among the essays Kadya left in YIVO, Kadya repeated the folk saying: "Better your own tatters than someone else's satins." This is the proud rejection of borrowed items that only the truly impoverished can feel. And Kadya had truly known poverty. It is of no consequence whether Kadya ever expressed herself this way when she herself was an immigrant. There is no doubt that she felt this way. The cultural world she moved in was alien; her physical world was full of borrowed items; and it was most disconcerting to live in a world where nothing at all was hers.

The passage quoted above is probably the most dramatic moment of the play. But as Shakespeare knew, a drama works well if it has some comic relief. And in this play, Kadya spiced her drama with some comedy.

The family Selma is marrying into is one of "ordinary folks": there are no rabbis, no great Jewish minds, not even a great secular scholar among the forefathers. For Selma's father, Abe, this lack of what is called "*yikhes*" in Yiddish (distinguished forebears) is a definite disadvantage. For Selma's mother, however, this is of no consequence. When her husband brings up this lack of *yikhes*, she says:

"Are you going to start carrying on about "*yikhes*"? I'm pleased that we've gotten there [planning a marriage]. If in fact we really have gotten there. With them [the in-laws, ZKN] it can still be "every Purim a new *megile*".

What Selma's mother is suggesting in this passage is that the in-laws can yet change their demands. On Purim, Jewish congregations read the *megile* (rolled manuscript) known as "Esther". But Selma's mom is suggesting that these folks can yet change the prescribed script on them. And then they will be forced to answer a new set of demands. Since the Yiddish-speaking audience could be expected to know what a *megile* is and which *megile* is read on the holiday of Purim, this outburst of Selma's mom was bound to call forth laughter.

This same scene was full of comic quips. Abe Kramer, Selma and Marvin's father (and Rivke's uncle), is in the insurance business. As might be expected, that profession colors all his judgments. In this business, fires are a major business expense. After all, in a fire an individual or a business loses all its belongings/stock. And if these are insured, the insurance company is forced to reimburse the customer for all that was lost. Thus "a real fire" is Abe Kramer's expression for an enormous outlay of money.

In the scene described above, Ida and Abe Kramer, Selma's mother and father, get to hear about the cost of the upcoming wedding of their daughter. The future mother-in-law spells out her expectations quite clearly. The Kramers will need to pay for a fine hall, a rabbi, a cantor, music, a master of ceremonies, and flowers. And all this is apart from her demand that the Kramers buy the couple the finest bedroom set that can be had. Once the mother-in-law-to-be departs, and the husband and wife are left to themselves, Abe Kramer groans: "A fire! A genuine fire!"

We have to imagine that the audience laughed here. And we know for a fact that the audience did laugh from time to time. In a letter that she wrote to Ida Maze, Kadya told Ida that the audience laughed in all the right places.[13]

But did the audience sometimes laugh in some of the wrong places? There is every reason to believe it did.

The New York Times review of this play claimed that Kadya "has a natural flair for comedy".[14] Was this play meant to be a comedy? By no means. As we know from Kadya's own testimony, the new-immigrant years in New York were the most miserable years of her life. And in this play, Kadya was doing her best to convey that feeling.

What made the New York Times reviewer dwell on the little bit of comedy that found its way into this play? The answer, I believe, comes from an unfortunate turn that Yiddish took in the US. Perhaps as a result of the success of the TV comedians of the mid-twentieth century, perhaps as a result of the discomfort that Jews felt as speakers of a "strange" non-English language, Yiddish in the US has come to be looked upon as an inherently comic language. The very sound of Yiddish is supposed to be funny. Indeed, this is considered such a funny language, that any string of words will cause an average American audience to burst into laughter, even when the semantic material has nothing even mildly comic about it.[15]

It is not clear whether Kadya had witnessed this phenomenon. It may well be that she simply did not travel in circles that were so Americanized. Nevertheless, she herself did not think she wrote a comedy.

She said in an interview:

"What interested me was the simple Jew, the average family [living] on Grand Street, its problems, and its daily struggles."[16]

There is no doubt that this was true. Kadya did indeed substitute the travails of an "ordinary", single, twenty-something-year-old for the travails of a famous, married, middle-aged writer. But the feelings of disorientation and culture shock that her heroine feels were also her feelings.

The reviewer of the Daily *Forverts*, the most well-known and most popular Yiddish newspaper of the time, thought that Kadya's aim was to

"show the disharmony between Jewish life in America and the vanished Jewish life in the "old home" that has been destroyed so tragically." [17] This reviewer did not see any need to address the few comic bits of the play. And he was justified. This is by no means a comic play.

Now to other changes in the play. In the novella, it clear that Jewish immigrants change/anglicize their names when they adjust to life in the US. Rivke of the novella accepts this unquestioningly. Abandoning the identifiably Jewish name "Rivke", she agrees to re-name herself "Rae". From the last line of that book, the reader realizes that the heroine has paid a price for this abandonment. But for her, the sacrifice was worthwhile: she has found love and acceptance and is no longer alone. But this is not what happens in the play. Here Rivke refuses to conform. She stubbornly sticks with her original, Jewish, name.

In the second act of the play, Mendel Pushcart, one of the regular visitors at her aunt and uncle's house, insists on calling Rivke "Rae". But Rivke will have none of it. She retorts with:

"Rae"? What's wrong with "Rivke"? In Lublin we considered it a fine name."

When Mrs. Kramer tries to claim that it makes no difference whether one keeps one's Jewish name or abandons it, Mendel Pushcart tries to call Rivke "Rae" once more. But Rivke does not give up easily. She responds with:

"But I beg of you, please call me by the name I was given."

This does not go down well with Mrs. Kramer. She is convinced that this sort of stubbornness will not serve Rivke well in her new home, and she says so:

"She's a stubborn one, that one. How a girl like that will manage in America, I don't know."

But Rivke is adamant. Her insistence pays off; the others give up, and her name continues to be "Rivke".

What make Kadya change this aspect of her story? Why was the young immigrant's easy acquiescence in the novella replaced in the play with a refusal to conform on this point?

If Kadya ever discussed this change with anyone, she left no evidence of it. There are no notes, no letters to friends discussing this issue, no crossed-out lines that have been replaced by others. Accordingly, we will have to surmise what we can based on the knowledge we do have.

There seems little doubt that personal name changes were common among Jewish immigrants in the early part of the twentieth century. Having come to the US in the hopes of bettering their economic status, new immigrants were anxious to learn from former immigrants, who had already acculturated. If a Jewish name could impede or deter economic contacts, then that name could be chucked, at least outwardly, and a new, American-sounding name could be adopted. When these immigrants became

Chapter Six: Return to the US: The first Decade 1952-1962   263

parents themselves, they generally gave their children two names: an American/English name, to be used in official documents and in dealings with non-Jews, and a Jewish name, to be used on specifically Jewish occasions, like being called up to the Torah, or being named in a Jewish wedding ceremony.

In her novel, written in 1912, about life among immigrants, Mary Antin says:

"With our despised immigrant clothing, we shed also our impossible Hebrew names. A committee of our friends, several years ahead of us in American experience, put their heads together and concocted American names for us all. Those of our real names that had no pleasing American equivalents they ruthlessly discarded, content if they retained the initials."[18] In just this way, retaining only the [r] sound of her "real" name, the immigrant "Rivke" of The Diary turned into "Rae".

Personal name changes were (and still are) very different for Jewish women than they were (and are) for Jewish men. Jewish men always have a "Jewish name". This is the name they are given at circumcision, when they "become Jewish".[19] Since girls have no comparable ceremony, there is no similar pressure for parents to give their daughters a Jewish name. And indeed, in parts of the Jewish Diaspora, there were women who simply did not have a "Jewish name".[20]

Jewish men are called by their Jewish name when the Torah is read in the synagogue on the Sabbath and on Jewish Holidays. During this ceremony, the named man either says a blessing aloud before the public reading, raises the Torah scroll for all to see, or rolls the Torah scroll and puts it away properly. Until very recently, when girls were given a place at Torah readings in some synagogues, girls did not get called on for any of these honors. Consequently, there was no need for a Jewish girl to have a Jewish name.

In the US, Jewish girls and women, then, either did not have, or were unaware of, their "Jewish names". If Kadya was insistent on having her heroine retain her "Jewish name" in the early 1950s, she must have had her reasons.

One possible explanation for this change in Kadya's attitude is simply the passage of time. As the years went by and Kadya saw how deeply even her Yiddishist circle of friends had assimilated, she became ever more alarmed. Determined to cling to every possible shred of Jewish identity, she was now unwilling to grant her heroine the luxury of shedding a Jewish name. Like the older Kadya herself, this newer "Rivke", aware that shedding a Jewish name is shedding part of one's Jewish identity, clings to her Jewish name at all costs.

Interestingly, studies done on naming practices among Jews in the early part of the twentieth century confirm that the passage of time did affect name-changing among Jews. Whereas immigrants of the very earliest part of the twentieth century shed their Jewish names quite often, the children born to these immigrants were "far more likely to share names with the foreign-born generation than with their native neighbors."[21] Perhaps the need to "fit in" was not as urgent; perhaps the tug of parenthood brought with it thoughts of generational continuity. Whatever the reason, naming practices did change over these years.

However, the issue at hand may be not simply the passage of time, but the passage of this particular time. The decade-plus that separates the writing of the novella from its re-fashioning into a play was not an ordinary decade; it was a momentous decade. In that decade, the thousand-year-old Jewish civilization in Europe was annihilated, the Jewish Socialist dream of the brotherhood of all mankind was proven to be a chimera, and an independent Jewish State of Israel was founded in what had been Palestine. These events may well have influenced Kadya's change of heart on the importance of keeping one's Jewish name.

If personal comfort and social adjustment were what mattered most for the great majority of Jewish immigrants to the US before WWII, (and indeed that was what mattered most), once the Holocaust had sundered American Jews from their European counterparts, a new national consciousness emerged among American Jews. All American Jews, even the most assimilated of them, realized that only an accident of geography had granted them life while their Jewish brethren in Europe had been slaughtered. And it is entirely possible that one of the effects of this new consciousness was a willingness to assert one's Jewish identity in the non-Jewish world.

For some Jews, this awareness may have elicited (or awakened) an emphasis on Jewish particularity. Were the German-Jewish men born as "Gershon" murdered even though they'd renamed themselves "Gephardt"? Why then, bring back "Gershon". One might as well stick with the genuine article; the faux, non-Jewish, names were ultimately useless.[22]

Among others in the Jewish community, reverting to those Jewish names was one way (perhaps even the only way) the living could honor and memorialize the murdered dead. There is no way of knowing if this was a consideration for Kadya. But for members of the Jewish community, naming children is a way of memorializing family members who have died.[23]

Finally, there is the emergence of the State of Israel. There is no question that this affected Jews world-wide. Simply knowing that a Jewish state existed somewhere (no matter how far away it might be), meant that a Jew could now walk and live among non-Jews with pride. For some Jews, part of this pride was the willingness to flaunt one's Jewishness for all the world to see. The former "Martins" and "Mortimers" whose Jewish name was "Moshe", could now revert to "Moshe" (at least within the Jewish world) as their grandfathers had been. The need to hide behind a neutral/non-Jewish façade had vanished.

Once again, naming studies prove there is something to this supposition. In an article entitled "Jewish Names and Names of Jews", Stanley Lieberson noted that the overlap between Jewish names and non-Jewish names declined in the 1950s. He suggests two possible factors: "the influence of the Holocaust on Jews living in the United States" and "the movement toward a homeland in Palestine, culminating in the establishment of the State of Israel."[24]

Paradoxically, the issue of personal names and the way they were handled in Israel in the early years of Statehood, may well have caused a counter-reaction in Kadya. Jews outside of Israel may have behaved "more Jewishly" after the establishment after the State of Israel. But that was not what was going on with Kadya. For her the issue may well have been a rejection of an Israeli norm.

Among the leaders and the elite of Israel, "Hebraizing" one's name was a desideratum: all the leaders of the young State of Israel changed their "Diaspora-sounding" names to different, "Hebraic"-sounding names. In fact, during the war of Independence, a commission put out thousands of copies of a book entitled "Choose Yourself a Hebrew Name!", intended to help soldiers choose an "appropriate" Hebrew name. What's more, all generals in the new army were told they had to abandon their Diaspora names and take on new, Hebrew names.[25] New immigrants to Israel were especially pressured. Some were re-named when they entered the country. Others simply bowed to social pressure as they acculturated into Israeli society.[26]

As we have seen, Kadya never for a moment thought of abandoning her Diaspora name. Although we have no direct evidence of her opinion of this rejection of Old World (Diaspora/Yiddishized) names in Israel, we have every reason to believe that this wholesale rejection of the Old World did not sit well with her. It may well be that for this very reason, on her return to the US, she insisted that her character retain her given, Jewish (Diaspora) name.

Just as Kadya's interest in retaining Jewish names changed in the decade or so that separated the novella from the play, so did her interest in retaining the Jewish Sabbath. In the novella, Friday evenings are reserved for card-playing. While this is a release from the pressures of the workaday world, there is nothing spiritual whatsoever about it. We have no indication in the novella that the Jewish Sabbath is observed at all. In the play, on the other hand, wee bits of Jewish awareness, and even of Jewish observance, creep in. While there is no mention of praying in a synagogue, we do hear about shops closing early "because it is the Sabbath tonight". What's more, the final words of the play, uttered by Selma and Marvin's mother (and Rivke's aunt), which, in its first version was supposed to be "Children, come, we're going to eat", became, in the final version:

"Well, children come! Your father is going to make *kidesh*"[the blessing on the wine that ushers in the family's Sabbath meal].

The lack of name-change as well as the appearance of the Jewish Sabbath in the play mirrored social changes that occurred in the US after the Holocaust. The audience at the play knew this from having lived through the changes, and with her sharp antennae for social change, Kadya knew this as well.

Now to the crucial issue of time-frame. The novella has a very clear time-frame. Rivke begins her diary in 1939. Since we know early in the novella that Italy has entered the war, and at its end, the US has not yet entered the war, the events of the novella range between 1939 and 1941.

The time frame of the play, on the other hand, is murky. In the play, as in the novella, Rivke is "a refugee". But what year is it? We are not told. In the play, Leyzer speaks of his "torture" in Europe. When did this happen? Once again, we are not told. While it is true that Jews were tortured in Europe even before the Nazis set up concentration camps, if the time frame of the play remains that of the novella, Leyzer's "torture" is unexplained and somewhat incongruous. Similarly, the switch from (1939-1940) "Palestine" and "the Land of Israel" of the novella, to simply (post-1948?) "Israel" of the play, is incongruous. Apparently, neither Kadya, nor the play's producer, found these incongruities problematic.

We have, then, four different items that point to a post-Holocaust time-frame for this play: the torture Leyzer underwent in Europe, the substitution of "Israel" for "Palestine" and "the Land of Israel", the retention of a Jewish name and the awareness of the Jewish Sabbath. But if the time-frame for this play is post-Holocaust, then Rivke, the refugee, is not simply a dislocated, unfortunate young lady. She is someone who witnessed the destruction of Jewish civilization in Europe. Why, then, is the Holocaust never mentioned?

Practically speaking, the answer is simple. Kadya had written the novella before the Holocaust. When she transferred the novella into a play, she simply lifted the plot and the characters and transformed the whole package into the format of a play. Admittedly, she made a few changes in the play. But she made no overt change in the play's time-frame.

As I see it, making Rivke into a Holocaust survivor was more than Kadya was ready for. She could, and did, give vent to her feelings about the Holocaust in poetry. But drama and poetry make different demands on the psyche, and Kadya was simply unable to bring herself to a dramatic expression of events that were so very painful.

Interestingly, even the critics did not notice that the time frame of the play was problematic. The Forverts critic who suggested that the play showed "the disharmony between Jewish life in America and the vanished Jewish life in the "old home", did not realize that the play's heroine, who found refuge in America, had apparently witnessed the vanishing of "Jewish life in the 'old home'"[27]. The critics, too, were unable to see the Holocaust as it hovered over that play, influencing events, but never mentioned.

This fatal flaw is an inherent feature of the play. It is one good reason for the play's early folding. But there is yet another, very practical, reason for the short run of the play. It can be called the demographic problem.

During the last decades of the nineteenth century and the early decades of the twentieth century, many Yiddish-speaking immigrants flocked to Second Avenue to see Yiddish plays. In those days, there were millions of Yiddish speakers in the NY area. In the 1950s, those immigrants were, for the most part, no longer around. If they were alive, they were likely to be living in Florida. Their children did not speak Yiddish, although they understood it- somewhat. The grandchildren of the immigrants, second generation Americans, did not, as a rule, speak Yiddish, and did not understand it either. Crowds did not flock to see this play, although Kadya's ever-loyal sister Dora came all the way from Philadelphia to see it. (She even brought along her son, Kadya's nephew Ben, who admitted to me that he didn't really understand what was going on.)[28] To be sure, there were new Yiddish speakers around: Holocaust survivors. But in the early 1950s, these men and women had all they could do to find housing and jobs. The new Yiddish speakers, frazzled, hassled and poor, could not possibly fill a Broadway theater. The play folded after a run of a month and a half.

A Third Iteration of Rivke Zylberg: Articles in the Forverts

Kadya's very first cycle of published poems was called *Froyen Lider*, women's poems, and the question of women's role in society held her attention throughout her life. By 1955, just about thirty years after the publication of *Froyen Lider*, she'd abandoned the militant, near-anger that colored her Warsaw poems, and she adopted a position of unprejudiced searching for patterns. What precisely was the role of women in society, she asked herself. And she came prepared with no ready-made answers. In an attempt to let her curiosity range freely, she took upon herself the writing of a weekly column in the weekend edition of the Forverts, devoted to this question.

Begun in 1955, this column contained biographical sketches of women. Sometimes these were women drawn from Jewish history, like the Biblical heroine Deborah, or the Talmudic figure, Bruria, the wife of Rabbi Meir.[29] Sometimes the women are of interest because of their connection to famous men; that was true of the mother of Sigmund Freud, and the wife of Benjamin Disraeli. And sometimes the women were in the news at the time, like Betsy McDonald, the author of a contemporary best-selling novel. For us, the most fascinating fact about this column is that Kadya wrote it under a pseudonym, and not just any pseudonym. These columns were written by one "Rivke Zylberg"!

While Rivke Zylberg of the novella and the play was Kadya's feminine persona lent to a young single woman, Rivke Zylberg of the Forverts is simply a woman writing about other women. It is as though in the first case the lens closes in on Kadya's attractiveness, while in the second case, the lens zooms out and considers only Kadya's gendered look at other women.

Because it gave her the opportunity to read widely, Kadya probably enjoyed researching the stories of these little-known women. These were not academic articles with footnotes and references; producing them at the pace of one a week, Kadya had no time for serious research. Nor was that her aim. What she wanted and presented were thumb-nail sketches, the results of her reading. Her New York archive gives no clue to her references, the books and/or articles she undoubtedly read, but it does have these sketches as they appeared in the newspaper. She turned out a potpourri of stories, some of them fascinating, others simply curiosities. Here are a few of them.

Yente di Nevite, Yente, the Prophetess is featured in one of these columns. This woman's husband (whose family name we are given) was a follower of the famous founder of Hassidism, the *Ba'al Shem Tov*. Yente once accompanied her husband on his visit to the great Rebbe, and when she returned, she was a changed woman. She separated herself from all doings with her husband; she immersed herself in a *mikve* (water that confers spiritual purity) three times (!) a day; she began to seriously study traditional Jewish texts. (Exactly how she managed to do this with no previous background, we are never told. But this is a folk story, so we are not supposed to raise doubts here.) Because none of this is normative behavior for a traditional Jewish woman of the 18th century, we would expect the *Ba'al Shem* to intervene and put a stop to this. But he does not. Instead he calls her "Yente, the Prophetess" and encourages her to keep up her "good works". And she does. A story is told of how she encouraged all the mothers in her town to contribute to the town's effort to marry off an impoverished young girl. They all follow her advice, and the young girl is successfully married off. The point here is: not only can an unusual, very independent woman choose to behave most unconventionally, but so great and respected a man as the founder of Hassidism approved of this woman and of her behavior.

A second story is simply called "Temerl". Here again we are given her (husband's) family name (Zabitkaver). This time we are told the heroine lived in Poland (We know nothing about the whereabouts of Yente, not even which of the East European countries she came from.), and we have an approximate date for her life: the late 18th and early 19th centuries. Temerl's family was wealthy, we are told, so wealthy, that her father was able to gift an entire estate to the Polish king, Stanislaw Panitavsk. In addition, he was able to support "thousands" of Jews who had escaped Cossack pogroms in 1794. Not only was Temerl's father wealthy; her husband was wealthy as well. And Temerl knew how to use this money wisely. She beautified the study houses of Prague and Warsaw, and she fought off the dangerous men of the Jewish Enlightenment in her own, rather unusual way. She bought the books of the "Enlightened" writer, Joseph Perl, in great quantities, and then burned them! This way, she saved believing Jews from the dangerous path of non-believers and helped keep them on the "right path".

One can't help wondering whether Kadya wasn't speaking a bit tongue-in-cheek here. Had she been writing this for the readers of the religious newspaper, *Der Tog*, her readers might well have agreed that what Temerl did was praise-worthy. The readers of the *Forverts*, however, were all in favor of Enlightenment. Whatever the case, Kadya was given free rein in this matter, and from all appearances, the reaction of the readers (if there was any) was not enough to stop Kadya from continuing these pieces. To return to Temerl: her son, Michael, was a musician who learned first in London and then in Paris, and her grandson was none other than the well-known French philosopher, Henri Bergson.

A far less conventional woman was Hannah Rokhl Verbermacher, also known as the Maiden of Ludmir. She was the only woman ever to behave, and win approval as, a female Hassidic Rebbe. She married twice and divorced twice, and very much like Yente, discussed above, she never lived with her husband as man and wife. She spent much of her time praying and studying traditional Jewish texts, and she did win a following among men. She left Europe for the Land of Israel and there she maintained a traditional Rebbe's court despite the disapproval of many traditional rabbis.

The pressure of having a deadline of one complete item a week meant that occasionally Kadya's hunt for interesting tidbits didn't turn up fascinating material. This happened, for example, when she did a piece on Treyne, the mother of the Vilna Ga'on. All she found were un-enlightening incidents such as the fact that Treyne nearly drowned as a child (but recovered, obviously), and the pious platitudes that Treyne was a *tsnu'e* and did good deeds.

A similar unsuccessful hunt was her attempt to find an unusual slant to the story of Chana Devora Spinoza, Baruch/Benedict Spinoza's mother. The woman died when her child, Baruch, was a mere six years old. If she influenced him at all, it was by her absence.

But there were times, when Kadya came up with unusual slants to unknown "back stories". This is what happened with her revelation that Walt Whitman's love of nature was something he picked up from his mother. Their joint interests, it turned out, made for a genuine friendship between them. That would make the letters between them a gold-mine for some doctoral student studying Whitman's poetry. Similarly, her investigation of the role that Letitia Bonaparte played in her son's life reveals that a stern, stubborn and determined mother reared a stern, stubborn and determined son. Once again, Kadya provided material for further research, this time for a psychological analysis of the relationship between Napoleon and his mom.

More than anything else, these short essays reveal a curious mind. It would seem that Kadya took this project upon herself for the joys of the hunt. As things developed, there were no predictable trends. Some mothers, wives, and/or daughters of famous men had a great influence on the men in their lives. Others simply did not. And as variable as men and women are, so were the influences of these women. As for the women who were featured as stand-alone characters in her column, each was, in her own way, independent and non-conformist. Long before the feminist movement called for focusing attention on women who dared to buck convention, Kadya single-handedly spot-lighted individual women who did just that: they dared to be different. In that respect, Kadya was a feminist, championing important, but largely forgotten (or ignored) brave women.

Kadya's Continued Productivity

In 1956 the Israeli theater known as "Ohel" performed a play Kadya had written in 1949. Entitled *Nokhn Got Fun Midber*, After God of the Desert, this is the story of Donna Gracia Mendes, a *converso* woman who managed her family finances with financial acumen and struggled to avoid the long arm of the Inquisition. The play had been performed in Buenos Aires in 1952. We are told it "was a great success" there, despite the fact that "not everyone understood everything."[30]

The dramatic tension in that play is twofold: there is the danger that the Mendes family will be tried by the Inquisition for maintaining their Jewish identity, and the danger that Donna Gracia's younger and weaker sister, will betray the family. For all that the play had potential, the critics did not especially like it. The costumes, they said, were laughable, the staging was not professional and the historical facts were stretched beyond recognition.[31] Like *A Hoyz Oyf Grend Strit*, this play was not a great success.

In 1957, the National Committee of Jewish Folk Schools, based in New York, helped fund a textbook written by Kadya entitled *Oyf Di Vegn Fun Tsiyon*, On the Roads of Zion. In the introduction to this book, Kadya says that "in previous generations, Jewish children were raised in an atmosphere[32] that was steeped in longing for the Land of Israel, for Zion."[33]

From everything we know of Kadya's childhood, this was certainly true for her family. Her father, almost certainly the person who influenced her the most, was a true lover of Zion. But in the late nineteenth and early twentieth centuries, when Kadya was growing up, a great many Jewish children were being raised in assimilationist families that wanted nothing to do with Zion, or with anything particularly Jewish, for that matter. What's more, as Kadya herself knew, some Jewish children were brought up in a secular system, committed solely to Yiddish culture and the Yiddish language. (This, indeed, was the program of the Folk School movement, the movement that helped finance her textbook.) The Land of Israel and the Hebrew language were simply not an important component of this educational system.

Kadya waxed eloquent about the Zionist "folk dream" in her introduction to this book. There was indeed such a folk dream. But most of these dreamers went out of their way to compose textbooks about Zion in Hebrew.

Which schoolchildren were the intended market for this textbook? In New York, the city with the largest concentration of Jews in the US, the Workman's Circle (known in Yiddish as the *Arbiter Ring*) schools were not interested in Zionist material. The Scholem Aleichem schools, also an after-school, supplementary school system which did allow some Zionist material into its curriculum, could not possibly have assigned such a textbook. Its students were in the system only for a few hours a week; they could not have devoted the time needed to assimilate the material in this textbook.[34]

The textbook itself begins with a chapter on Jerusalem, headed by a quote, in Hebrew, from the prophet Isaiah. This quote was not translated into Yiddish. Was there anyone among the students using this textbook who could dope out a verse from Isaiah in its original Hebrew? That is doubtful. Although there was a "Zionist Workers" section of the National Folk schools, and its head did in fact have a say in the making of this textbook (as evidenced from the few paragraphs allotted to him in the beginning of this book), there was no way these schools could teach the Hebrew Bible if their students knew only Yiddish, and a smattering of that, to boot. Biblical Hebrew can be taught, but in order to understand the poetry of Isaiah, students need to spend many hours learning Biblical Hebrew. And very few Yiddish-language school systems (if any) did that.

The Folk schools were, by definition, secular, and the students who attended these schools belonged to secular families. As such, they were not familiar with or exposed to, Jewish observance. What were they supposed to make of the passage in this book that says: "God's presence (*di shkhine*, in Yiddish) dwells in Jerusalem. Jerusalem is holy." ? For Kadya, this was not new. Five years earlier, she had published a collection of poems entitled, "Angels Come To Jerusalem". But for the secularists of the Folk School movement, this passage bordered on anathema. The world-view of these children did not include God (not a Jewish God, and not any other god.); nor was a word like "holy" in their vocabulary. It was a term neither they, nor their teachers, were in the habit of using.

How did Kadya get away with this? One can only suppose that her bona fides as a writer of children's books was so great, that her publisher gave her carte blanche, and did not dare interfere with the content of her book. It is also possible that the secular parent body, more concerned with the social advantages of the Folk school (where Jewish children socialized with each other), than with the content of the textbooks assigned in these schools, were entirely unaware of what their children were supposed to be reading.

The first one hundred or so pages of this textbook are an excellent overview of the history of the Jewish attachment to the Land of Israel. In her inimitable way, Kadya chose just those tidbits that are of dramatic excitement: the Talmudic rabbis who made every effort to keep the memory of Jerusalem alive even after it had been destroyed, the extraordinary customs Jews continued to observe in order to keep alive the memory of the land they had left, the later rabbis who visited the Holy Land and were attacked, and sometimes killed, just for wanting to visit the Holy Land. Portraits of the cities of Israel are painted here lovingly, each city together with the folk stories that accrued to it (Jerusalem, Safad, Tiberias), and well-known Jewish thinkers and writers, like

Yehudah Ha-Levi[35] and the *Ramban*[36], each of whom traveled in dangerous times just to be in the Land of Israel.

But that is only the first third of the book. The next two thirds are riddled with a prejudiced view of the history of Zionism. Here we find what is essentially the Socialist (Labor Party's) view of the events leading up to the establishment of Israel. We hear about the pioneers who founded collectivization and the kibbutz movement, but nothing about the many more petit bourgeoisie who founded and populated the city of Tel Aviv and made it into a thriving, modern metropolis. The *Haganah* and the *Palmach* are discussed in detail; they were, after all, the military arms of the ruling Labor party. But there is no mention of the *Etzel*[37] movement, the historically important military arms of the Opposition party. Ze'ev Jabotinsky[38], a prominent Zionist and theoretician in his own right, but a leader of the Opposition, is mentioned only once, and then for his one-time cooperation with Trumpeldor[39], a man who is only a footnote in the history of Zionism.[40] All of Jabotinsky's works and his deep influence are ignored. Most shockingly, even in the late 50s, after she knew all about Communism in the Soviet Union and about the infamous sign above the entrance to Auschwitz-Birkenau, Kadya quoted without comment (or criticism) the slogan that "Work will bring about the Messiah".[41]

Kadya published another book in 1957, this time a collection of short stories, entitled: *A Shtub Mit Zibn Fenster*, a House with Seven Windows. From the introduction that Kadya wrote, we know that she considered this her reflections on Jewish life in her time: life in Europe before the Holocaust, life in the US right before and after the Holocaust, and life in the newly established State of Israel.

It is no accident that Kadya chose the word "house" as a metaphor for Jews. These people are often referred to in the Hebrew Bible as "the house of Israel". [42] As for the number seven, it could almost be considered **the** "crucial number" in Judaism. After all, Jews count seven days in order to get to the Jewish Sabbath, the sanctified day of the week. In the Land of Israel, the land itself gets a "sabbatical" and is supposed to be allowed to rest every seventh year.[43] And when seven times seven (forty-nine) years have passed in the land of Israel, the Bible tells us, the folk is enjoined to declare a "Jubilee Year", when the land rests, and all the slaves are to be set free.[44]

Speaking of the losses and gains that came with the transference of Jewish life from Europe to the US, Kadya says in that introduction that these "losses and gains are both tragic and comic."[45] She adds, "Perhaps that's why I wanted to call this book "A House with Seven Windows": light and shadows enter each window."[46]

The losses may have been both tragic and comic, but the stories themselves are neither tragic nor comic. For them to be tragic, the reader would have to empathize with the characters deeply, and that never happens. For them to be comic, there would have had to be authorial abandon and detachment, and that, too, does not happen.

But the stories are accurately observed, and even biting. Sometimes they are thought-provoking, and occasionally they are amusing. There is even a group of feel-good stories.

Less than a third of the stories (sixteen out of fifty-seven) are set in Europe, and even these are occasionally told in a flashback by a Jew now living in the US. It is these stories that tend to be feel-good stories. Here characters are one-dimensional, and often (though not always) virtuous. The setting is the traditional shtetl, the small, one-horse town where Jews lived a traditionally Jewish life. Characters here embrace Judaism reflexively. This is shtetl life as Kadya knew it when she was growing up. It is true that when World War I overtook Europe, and Kadya began her wandering across the borders of Eastern Europe, this world was crushed and began to disintegrate. But for Kadya this world is still alive. She presents it here as she remembers it, or, what amounts to the same thing, as she would like to remember it.

The stories set in the US are cast in an entirely different light. Here Kadya is almost ruthlessly clear-sighted. In some of these stories we get a swath of immigrant life. This is the case in the string of five related tales that go under the general title: "In a Brownsville *Kretchma*". The word "*kretchma*", retained even in the English translation, is the Yiddish for "inn" or "pub". In Eastern Europe, (as in modern England), this was a place for social gathering as well as social drinking. And in Brownsville, the area of Brooklyn in which East European Jews congregated in the first few decades of the twentieth century, the pub served the very same purpose. Like Isaac Babel's Benya Krik, the man who controlled Jewish activities, legal and illegal, in early 20th century Odessa, Nyoma Khurgin controlled Jewish society in Brownsville. And like Isaac Babel, Kadya paints a broad canvas: petty clashes, personal vendettas, fellowship and community, all pass through the watchful eye of the agreed-upon community leader.[47]

But most of the American Jewish stories in this collection are about individual immigrants and their problems. These immigrants have cast off Jewish tradition along with Yiddish and their original Jewish names, and they pay dearly for that. They often lose their humanity in their frantic race to acquire riches. More than one character has a pathological relationship to money: it is the measure of all that is good in life. Whoever has acquired wealth, is to be revered, and whoever has not, is worthy of neglect, or worse, contempt. Admittedly there are occasional exceptions: unexpected and unrequited kindnesses are sometimes showered on total strangers. But these are the exception, not the rule.

The saving grace that was offered by the social gatherings of *landslayt* (residents of the same home-town in Europe) is another theme that appears in these stories. It is true that these gatherings were sometimes a source of friction and an arena in which personal grudges came to the fore. But for all that, these gatherings also served as a balm for the psyche, a reminder of the lost world, and a venue for rekindling memories and lost personal connections.

The State of Israel plays a fascinating role in this collection. Only four stories feature Israel: the title story, the first in this collection, the penultimate story, set entirely in the young state, and two stories found in the middle of the collection, both

Chapter Six: Return to the US: The first Decade 1952-1962 279

of which deal with inter-generational tension: young American Jews who want to "ascend" (immigrate to Israel) versus their unhappy, "Zionist" parents.

The first story is only marginally related to Israel. Its heroine, a determined, married woman, leaves her husband in Europe, while she and her children "ascend", or immigrate to Israel. Only its final paragraph tells us that the heroine's "house, with seven windows stands in Rosh Pina."[48] The penultimate story, "Godl the Shoemaker in Rehovot" features a European-born shoemaker and his wife who are baffled by the mores of their newly adopted land. Here their independent daughter does not need a dowry, and their son, an officer in the Israeli army, returns home and announces his intention to join a kibbutz. The couple remain bewildered and bemused, and yet somehow hopeful.

The two stories about American Zionists are especially illuminating. In both stories the parents actively support Israel. They are members of a Zionist organization; they donate money to projects in Israel; their social networks require an expenditure of time and energy on these Zionist activities. And yet, when their children announce an intention to actually live in Israel, the parents are jolted into disbelief and apprehension, if not outright disapproval. In one story, (entitled "Married Off") the parents manage to deflect their son from immigrating by luring him into a relationship with a local, marriageable young lady.

But in the other story (entitled 'On the Eve of the Journey"), the parents reluctantly come to realize that they cannot blame their son for wanting to act on a program they have been so strongly advocating. Here Kadya is both clear-sighted and honest. Never a parent herself, Kadya was not faced with this exact situation. Nevertheless, she, like most American Zionists, was happy to promote a course of action that was appropriate for others, but not for herself.

As we saw in the selection of women she chose to feature in her once-a-week column in the *Forverts,* Kadya admired strong, independent-minded women. The stories in the collection occasionally involve such women. In two of these stories, ("The

White Wedding Dress" and "The Queen"), the first set in Europe, and the second, set in the US, we find women who agree to marry men even though they are fully aware that their husbands-to-be do not really love them. In both cases, the women have assessed the consequences of speaking up, and have decided against it. It is clear to the reader that their decision is a conscious one. But their motivation is never clarified. Are they afraid of the social ostracism that comes with being an unmarried woman? Perhaps they are afraid of being lonely? Kadya leaves these questions hanging; it is the reader's job to answer them.

A woman's need for control over her earned income is the theme of yet another story, one entitled "The Fur Coat". Here a husband's attempt to prevent his wife from spending money on herself results in the break-up of their marriage. The wife simply walks out on her husband and begins a new life as a single woman.

Two other stories deal with the gender-generated consequences a woman faces when she chooses to use her abilities at work. In one story ("Lunch"), a simple operator "rises" to become a fashion designer, while her husband remains at his lowly, poorly-paid position in the factory. The husband resents his wife's success, and their marriage suffers, but does not fall apart. The wife, at least for the length of this short story, tries to have both: a successful career and a workable marriage.

We saw earlier, that Kadya sometimes endows her heroine with the guts to walk out on a man who tries to control her. A second such character appears in the story entitled "Elaine". Here a young woman's fiancé insists that she quit her job in a chemistry lab if she wants to marry him. The young woman is not intimidated by his threat. She breaks off her engagement, and instead, marries the professor who runs the lab she works in.

Either of these stories would have made the kernel of a fascinating, feminist novel. Will the fashion designer preserve her marriage? That depends on whether a resentful husband can learn to appreciate, or maybe even be proud of, his wife's talent. Can the young woman who married a chemistry professor keep both: her career ambitions and her working marriage? That depends on how her husband reacts when there is a conflict between his wife's two roles.

But Kadya did not write these novels. She raised these questions in a kind of embryonic feminist short story, but left the working out of such questions to feminists of a later era.

The Appearance of *Svive*

For years, Kadya had dreamt of starting a literary journal.[49] It was to be her ersatz milieu, a kingdom of poetry and ideas, a forum for Jewish creativity that would create in the US a would-be Warsaw literary club. This was what she meant when she spoke of a "*svive*", literally, a [Jewish/artistic] milieu.

Twenty-three years earlier, when she complained to her friend Melekh Ravitch that the US was missing such a *svive,* he chided her:

"Kadya, feh! Why are you complaining about America? If there is no *svive* there, that's your fault and the fault of thousands like you who don't create this *svive.*"[50]

That criticism struck deep because Kadya knew it to be true. Recall that Kadya and Bashevis Singer did establish and co-edit a literary journal called *Svive*. But only seven issues were printed before it became defunct. Then Kadya relinquished her editorial role and began writing poetry, her refuge from despair. When the war was over, she attempted to live in Israel and establish a literary journal there. Once that project collapsed and she returned from Israel at the end of 1952, the idea of editing a literary journal in the US re-surfaced once more.

It is probably no accident that Kadya kept none of the correspondence between herself and Rokhl Korn for the years 1955 through 1958. In those years, she put on her play, and saw it fold up in a rather short time, and she began writing a weekly column for the *Forverts*. 1957 saw the publication of two of her books (On the Paths to Zion and A House with Seven Windows), both of which must have taken up much of her time. By 1958, she was a bit more relaxed, and ready to resume her careful record-keeping.

In 1958, Rokhl Korn, one of Kadya's most long-standing literary friends, wrote her:

"Everything is conspiring against us. We are not even allowed to sink. Over time we are being eaten up by a parasite that stealthily invaded us while we were despairing, and it disturbs the organism like a worm that lies under the bark of a tree."[51]

As Korn saw it, Yiddish writers, no longer subjected to external persecution, were now suffering from a self-inflicted lassitude. This was the "worm under the bark" of the Yiddish tree of life. She saw the need for change and urged Kadya to take action. In the aforementioned letter she says:

"And that is why we need a periodical and a press that will be run by a group of responsible and non-affiliated people to whom the [Yiddish] word is dear...After all, someone has to do something. 'It's burning, Jews, it's burning.'"[52]

The "non-affiliated" part of Korn's suggestion is crucial. By 1960, Yiddish writers knew full well what had happened to their fellow writers in the Soviet Union. Outside of Russia as well, political involvement could lead to problems.[53] Accordingly, the two friends wanted to stay clear of politics. If Kadya were to be the editor of a new journal, she would make sure that the only criterion for inclusion in her journal was artistic quality.

By the time the decade of the sixties began, Kadya and Simche's life had taken on some security. Because Simche's income was secure, Kadya was able not just to take on the herculean task of editing a literary journal single-handedly, but also, just to relax. In her letters to Rokhl Korn, she suggests resting daily, something she was able to do with her independent schedule. She invited woman friends over, and with them, and apparently only with them, felt comfortable enough to "whoop it up".[54]

Kadya had been back from Israel for a bit more than seven years when she decided to take upon herself the editorship of a literary journal called *Svive* in 1960.

Chapter Six: Return to the US: The first Decade 1952-1962

Apparently, the idea was bruited about in the small world of Yiddish literati, even before one issue was printed. An undated note she received from the Yiddish linguist Max Weinreich, found in the YIVO archive, says much about her acculturation to life in Israel and its influence on her Yiddish. Weinreich tells her he has heard she wants to call this journal *Sviva* [note the last vowel ZKN]. But that would not be correct, he points out. That may be how the Hebrew word is pronounced in Israel, but that word, in its Yiddish Diaspora adaptation, is pronounced *Svive*. If Kadya answered this note, she left no copy of it in her archive. But she did listen to Max Weinreich: the official name of her journal was *Svive*, just as Max Weinreich suggested.

Kadya was the ideal candidate for editor for another, more important, reason. To run a journal, one needed not just contributors and a discerning editor, one needed, above all, access to a printing press. And Kadya had such access. Best of all, it was nearly free of charge.

Simche worked at a printing press that printed Yiddish. He was not the owner of the publishing company; he was a Lino-type-setter.[55] From what Kadya tells Rokhl Korn in her letters, it is clear that she and Simche went back to this printing press after the company's closing hours to print out the copies of *Svive*. Quite probably, the couple had to pay for the expenses incurred: electricity and some wear and tear of the machines. They also needed to pay for paper, ink and distribution/mailing of the journal. But they did not need to provide the (quite expensive) machinery, and they did not need to pay a type-setter. Simche did the type-setting. Since Kadya did the correspondence, editing, proof-reading and book-keeping on her own, the subscription fee needed to cover only what the printing company charged them for using the machinery. The address provided for subscribers is Kadya's address: 570 Grand Street. Essentially, this was a literary journal put out by only one person: Kadya.

Kadya was as networked as anyone could be in her time. She knew writers from her days in Kiev, but more importantly, from her years in Warsaw. Those who had survived the war years, were scattered all over the globe. Among those were writers and critics in Israel. She and they had strong bonds, and she could now appeal to them to contribute to her new journal. She had toured the US and Canada often enough to have made friends in virtually every major North American city with a large Jewish population. The producer of her Broadway play came from Argentina; her friend Melekh Ravitch had lived in Australia. She and her work were featured in newspapers in South America. The list of writers and critics with whom she communicated ran into the hundreds. From the responses she received that are cataloged in the YIVO archive, it is clear that she asked strategically placed friends and colleagues to spread the word that she was putting out a literary journal and wanted contributions. And she got material. Each number of her quarterly journal ran to something like ten pages. Mostly the offerings were poems and short stories. But there was nearly always one (sometimes more than one) critical article.

In the nearly fifteen years that *Svive* was printed (1960-1974), its only competitor was *Di Goldene Keyt*, The Golden Chain, printed in Israel, and funded by the *Histadrut*, the Labor party's workers' union. That publication had guaranteed financial backing, and a cadre of assistants and proof-readers. The Israeli publication had many more entries (and pages), but it was a subsidized publication. Kadya's venture, though much smaller, was nevertheless of equal quality. Many of the writers and poets who published in the Israeli journal also published in *Svive*. Unlike its Israeli competitor, though, Kadya's journal had no public funding. Indeed, it had no outside funding at all. And it had no staff whatsoever. All it had was Kadya, and her reliable partner, Simche.

Once she took upon herself the editorship of her journal, Kadya went on a never-ending search for subscribers. Nearly every letter she received from Dora, her ever-loyal sister, contained names and addresses of new subscribers. Dora snagged them and got their addresses and Kadya proceeded to send them her journal.

The very same thing happened with Rokhl Korn. She, too, was on the look-out. Whenever she met new people who had not yet subscribed to Kadya's journal, she got their agreement to subscribe, and sent Kadya their names and addresses.

A year after she started putting out *Svive*, Kadya wrote to Sarah telling her about the first year's success of the journal. The enterprise had only a "minimal deficit" and that was without the help of any organization or charity of any kind."[56] Ever the advisor and dear friend, Sarah wrote her the next year giving Kadya some business advice. She suggested that Kadya print out receipts to be sent to subscribers; it looked more professional than hand-written receipts. What's more, thinking that she might know of potential subscribers who had not already been approached, she asked Kadya to send her a list of subscribers.[57] Like Dora, Ida Maze, Rokhl Korn and the Drosts, Sarah did everything she could to ensure Kadya's success with *Svive*.

Kadya herself was delighted and a little bit surprised at her own success. She wrote to Rokhl Korn:

"We should be congratulated. *Svive* has elicited a very good response in our sleepy, dejected literature-world. It's simply a miracle. In the book business of New York it is considered a "best seller"…People are buying *Svive*. They come, but not in the hundreds. No one stands in line, no one is banging down the door, but a few tens of copies are already on their way."[58]

For all its popular success, *Svive* was not immediately heralded by the Yiddish establishment, or so Kadya maintained. It is impossible to know which "culture-institutions" Kadya was referring to in the following passage. Nevertheless, it is clear that in her estimation, the "establishment" was more interested in dwelling on the past than in recognizing and encouraging contemporary creativity. She wrote to Korn:

"It is interesting to note that our culture-institutions did not even raise an eyebrow over *Svive*. As long as they discuss "treasures" [of the past]"[59]

She herself contributed articles and stories, often signing with her initials only: K. M. As was the case when she was the editor of *Heym*, she gave her husband Simche a forum for his efforts. He wrote historical essays, always under the name of "Simche Lev". Since the Yiddish reading public was tiny, it is almost certain that everyone knew Simche was Kadya's husband. But as had been their habit since their marriage, Kadya and Simche went under different family names.

As it turned out, this journal gave Kadya a forum for her autobiography. It is not clear at all that she intended originally to convey there the sweep of her whole life. From the title: "*Fun Mayn Elterzydes Yerushe*", From My Great-grandfather's Legacy", it seems as though Kadya intended only to give a snap-shot of her early life in Europe. But once she began, she didn't stop there.

Rokhl Korn, Kadya's long-time friend from Warsaw, truly enjoyed reading this memoir and told Kadya why she liked it. In a letter dated April 20, 1965, she noted:

"Your story about your great-grandfather's legacy is exquisite. I truly enjoyed reading it and at the same time, I was upset that it ended so soon. I could have read on and on." A few months later, Korn continued her praise of the memoir: "Your story about the great-grandfather's legacy has in it the lightness and warmth of a wonder-tale. All the aunts and uncles have become familiar to my eyes because they are described with such a highly artistic pen that they seem to have been caught *in flagrante* with their destiny."[60]

Kadya viewed her memoir as a form of private consolation:

"When things go hard with me and thousands of teeny things disturb me— then I resume writing a chapter of "My Great-grandfather's Legacy." I run away for a short time to a greener world, when the surroundings were purer... and I was younger..."[61]

An Anthology Of Holocaust Poetry

In 1962 Kadya published an anthology of Holocaust poetry, entitled "*Lider Fun Khurbn*", Poems From the Destruction". It is noteworthy that Yiddish poets tended to use the term "*khurbn*" (pronounced "*khurbm*" in Yiddish) rather than the word "*shoah*".

Chapter Six: Return to the US: The first Decade 1952-1962

The Hebrew term "*shoah*" is used in the Bible for a conflagration, or a disaster that comes with fire. In time it has come to be a synonym among English speakers for the destruction of Jewish civilization in Europe during World War II. While the reference for the word "*khurbn*" is exactly the same as the reference for the word, "*shoah*", the former term, *khurbn*, is weighted with centuries of Jewish history. For Jews, the destruction of the Temple in Jerusalem and the loss of Jewish sovereignty associated with it, for the first time in 586 BCE, and for the second time in 70 CE, all of that and the forced exiles and murders of the Diaspora, are all connoted by the word "*khurbn*". The rabbis decided on three separate fast days in the Jewish calendar, in memory of the "*khurbn*". The Jewish bride-groom breaks a glass under his wedding canopy in memory of the *khurb*n, and when a Jew builds his house he is enjoined to leave a small spot unfinished in memory of the *khurbn*.[62]

This anthology that Kadya put out includes the poems of sixty-three Yiddish poets. Of these, the first eleven in the collection are poems of "*kedoyshim*", literally holy-ones, figuratively, martyrs, who died/were murdered/starved to death before the end of WWII. Each of these gets a short biographical note, telling the reader where the poet lived, and, if it is known, how (s)he came to die. The following fifty-plus poets came from all over the world. Some, like the great poet who lived in Israel after the war, Avrohom Sutzkever, were only poets. Others, like Kadya's friends from Europe, Melekh Ravitch and Rokhl Korn, also wrote in other genres. Even Kadya's nemesis in Warsaw, A(ha)ron Zeitlin, appears in this book. There is no archival record of their correspondence over this contribution. The collapse of the Jewish civilization they had all known in Europe, was so overwhelmingly horrific, that it wiped out petty, personal differences. It is impossible to imagine any Yiddish poet, even Kadya's one-time enemy, A(ha)ron Zeitlin, turning down Kadya's request to contribute a poem or two to a volume on this topic.

Kadya was eminently fair in her editorial decisions. Most poets contributed two or three poems; some contributed only one, and a few contributed as many as four.

Kadya herself chose three of her own poems for this volume. It is a testimony to Kadya's networking that she was able to spread her net so widely. Because the US and Israel were the two main places to which Jews fled after WWII, the great majority of the poets in this volume are from either the US (and Canada) or Israel. But among the poets, there are also representatives from Buenos Aires, from Mexico City, from Paris and from London. Since Kadya's anthology was published in 1962, there has been no other Yiddish-language anthology that matches the breadth and the depth of the poems on the Holocaust found in this collection.

A surprising element in this book is the piece that precedes the introduction. There one can find the words of the prayer, the most well-known of the 13 tenets of Jewish belief[63]. In English translation, the words of this prayer are: "I believe, with a total belief, in the coming of the Messiah. And even though he is procrastinating, nevertheless I believe he will arrive, and I will wait for him every day". As I understand it, this prayer was included in Kadya's book because it was sung by the liberated Jewish prisoners of the concentration camps.

This song, sung to a haunting melody, was put onto a 78 RPM record and sent to my parents in New York by my uncle, who was a sergeant in the US army during WWII. He sent photos of himself with the liberated prisoners, along with this record. Though I myself was not yet born, and so did not hear the recording, my parents and my sister did. As they tell it, they listened to that record and cried. My parents cried out of feelings of angst, and my sister, then a child, cried because my parents cried.

Perhaps Kadya's knowledge of the powerful song sung by the liberated prisoners of the concentration camps persuaded her to include this prayer in her book. She left no record of why she chose that song/prayer for her anthology of Holocaust poems. There is no question that many of the poets in that collection did not agree with the words of the song. However, after the Holocaust/*khurbn* and the establishment of the State of Israel, most were ready to believe the new Jewish State of Israel that came into being so soon after the Holocaust, was, if not the precursor to the coming of the

Messiah, then at least as close as the Jewish people were going to get to the national deliverance promised by the Jewish Messiah.[64]

NOTES

[1] In a letter written to Ida Maze, Kadya says she and Simche were allowed to exit the country with $14 each. Why she should have gotten an "extra allowance" of $4 per person is unclear. What is clear is that even with this added "generosity", the couple was strapped for cash when they arrived back in the US.

[2] This apartment, at 602 East 171st Street, was a fine piece of real estate at the time. Ownership of it gave Kadya a kind of financial security that made their return to New York not much of a financial risk.

[3] See Kathryn Hellerstein's "Finding Her Yiddish Voice: Kadya Molodowsky in America" Revue d'Etudes Anglophones, no. 12, Spring, 2002, p. 55. On that same page, Hellerstein says "I do not have any evidence that Molodowsky ever lived in Brownsville." That is rather surprising. In the memoir Kadya wrote *in Svive*, no. 38, January 1973, she tells the reader on page 58 that she and Simche lived in Brownsville after he arrived in the US. And on pages 59 and 60, she goes on to describe what life in Brownsville was like at the time. Ironically, in Brownsville she lived on a street called "Herzyl Street". From letters addressed to her that can be found in the Makhon Lavon archive, we know that her address there was: 231 Herzyl Street.

[4] See end-note iii above, p. 65. Hellerstein gives a detailed account of this poem in that article.

[5] This is a complex of housing co-ops built by and for the members of the Amalgamated Clothing Workers Union.

[6] Her address there was in 602 East 170th St.

[7] For all that the Bronx still had a Yiddish-speaking elite, the Bronx was "removed" from the center of things, and Kadya preferred being in the center.

[8] This letter, dated April 20, 1953, was left in the YIVO archive.

[9] One can't help wondering if "Red" was dropped as a name because of its political associations. In the early 1950s, there was a "Red Scare" and for most Americans, the name "Red" was anathema.

[10] See Yechiel Szeintuch's book: <u>Aaron Zeitlin and Yiddish Literature in Interwar Poland: An Analysis of Letters and Documents of Jewish Cultural History</u>, Magnes Press, 2000, letter n. 62, p. 228.

[11] *Svive,* no. 37, September, 1972, p. 59.

[12] The situation is a bit more complex than the simplistic situation I am presenting. Someone who has learned only Yiddish, can dope out the words of a Hebrew text, (especially if the text comes with vowel points), but cannot generally understand

what is meant. Yiddish is an Indo-European language while Hebrew is a Semitic language. Although the two languages share some vocabulary and some grammatical forms, they are nevertheless so different that a Yiddish reader and speaker cannot understand a Hebrew text without some knowledge of Hebrew grammar.

[13] This, in a letter, found in the Ida Maze archive in Montreal. By December 5th, 1953, when this letter was written, the play had closed down. Apparently, Ida had tried to console her. In response, she told Ida that the audience was pleased but the theater had financial difficulties.

[14] New York Times, October 10, 1953, p. 12.

[15] I myself was at an academic conference on Yiddish in the twenty-first century at which a well-known linguist played recordings of half sentences said in a mixed Yiddish-English creole. He expected the audience to laugh, even though there was absolutely nothing funny about the conversation. For him, the very sounds of Yiddish were supposed to elicit laughter. Neither I, nor any of the other Yiddish speakers in the audience, found the material at all funny.

[16] From an article entitled "What Kadya Molodowsky Says About her Play", *Der Forverts*, October 10, 1953, p. 8.

[17] *Der Forverts*, October 14, 1953, p. 4.

[18] Mary Antin, The Promised Land, p. 187-88. Originally published in 1912 by Houghton Mifflin, this book was republished in 2012 by Penguin Books.

[19] Because the act of circumcision confirms the Jewishness of a boy, the verb in Yiddish for "circumcising": is "*yiddishn*", literally, to make Jewish. Strictly speaking, though, even an uncircumcised boy is Jewish if he is born to a Jewish mother.

[20] Personal communication. I have this from a woman who was born in the Alsace Lorraine region into an orthodox Jewish family. However, in Eastern Europe, most girls and women did have a Jewish name.

[21] Susan Cotts Watkins and Andrew S. London, "Personal Names and Cultural Change: A Study of the Naming Patterns of Italians and Jews in the United States in 1910", in *Social Science History*, vol. 18, no. 2, summer 1994, Cambridge University Press, 1994, p. 185.

[22] This argument is hard to prove, mostly because Jewish men continued to present themselves to the outside, non-Jewish world with non-Jewish names. They resorted to their Jewish names only when they were in "comfort zones", among other Jews.

[23] In this, the Ashkenazic Jewish community (those whose ancestors came from Eastern Europe), differs from the Sephardic Jewish community (those whose ancestors were expelled from Spain and Portugal). Ashkenazic Jews name their children only for family members who have died, while Sephardic Jews name their children for living family members.

[24] Stanley Lieberson "*Jewish Names and the Names of Jews*" In: Demsky A These Are the Names: Studies in Jewish Onomastics, Vol. 4. Ramat Gan: Bar-Ilan University Press, 2003, p.160.

[25] See *he.wikipedia.org/wiki/*עברית

Chapter Six: Return to the US: The first Decade 1952-1962

[26] Ibid.
[27] See footnote xvii.
[28] I spoke to Ben, Kadya's nephew, on the phone twice. I heard from him that his mother took him to see Kadya's play on Broadway.
[29] See: https:/en.wikipedia.org/wiki/Bruriah
[30] This is what one Max Berliner wrote to Kadya in February of 1952. The letter is in the Makhon Lavon archive.
[31] See the review in *Ma'ariv*, of Friday March 16, 1956.
[32] Here she uses that crucial word, one that packs a punch for her: *"svive"*, a word that I've translated here as "environment".
[33] See On the Roads to Zion, New York, 1957, p. 5.
[34] I am grateful to Rukhl Schachter for her contribution on the curriculum of the different schools that advocated Yiddish literacy.
[35] See: https://en.wikipedia.org/wiki/Judah_Halevi
[36] See: https://en.wikipedia.org/wiki/Nachmanides
[37] See: https://www.jewishvirtuallibrary.org/background-and-overview-of-the-irgun-etzel
[38] See: www.jewishvirtuallibrary.org/ze-ev-vladimir-jabotinsky
[39] See: www.jewishvirtuallibrary.org/joseph-trumpeldor-1880-1920
[40] For more on Trumpeldor, see https://www.jewishvirtuallibrary.org/jsource/biography/trumpeldor.html
[41] On the Roads to Zion, p. 156.
[42] See, for example, Jeremiah, chapter 31, and Ezekiel, chapters 20 and 36.
[43] See Exodus, chapter 23, Leviticus, chapter 25, and Deuteronomy, chapter 15.
[44] See Leviticus, chapter 25, verses 8-15.
[45] See A House with Seven Windows, English translation Syracuse, NY, 2006, p. xi.
[46] A House with Seven Windows, p. xii.
[47] Naturally, there are differences. For one thing, Benya Krik is clearly a criminal, and Nyoma Khurgin is not. A comparison of the two characters and their genre deserves a fuller treatment than I can give it here.
[48] A House with Seven Windows, p.6.
[49] As early as 1942, she spoke of starting a "small literary journal". This, in a letter found in the Makhon Lavon archive, dated October 26, 1942.
[50] This, in a letter dated December 10, 1937, written in Buenos Aires, and found in the Makhon Lavon archive.
[51] This, in a letter dated October 28, 1958, found in the Montreal archive.
[52] The words "It's burning, brothers, it's burning" are the opening words of a famous song, written in Yiddish by Mordecai Gebirtig in 1938. The reference then was to the oncoming Holocaust. Korn is using the very same words to suggest that the situation in the Jewish world in the Diaspora is truly dire.
[53] The McCarthy era in the US had ruined the careers of those termed "fellow travelers". See: https://en.wikipedia.org/wiki/Fellow_traveller

[54] In a letter written on December 21, 1949, found in the Montreal Jewish Public library archive, Molodowsky explains that she was unable to visit Korn because she was not feeling well: "But since the world is not all that big, we will, please God, yet see each other - there or here, and we will yet whoop it up [*mir veln nokh hulyen*]."

[55] In one of her phone-books, found in the Makhon Lavon archive, Kadya has Simche's phone number at a place called the Futuro Press. It seems clear that Simche worked there before they left for Israel. It is not clear whether he worked there after they returned from Israel.

[56] This, in a letter dated September 22, 1961, found in the YIVO archive.

[57] This, in a letter written in January of 1962, found in the YIVO archive.

[58] This, in a letter dated September 12, 1960, found in the YIVO archive.

[59] Ibid.

[60] This, in a letter dated July 20, 1965, found in the YIVO archive.

[61] This, in a letter dated February, 19, 1968, found in the YIVO archive.

[62] See also: http://www.daat.ac.il/encyclopedia/value.asp?id1=3323 and http://cms.education.gov.il/EducationCMS/Units/Moe/Hurban/Minhagim/.

[63] These principles, formulated by Maimonides, can be found in most Jewish prayer books after the morning service. See also:
https://he.wikipedia.org/wiki/עיקרי_האמונה_היהודית

[64] One of the many differences between Judaism and Christianity is the importance placed on belief. For a Christian, to be religious is to believe (in Jesus). That cannot be said for Jews. One does not lose membership in the Jewish people if one does not believe in God. To be sure, religious Jews generally do believe in God, but one can be a non-believer and still be a Jew. Another difference between Christianity and Judaism is their different understanding of the nature of the Messiah. For Jews, not only will the Messiah bring about lasting peace for the entire world, he will also see to it that all the world's Jews return to their ancestral home in the land of Israel.

CHAPTER SEVEN: THE US (1963-1975)

Wherein Kadya is left "...to the mercy/ Of a rude stream"

Final Books

In 1965, three years after the publication of her anthology of Holocaust poems, Kadya published her own last collection of poems. It was more than 200 pages long and entitled *Likht Fun Dornboym*", Light from the Thorn-bush. The reference here was clearly to Exodus, chapter 3 verse 2, which speaks of the wondrous thorn-bush that Moses saw: a thorn-bush that was on fire, but was not consumed. This was an apt metaphor for the state of the Jewish people in 1965. It was a people that had experienced a horrible conflagration, but was nevertheless still alive.

It is no accident that this book was published in Argentina by the Yiddish speaking *Po'alei Tsiyon* (Labor Zionist) publishing house. In the US at the time, there were Zionist-leaning educational systems, and Yiddishist-leaning educational systems. But there was no system that was both Yiddish speaking and Zionist. Buenos Aires had such schools. In addition, this educational stream had its own publishing house.

Of the two hundred-plus pages in this book, forty-five were one long narrative poem entitled "*Der Shteynhaker fun Risho*n", The Stone-Cutter from Rishon [*Le-Tsiyon*]. This was essentially an expansion of a poem found in Kadya's previous book. Another thirty-five pages, part of a section called "*Yerusholayim*", Jerusalem, were mostly poems that had already appeared in Kadya's previous book of poetry, *In Yerusholayim Kumen Malokhim*, Angels Come in Jerusalem.[1] Thus, nearly half this book were reminiscences from Kadya's three-year stay in Israel. This is what made Buenos Aires the ideal venue for publishing this book.

But the poems devoted to life in Israel are by no means all that can be found here. There is a poem here entitled "*Viduyim*",[2] Confessions, which is telling. Its opening lines are:

"*keyn lider shrayb ikh nit/ikh zog viduyim*", I don't write poems/I give [literally, say] confessions.

Clearly, the reader cannot take Kadya literally here. Her poems about Moses and Aaron, Jonah, and King Solomon, are obviously not confessions. Nevertheless, when Kadya assumes the persona of the first person, even when she is not speaking literally, and often she is not, there is still a kernel of personal experience behind her persona.

We have every reason to believe that the two poems in this collection which speak of her husband, convey her genuine feelings for him. The first of these poems, dated 1959, is entitled "We Are Now Like Two Grey Doves".[3] In addition to being grey, the couple in this poem are quiet, loyal and smart. And when they have free time, they read Psalms together. Admittedly, they have inconsequential tiffs over the need for a sweater, but the two have reached a comfortable state of accommodation. This is not all that surprising. After all, at this point, Kadya and Simche had been married for over forty years and they had, it would seem, come to a comfortable accommodation.

What is very surprising is that Simche has acquired a taste for reading Psalms. Is this the man who helped the Communists of Paris in the early 1930s? Is this the man who was a card-carrying member of the Communist party in Warsaw?

It is indeed. Like many other Jews of his time, Simche had a change of heart. We know for a fact that this is so from archival material that Kadya left in New York. In 1960, one year after this poem was written, the Yiddish speaking Los Angeles Community Center invited the couple to speak. Kadya's topic was "The Web of Folklore in Artistic Work", not at all a surprising topic for her, while Simche's topic was "The Literature of a Torah Folk"! There is no question that Simche had little (or nothing) to do with Torah when he was a young Communist. But he was no longer

Chapter Six: Return to the US: The first Decade 1952-1962

young, and at this point, thirty years after his involvement with Communism, he saw Torah as the hallmark of Jewish identity.

The second poem in which Kadya mentions Simche is entitled "A Captive".[4] Here are its first two stanzas:

> I convinced my husband / To give me bread. / Now I stand a captive / In my speech,
>
> I see how he drags the weeks / Like a chain / And I stand a captive / In my speech.

This is the only time that Kadya spoke publicly of the price she and Simche paid for their arrangement. To be fair, Simche owed Kadya his life. Nevertheless, Kadya would have liked to be able to contribute substantially to the family income, and she did not. Because her earnings were meager, the two of them were financially dependent on Simche. It is this dependency that makes her "a captive".

This collection has any number of poems in which Kadya displays her mystical longing for a union with God. In one poem, entitled "*Oyf An Indzl*", On An Island,[5] she says:

> *ikh bin poshet bay got oyf a vayl,* I'm simply with God for a while.

Similarly, she says in a different poem:

> "*Ikh benk shoyn lang tsu milder hant fun got*",
>
> For a while now, I've been longing for God's mild hand".[6]

This talk of God should not be confused with a traditionally Jewish/religious attitude. There remains in her poetry the Romantic, non-submissive, voice of the self-aware poet that a truly religious person would be reluctant to assume. This surfaces in her poem entitled "*Dos gezang fun shabes*", the Song of the Sabbath. The first few lines could be taken from the notebook of any traditionally orthodox Jewish poet:

> *Di grinkayt fun berg– / iz di grinkayt fun shabes. / der zilber fun taykh– / is der zilber fun shabes. / der gezang fun dem vint –/ iz dos zingen fun shabes.*

The greenness of mountains– is the greenness of the Sabbath. / The silver of [a] stream – / is the silver of the Sabbath, / The song of the wind - / is the song of the Sabbath.

But for a genuinely religious person, the last line of this poem would be somewhat inappropriate:

"*un dos gezang fun mayn harts– / iz der eybiker shabes.*
And the song of my heart– is the eternal Sabbath."[7]

Religious Jews do speak of an eternal Sabbath,[8] but that is a gift from God, and it is something that must be earned. To suppose that a flesh and blood poet necessarily has this great spiritual gift, and that this gift comes together with the calling of a poet, is to be guilty of hubris, and to put one's self at the outer reaches of the religious world. But that was fine with Kadya. She was not a traditionally religious person.

For all that there are many poems in this collection in which Kadya assumes the voice of a poet seeking the rest of an older person, one can still find here the mischievous, charming voice of a younger woman. One such poem is called *"Mayn Shprakh*, My Speech. Here Kadya confesses that she has a special speech all her own and it is called "white speech".

It has "no script/ And no tongue/ can discover it".

It is silent speech that is used when Kadya encounters "evil scorn" or a "nasty roar". When confronted with this sort of nastiness, then, Kadya's white speech kicks in. It speaks even while her lips are sealed.[9]

There is a poem in this collection, written in 1963, eleven years after Aizik's death. It is entitled "*Dos Likht Fun Dayn Tish*", "The Light of Your Table", and its dedication note reads: At My Father's Grave". At this point, Kadya had dedicated a collection of poems to her father, (this was her previous collection, entitled "*In Yerusholayim Kumen Malokhim*", Angels Come in Jerusalem), but she had not spoken publicly about him in any of her poems. Finally, she did so.

Here, addressing her father (so to speak) directly, she says:

"*es shyant nokh dos likht fun dayn tish*", the light of your table still shines.[10]

Understandably, in the mind of the child, the parent never dies. But the connection between Kadya and her father was far deeper than the lasting memory of her father bent over his table "learning Torah". In her mind's eye, Kadya stands near her father's bent shoulder and the two of them at first communicate wordlessly. Then all her father says is: "*gey shlofn, mayn kind, s'iz dayn bet a gegreyte*", Go to sleep, my child, your bed is ready. That takes a few seconds, or as Kadya puts it: "*a rega*", one minute. And after that magical moment, Kadya says: "*kh'bin in ru fun a heym*",[11] I am in the peace of a home.

Here, finally, Kadya confesses the truth: only in the loving presence of her father, her true soul-mate, did she ever know the peace of a home. It is not accidental that Kadya called the journal she edited in Israel "*Heym*", home. She and Simche were supposed to make/find a home in Israel, but that never happened. Looking back at the seventy-plus years of her life, Kadya admits that only in her father's presence did she find the peace and protection of a home.

The most well-known and most quoted poem in this collection is undoubtedly the poem "*Oyf Di Papirene Brik*", On the Paper Bridge.[12] This is the third time Kadya wrote a poem which speaks of a "paper bridge".[13]

The first poem, written in Warsaw in 1930, before WWII, speaks of bridge that leads to happiness. In that poem, entitled "My Paper Bridge", the speaker tells of the poverty of her surroundings and the personal dreams she had that did not come to pass. The second time the paper bridge appeared as a theme, the poem was entitled "A Poem to the Paper Bridge". Kadya was then living in New York. It was 1942, and WWII had not yet ended. It is easy to imagine what Kadya meant when she said in that poem that she had seen "How illustrious cities become Sodom".[14] There Kadya spoke of being led to a land "built with honest hands"[15], where "a sapling still blooms."[16] It would seem she was beginning to think of living in the land of Israel.

This third poem, the final variation on the paper bridge theme, is more enigmatic than the first two poems on this theme. By now the war has been over for quite a while, and the State of Israel has been established. But has that brought Kadya personal happiness? Clearly, it has not. But how to find happiness is no longer the question. The question now is finding a sense of purpose.

In this third variation on the theme, the poet speaks of callings she might have had- but didn't. She wanted to be a servant-girl, but was told she could be the servant-girl only of the Patriarch Abraham. She wanted to be a seamstress, but was told she could be the seamstress only of King David. And when she said she wanted to adorn stars, she was sent to cry with the Matriarch Rachel. With no calling that suited her, she returned to the paper bridge, where the righteous are silent, and what she heard there and what she saw there, well, she's not saying.

This poem has some intertextual references that need to be explicated. The Patriarch Abraham had a concubine, Hagar, a kind of half-servant, whom he sent away to live in the desert; no one would want to be *his* servant-girl[17]. About King David, we are told that "he tore his clothes"[18]; no one would want to be *his* seamstress. As for the Matriarch Rachel, the prophet Jeremiah says about her: "A call is heard in Rama (alternatively, in high places), a bitter sobbing, Rachel is crying over her children. She refuses to be consoled, for they are gone."[19] But for all that Rachel cries over her children's exile, she is ultimately consoled, for the prophet says in the very next verse: "Stop your voice from crying…For there is a reward for your deeds. Your children will return to their boundaries." [translation my own ZKN]. Perhaps the poet did not join the Matriarch Rachel, then, because the promised return from exile had begun; there was no longer a need to cry. We know for a fact that Kadya felt she was indeed witnessing the return to the land of Israel that the prophets of Israel spoke of. The book of poems she composed while in Israel speaks repeatedly of this sense of witnessing the realization of that prophecy.

Having rejected all the options given her, why does the poet join the righteous who are silent? As I see it, the answer to this question is to be found in the story of the one righteous Biblical figure who, we are told, is deliberately silent: Aaron the High Priest. Aaron's two sons, Nadav and Avihu, were killed by God; what the two did to deserve this punishment, is not clear. When, immediately after their death,

Chapter Six: Return to the US: The first Decade 1952-1962

God tells Aaron: "I am sanctified by [the deaths of] those close to Me", Aaron remains silent. [20]

Kadya, like virtually all men and women who were witness to the Holocaust, felt that the Jews/the Children of Israel had suffered cruelly at the hands of God.[21] As a younger woman, Kadya had railed against God in response.[22] Now that she had mellowed, she took an example from the righteous, whose response to the horrors of the Holocaust is to remain silent. This interpretation of Kadya's last Paper Bridge poem has the poet undergoing a flip-flop: from anger at God, to the silence of the righteous. But Kadya's life is full of switches of this sort. She began as a member of the Zionist, pro-Hebrew camp, then switched allegiance to the Socialist, pro-Yiddish camp. Then, she swerved once more, back to the Zionist camp, albeit with a pro-Hebrew and pro-Yiddish stance, and an ideology that was both Zionist and Socialist. My interpretation of this poem simply has Kadya undergoing one more switch.

In 1967 Kadya published her last book intended for adults. Entitled *Baym Toyer*, At the Gate, it was a novel set in Israel in the early years of statehood. Essentially, it was a novelistic working of the play *Oyf Eygene Erd*,[23] the play about life in an immigrant tent-city (called a *ma'abara* in Hebrew), that was never published or performed. The manuscript of that play can be found in the YIVO archive, and a comparison between it and the published novel is worthy of scholarly attention.

The main characters in the two works remain the same, but in the novel, the canvas is broader. The secondary characters that have been added allow Kadya to present sketches of colorful characters whom she undoubtedly saw first-hand. After all, in the three years that she spent in Israel, she toured these camps under the auspices of *Mo'etset Ha-po'alot*, and she got to see the camps and speak with their residents. The *Te(hi)lim Zoger* (Psalms reciter) who sits and recites Psalms all day, the engineer who is so devoted to his work that he cancels a long-awaited trip in order to oversee repairs on a construction site, the single young women, who waver between wanting to find someone to marry and wanting to find a profession that will ensure them financial security: all these found their way into this novel.

There are clearly two sets of population here: the "old-timers", who run the camp and do their best to help the newcomers adjust to life and acculturate in Israel, and the new immigrants (or "*olim*", as they are called in Hebrew), the camp residents, who are uprooted, bewildered and clueless about life in Israel. In this camp, the majority of the residents are Holocaust survivors. Nevertheless, there are also others: Moroccans and Yemenites.

The novel describes courses for immigrant young women that were organized by the "old-timers", and *Mo'etset Ha-po'alot* really did run courses for young women like the ones described in this novel. The self-sufficiency that came with acquiring a profession was crucial for these single women. As a hard-working, poor, young woman during the inter-war years of Warsaw, Kadya had seen penniless women sell their bodies to get by. She was pleased to see this could be avoided in Israel. In the immigrant tent-camp, the young were offered courses in book-keeping, in toy-making and in sewing. In Kadya's novel, the heroine takes a sewing course.

The novel's heroine, one Tsivya Greenberg, is not unlike Rivke Zylberg of The Diary. She is a twenty-something, good-looking, single young woman. She is neither highly educated, nor especially talented. But she is sensible, proud, naturally intelligent, and of an independent mind. She arrives alone in Israel because her family was murdered in the Holocaust. But she does not, and cannot, speak of what happened. She is too busy trying to adjust to her new life in a new country. She has no reserves of emotional energy for more than that.

In the very first chapter of the novel, Tsivya meets, and is attracted to a handsome young native Israeli named Yair. The reader knows right away that the plot structure of this novel will be: couple meets, couple undergoes difficulties, and (ultimately) couple gets together. That is, in fact, the skeletal structure of the novel's plot.

But Kadya throws a monkey-wrench into this tried-and-true plot line. Feminist that she was, she did not construct the Disney-like happy end of a couple riding off together into the setting sun.

Chapter Six: Return to the US: The first Decade 1952-1962

In the year that the young women spend in their sewing course, Tsivya distinguishes herself as a tireless worker. She wins the trust of (most of) her colleagues and the respect of the course's teachers and planners. As a result, she is chosen as the assistant manager of a store that will sell the finest products that the young women produce. This is a position of great responsibility and she feels both challenged and privileged at the prospect of proving herself in this job.

But it is exactly at this point, at the novel's end, that Yair finally confesses his love for Tsivya and suggests that the two marry. He wants Tsivya to come live with him in the kibbutz he has helped found. Tsivya is conflicted. She loves and wants to marry Yair, and, in theory at least, she wants to live with him. But she is not prepared to give up the challenge she has been offered. Conflicted, she tells Yair she cannot leave her new job.

This leaves Yair, and the reader, wondering. Will this couple ever live together? If so, which of the two will cave in and join the other? There is a suggestion that the two will realize their love, but how this will happen is left for the reader to decide.

Though bereft of the fanciful flights of imagination that characterize her children's stories, this novel is interesting for other reasons. It shows us that throughout her long career, Kadya did not give up thinking about women's (one could say "feminist") issues. There is no question that in Kadya's view, couple-hood is valued and is of crucial importance. But so, too, is personal fulfillment. Can a woman have both at one and the same time? Kadya asks this question, but she does not provide a clear answer.

The World Impinges

1967 was also the year of the Six-Day War in Israel. Kadya may have left Israel, but in a very deep sense, Israel never left her. She had many friends there, as well as many colleagues. As someone who had lived through the Holocaust years as a helpless bystander, unable to save the people she loved, she was plagued by the thought that she might once again have to stand by helpless while the people she cared about were harmed, or even killed. Her worry over the fate of Israel, in general, and her friends in particular, was genuine. But this time the tension was short-lived. It was a relief to her when Israel won that war and the danger passed. Then Israel went back to its role as the potential Jewish homeland, a place of potential refuge, but actual discomfort.

Once the war was over, there were countless discussions on what, if any, territory should be ceded to the Arabs, and under what conditions. All this was something Kadya and her friends watched and listened to with great interest.

In a letter dated March 4, 1968, Kadya told her friend Rokhl Korn:

"The issues of Israel do not leave my mind. We are faced once more with an exodus from Egypt [in Yiddish: *yetsi'as mitsrayim*] – and all this in our generation."[24]

No matter what happened around the world, Kadya and her friends always wondered what effects the events would have on the State of Israel. In 1968, when it seemed that the Czechs, (then ruled by a puppet government, under the influence of the Soviet Union), might free themselves of the Soviet grip, Rokhl Korn wrote to Kadya:

"If the Czechs were to manage (even for the interim) to tear themselves out of Russia's paws, that would have a good effect on Israel's stand."

At the time the Soviet regime was supporting Israel's Arab neighbors militarily and diplomatically. Any setback for Soviet Russia, therefore, was seen as a positive development for Israel. Ultimately, Soviet tanks rolled onto the streets of Prague and crushed the revolution. Rokhl Korn, who had hoped that the Soviets might back down, even temporarily, was shocked at the world's acceptance of Soviet power.

In a letter to Kadya she asked:

"Where is decency, justice, humanity?"[25]

The late 1960s were also the years of the student unrest and "rebellion" in the United States. Kadya and her friends were not connected to a university or any

Chapter Six: Return to the US: The first Decade 1952-1962

academic institution, but the phenomenon sparked their interest. In a letter dated August 27, 1968, Rokhl Korn told Kadya:

> "If I were a bit younger, I would belong to the "hippies." They are the only ones who try in an odd fashion to tear themselves away from the nails of civilization."

It is instructive that we have no evidence of Kadya agreeing with this opinion. Possibly because she lived in a larger city (New York, not Montreal) and one which was, so to speak, in the eye of the storm, she got to see the anachronistic, truly destructive aspects of the movement. Perhaps she had had her fill of "revolutionary movements" and had seen what terrible damage they could inflict.

In the old days, it was Simche who had truly "belonged" to the movement. But, as we have seen, he had undergone a change of heart. It is not surprising then, that Kadya responded to her friend Rokhl with:

> "About this Simche categorically declared that under no circumstances would he ever become a hippie."[26]

Why were Kadya and her friend Rokhl so interested in this movement? For one thing, it resurrected in their minds what was probably a treasured, almost dormant, period in their lives: the years in which they were actively engaged in joining a crowd. That, as Elias Canetti has shown, is heady stuff in and of itself.[27]

The "high" becomes even greater when the crowd appeals to one's sense of justice. For the young Kadya in Warsaw, the issue was justice and fair pay for workers in general and for the teachers in the Jewish community, in particular. The issues at hand in the student movement of the 1960s were by no means the same.

The students were not working without pay, as Kadya had been in Warsaw. Nor were they doomed to live in hovels and subsist on a bit more than a starvation diet, as Kadya and Simche had in Warsaw. Perhaps that is what Simche was thinking of when, as Kadya reported it, Simche said he did not share Korn's empathy for the hippy "revolution" of the sixties.

The students did speak of justice. They wanted justice for Americans of color, who were being discriminated against in the South, and they wanted to change the role of women in society. Each of these issues took on its own trajectory of protest and both were overwhelmed by the protests against American military involvement in Vietnam.

Kadya was familiar with the conviction that the status quo regarding women needed changing. She had felt strongly about the need to change the status quo on feminist issues since she began publishing her work in Warsaw in the 1920s. During the mid and late 1960s, the tide of history finally caught up with her.

But by the time the non-Yiddish speaking women of the US became aware of the problems that Kadya had pondered over most of her life-time, the cultural gap between them and Kadya had become an impassible chasm. They were thoroughly American; she was an immigrant in the US They were totally acculturated Americans; she was a cultural outsider. They were monolingual English speakers; she was a multi-lingual, native Yiddish speaker. They had never heard of her and were unable to read her large body of work; she was not used to their lingo. It never occurred to them to reach out to her to get her input on their movement and its aims. For her part, she was engrossed in her own project: giving voice in her journal to the poets and writers who still felt moved to write in Yiddish. For her, the editing and publishing of *Svive* was a mission.

The Beginning of the End

In December of 1966, Simche had a heart attack and was hospitalized. Sarah Dubow, still one of her closest friends, wrote to her:

"How does it happen that a handsome, healthy man like Simche should lie in the hospital with a sick heart? It doesn't suit him."

Knowing how dependent Kadya was on Simche in putting out *Svive*, she continued:

"Who will help you now to put out *Svive*...?"[28]

Clearly, all of Kadya's friends knew that the printing of *Svive* was a two-person affair: Simche at the type-setting and Kadya doing the editing and proof-

Chapter Six: Return to the US: The first Decade 1952-1962

reading. Apparently, Simche was released from the hospital before the next issue of *Svive* needed to be type-set.

It is time to re-consider Sarah Dubow place in Kadya's life. There seems little doubt that the two women were close when they were both in Warsaw. It also seems clear that this friendship was a deep one. When Kadya needed help or had setbacks, she confided in Sarah. Nevertheless, the two women's paths diverged. With Sarah in Chicago and Kadya in New York (or Israel), there was little opportunity for their intimacy to take on a face-to-face, one might say in their case, a hand-to-hair aspect. Over time, Sarah's fortunes soared. She moved into an upper-class neighborhood[29], and her milieu changed. This in no way prevented her from keeping up her friendship with Kadya. The two women corresponded, and almost certainly spoke on the phone. But at the end of her life, Kadya's friendship with Sarah was based more on pleasant memories than on real-time shared experiences.

Kadya's friendship with Rokhl, her most long-standing literary friend, also underwent changes. Rokhl regularly sent Kadya her works for inclusion in *Svive* and Kadya was always pleased to include them in her journal. But the relationship between them had a serious break-down.

It happened one time that an error of lay-out occurred, and Rokhl's poem was printed with the heading and numerals misplaced. Rokhl exploded with anger.

Kadya could have fobbed responsibility for the error onto Simche. After all, it was he who did the type-setting. Nevertheless, it was she who did the final proof-reading, and she should have corrected the typos. Ultimately, it was she who let the errors slip by. Kadya did her best to mollify her friend. She apologized profusely, and when that did not help, she apologized again. So important was this relationship to her, that she left in her archive three different versions/carbon copies of the letters she sent desperately trying to appease her friend.[30]

It may have been the intervention of Melekh Ravitch that helped patch up this rip in the fabric of their friendship.[31] He was a friend of both women, and a natural choice for mediator. In any case, it took a while, but eventually Rokhl calmed down. The two women continued to correspond as though nothing at all had happened.

It is not clear exactly when Simche retired; Kadya left no record of that. But his heart attack was the beginning of the end of Simche's good health. He did get out of the hospital, and he did travel with Kadya when she went to Israel to receive a prestigious award a few years later, but his health was clearly declining.

Kadya's children's poems and stories in rhyme are what she is most remembered for today. She published four collections of children's poems and stories in rhyme. The first, called *Mayselekh*, (Little Stories), was published in Warsaw in 1931. All the other collections were published in New York. The second, called *Afn Barg* (On the Hill), was published in 1938. The third, called *Yidishe Kinder* (Jewish Children) was published in 1946, and the fourth, her last poetry book for children, was called *Martsepanes* (Marzipans), and was published in 1970.

The first collection contained twenty-three poems. Among these were poems that are now considered "classic", poems that have found their way into subsequent collections. These include "Olke" (and Her Blue Parasol), "The Story of the Washbasin", and "The Story of The Coat (Made of a Dark Material)".

The second collection was published by the Jewish Cooperative Book League of the International Workers' Order. The year of its publication, 1938, was the same year that Kadya's play "*Ale Fenster Tsu der Zun*" All Windows Facing the Sun", was published in Warsaw. Like that play, *Afn Barg* On the Mountain, shows clear signs of Kadya's Communist leanings. Only in 1938 did Kadya publish a book of hers with a Communist press.

It is difficult now for Westerners to understand the hold that Communism had on intellectuals during those years, even in Western Europe. George Orwell, writing about Communism in England said: "Between 1935 and 1939 the Communist Party had an almost irresistible fascination for any writer under forty."[32]

The economic hardships in Eastern Europe were far greater than they were in England, and the fascination with Communism in Eastern Europe was concomitantly greater. The year 1938 was the year Simche joined Kadya in the United States. Simche, we must keep in mind, had been a member of the Communist party in Poland. It took a while for this influence to fade away.

Chapter Six: Return to the US: The first Decade 1952-1962 307

To understand how this Communist influence can be seen in *Afn Barg*, we need to know about the influence of Hebrew on Yiddish, and the spelling conventions of both languages. Hebrew and Hebrew-Aramaic are an integral part of the Yiddish language. For example, the seventh day of the week, or Saturday, is the Jewish "Sabbath"; that is called "*shabes*" in Yiddish. For centuries, this word was spelled in Yiddish exactly the way the Hebrew word is spelled: שבת. Essentially, this word is spelled with three consonants: the first consonant is [sh]; the second consonant is [b]; the third consonant is [s]. Note that there are no vowels in this Yiddish spelling. That is because the written Hebrew word indicates no vowels between the consonants. Put differently, in Standard Hebrew orthography, vowels are not indicated. They are understood by native speakers who know the words and can insert the proper vowels from clues about the word in its context. This is how Hebrew-derived words were spelled in Yiddish from the inception of Yiddish writing until the early 1930s in the Soviet Union.

At that time, in an attempt to uproot Jewish nationalism from the Jewish citizens of the Soviet Union, Stalin decided to de-Hebraize Yiddish. In order to do this, he promulgated a new orthographic system for Yiddish in the Soviet Union.[33] In this new orthographic system, every vowel that had been "left out" of the Hebrew spelling, was given a symbol in the Soviet spelling. Thus, the Hebrew word for "*shabes*", which used to be a three-symbol word (all of these symbols, consonants), would now be a five-symbol word, consisting of three consonants and two vowels: 1) [sh], 2) [a], 3) [b], 4) [e], 5) [s]. What's more, under this new system, Yiddish spelling was "simplified". Whenever there were two consonants in Standard Yiddish orthography that had the same pronunciation, (as the letters "s" and "c" sometimes do in English), the new system had only one symbol for this sound. So, while in Standard Yiddish some [s] sounds were spelled with the symbol called "samekh" [ס] while others were spelled with the symbol called "sof" [ת], under the new system all [s] sounds were spelled with the symbol [ס]. Thus, whereas the spelling for "*shabes*" had been שבת in the Standard orthography, under the new system the proper spelling was שאבעס.[34]

This new system took hold exclusively under Communism. Nowhere else in the Jewish world did Jews agree to de-Hebraize their Yiddish. This Communist-ordained orthographic system is the one that is found in Kadya's 1938 collection of children's poems. It would seem that funding for this book came from sources that had Communist leanings. Accordingly, the rules of orthography in this book followed Communist dictates.

Of the twenty poems featured in this second collection, nine are new. We get a glimpse of Kadya's new world from these new poems. One of these is dedicated to Edith Litman, Kadya's niece (Dora's daughter), whom Kadya saw regularly when she visited her sister and father in Philadelphia, and one is about a letter that follows a Jewish worker as he travels (as Kadya did) from East Europe across the ocean to New York.

The third collection, published after WWII, shows no sign of Communist involvement. By this time Kadya and Simche, and indeed much of what was left of East European Jewry, were "cured" of their infatuation with Communism. This collection contained twenty-six poems, of which fifteen were new. Fifteen years after she won a prize for her children's poems and stories in Warsaw, Kadya continued to produce new poems and stories in the US that were every bit as charming and whimsical as the ones she had created when she was young.

In this third collection, we find a poet that has acculturated. Her poems have "new" Yiddish words, borrowed from English. In its travels around the world, Yiddish had always been comfortable borrowing new words from languages with which it was in contact; change of this sort is one indication that a language is alive and well. In this vein, Kadya used words like the newly Yiddishized word [truk], for "truck" and the "Yiddish" answers: [alrayt] and [okay]. One poem in this collection is called "Children From East Broadway"; in one poem we are told that a child must have his Teddy Bear, and one poem speaks of "all of Brownsville".

This collection ends oddly. Its last Yiddish poem is an unfortunate ditty entitled "The German, May His Name be Blotted Out". The lilting rhythm of this poem is totally at odds with the horror of the Nazi crimes. Its very general descriptions lack the particularity that gives weight to truly felt tragedy and its lack of sublimation leaches out all poetic force. But this poem is not the last one in this collection. It is followed by one more poem, this time, a poem entirely in Hebrew. For some reason, Kadya decided to end this collection with the Hebrew translation of her poem "*Efent Dem Toyer*", Open the Gate, or in Hebrew, "*Pitkhu Et Ha-Sha'ar*". Kadya commented in a foot-note to this poem that the very fine translation into Hebrew was done by Fania Bergshtein.

In 1970, Kadya published her fourth and last book of children's verses and stories. Entitled *Martsepanes*, Marzipans, this last children's book, put out nearly forty years after her first book for children (thirty-nine years, to be exact) contained nearly three times as many poems as her first book.

To be sure, some of the poems in this collection were oldies but goodies, among them the story of the hand-me-down coat, the story of the wash basin and the story of Olka and her blue parasol. Nevertheless, there were fifteen new poems and stories in this collection.

Kadya had an instinctive sense both for the music-in-language that children love and for the contemporary realities of the Jewish people. One of the new poems in this collection is called *Di Zun un Der Foygl Tsipilili*", "The Sun and the Bird Tsipilili". The bird's name appeals because it rhymes; children love sound repetition. But apart from that, "Tsipi" is the nickname for the Jewish name "*Tsipo(y)re*, which means "bird" in Hebrew, and "Lili" sounds like the refrain of a song, and rhymes with "Tsipi". Another one of the new poems in this collection is called: "Tomy, Bomy un Semy". These boys' names share a half rhyme, of course, and that is important. But of these three names only "Bomy" would have been known to Yiddish speakers in Europe. It is an endearment for the Hebrew-derived name "*Avrohom*".[35] The other two names are New World names. ("Semy" is how Yiddish speakers would say the name "Sammy".) This book was after all, intended for an American (or an Anglo) audience, where "Tommy" and "Sammy" fit in perfectly.

There are three Jewishly themed new poems in this collection: "Blintses", "*Ester HaMalke*" (Queen Esther), and "*Shalekh Mones* (literally, sending of portions, actually, food packages sent to friends and family). Blintses are usually connected to the Jewish holiday of *Shvu'es*, while Queen Esther and the sending of portions are connected to the Jewish holiday of Purim. For most of the secular Yiddish-speaking public in the US, Jewish identity was intimately connected to Jewish gastronomy. To be Jewish was primarily to eat Jewish food. The choice of "Blintses", then, for a poem, was a brilliant choice. It resonated with the Jewish public that this book targeted. As for the two other Jewishly themed new poems in this collection, they were bound up with Purim, the one Jewish holiday whose theme is Jewish identity in the Diaspora. Kadya was a writer who knew her audience intimately.

Kadya divided this last children's book of hers into four sub-sections: 1) Wonder of Wonders, 2) Stars Fall, 3) On the Hills of Judea, and 4) Young School Boys. All of the poems in section 3 are about Israel.

Kadya must have felt strongly about her poem "Angels Come In Jerusalem"; she published it four times. It appeared first in *Di Goldene Keyt* before she left Israel in 1952[36]; it was the title poem as well as the name of the book she published in New York when she returned at the end of 1952; it appeared again in her collection of poems for adults, "*Likht fun Dornboym*", Light of the Thorn Bush, and it appeared one last time, in her fourth book for children, *Martsepane*s (Marzipans).

Some of the poems in the third section (On the Hills of Judea) are clearly children's poems. This is the case of the poem "*Ekhod Mi Yode'*a", (Who Knows One?). Its inclusion in the adult collection "*Likht Fun Dornboym*", Light of the Thorn-Bush seemed surprising; its inclusion in this children's book, on the other hand, seems quite natural. There are other cases, however, when the reverse is true. Inclusion in a book of adult poems seems natural, while inclusion in a book for children seems puzzling. This is the case of both poems that have the word "Jerusalem" in their title. One poem is entitled simply "Jerusalem", while the other is the much-printed "Angels Come In Jerusalem".

No one knows what children make of notions like "holiness". Assuming these notions are descriptions of experiences that are spiritual, there is every reason to suppose that children may have such experiences. However, it is quite clear that they do not have the ability to discuss these experiences using abstract language. Do they understand these notions when they read about them in a book? Kadya must have thought they do. It was her decision to include poems about the holiness of Jerusalem in a collection intended for children. Apparently, she felt it made sense for children to hear about holiness, as well as to hear about the connection between holiness and Jerusalem.

It is a fact that nowhere in the world is Kadya's poetry as well-known now, in the 21st century, as it is in Israel. But there her poetry is known in its Hebrew translation.

Some of the youngsters who enjoyed Kadya's Yiddish poetry as children in Europe, made their way to Israel and became known as writers of Hebrew themselves. Remembering her poems with fondness, they lovingly translated them into Hebrew. The most well-known of these Hebrew translations is a collection of poems entitled "*Pitkhu Et Ha-Sha'ar*", Open the Gate. Its translators were the crème de la crème of the Hebrew writers of their day: Leah Goldberg, Nathan Alterman, Fanya Bergstein, Avrohom Levinson and Ya'akov Fichman. Not only was this book reprinted over and over again in its entirety, individual poems within it made their way into literature books for school-children and popular anthologies of children's poems in Hebrew. Six other collections of Kadya's poems found their way into Hebrew translations just between 1986 and 2006.

Kadya was especially fortunate. Her Hebrew language translators were blessed with a wonderful sense of the unique features of both Hebrew and Yiddish. They knew how to transmit the cleverness of Yiddish into a different, but equally clever, form of Hebrew.

Here is an example of how this worked. One of the all-time favorites among Kadya's poems is, in Yiddish: "*Olke mit der Bloye Parasolke.* In Hebrew this poem is called: "*Ayelet im Shimshiya Kekhalkhelet.*" For one thing, the Hebrew translation has a girl's name that rhymes with the last word of the title. Thus the Yiddish: ***Olke***: *Paras****olke*** is paralleled by the Hebrew: *A****yelet***: *Kekhalk****helet***.

In addition, the translator got as close to a rhythmic match as is possible for two languages that stem from different language families:

Yiddish: / -   - - / -   - - / -

Hebrew: - / - [-] - - /   - - / -

Finally, in what comes close to a stroke of genius, the Hebrew translation mirrors the original Yiddish even at the level of word-formation. A literal translation of the Yiddish noun and its adjective, "a blue parasol" into Hebrew would have been "*shimshiya kekhula*". But recall that the Yiddish word for "parasol" has a diminutive –*ke* tacked onto it, so that it becomes "*parasolke*". In order to mirror this, the Hebrew translation also uses a diminutive. It takes the last word of the phrase, the Hebrew word for "blue", and adds a diminutive. Whereas the Yiddish diminutive,-*ke*-, stems from the Slavic component of Yiddish, the Hebrew diminutive can be traced as far back as Biblical Hebrew.[37] In Hebrew, a diminutive is conveyed by what linguists call "partial reduplication": the consonants of last syllable of the adjective are repeated. Had the Hebrew adjective been modifying a masculine noun, the diminutive form for the Hebrew word "blue" would have been "*ke-khal-khal*". But since the adjective "blue" is modifying a feminine noun, we have here the feminine diminutive form of the adjective "blue": *ke-khal-khelet*. This gives us a rhyme match, a rhythm match and a word-formation match. No translation could be better.

In her last book of poetry, Kadya admitted openly that she was, if not the last of her kind, then one of the last of her kind. She included in that last book a poem she had written in 1947, in which she said:

"I am a spark/ Of a burnt-out fire".

This theme repeated itself in a poem she wrote in 1960, in which she said:

"I am an echo/ Of an orchestra that's disappeared."[38]

Finally, in the first line of one of her later poems, she says:

"I am perhaps the last of my generation." [39]

It is not as though there were no longer individual speakers of Yiddish in those years. There were such speakers. There were then, as there are now, whole

Chapter Six: Return to the US: The first Decade 1952-1962   313

communities of Hassidic Jews whose everyday language was/is Yiddish. But these Jews were not about to buy, read or recite Kadya's poetry. They were (and are) a world apart. What had disappeared were secular communities that functioned in Yiddish.

Kadya Receives Awards

In the 1960s, world-wide Yiddish readership of Kadya's books was dwindling, but international recognition was forthcoming. In the decade between 1961 and 1971, Kadya received every prize that could possibly be awarded to a Yiddish writer. In 1965 she received the Yiddish literature prize awarded by the Jewish Book Council; in 1966 she shared with A. Tabachnik the N. Chanin prize, awarded by the Arbiter Ring in New York; in 1967, she received the Tsvi Kessel award for Yiddish literature, awarded in Mexico City. And in 1971, she received along with three other Yiddish writers, the Itzik Manger prize in Israel. This was the most prestigious of all prizes that could then be awarded to a Yiddish writer.

In explaining the rationale behind choosing Kadya, the jury said:

"The jury is impressed with her unornamented sincerity and the heartfelt sense of responsibility in her poetry".

When they said this, they were almost certainly referring to her early poetry describing the poverty and misery of pre-Holocaust Warsaw (this accounts for her "sense of responsibility"), and to her pained response to the Holocaust in poems like "Grace-Granting God" (this accounts for her "unornamented sincerity"). The jury didn't need to give examples; the audience at the ceremony was able to figure out which phrase of the jury corresponded to which part of her oeuvre.

The jury then pointed out that "two or three generations" of Israelis had been brought up on her poetry. This was most definitely true. The jury did not point out that Israeli children learned Kadya's poetry not in the original Yiddish, but in its (excellent) Hebrew translation. The unfortunate part of the reality, the one they chose not to mention, was that as a rule, Yiddish was not taught in Israeli public schools.

In fact, the school system did everything it could to reinforce a Hebrew-only policy in the public schools. The good news was what the jury chose to celebrate: Kadya's poetry lived on, even if it was in translation.

Next the jury pointed out that Kadya was in a manner of speaking realistic.

"She saw that Dzshike street[40] was poor and filthy and a victim of injustice."

While there is no question that this is an accurate picture of the Warsaw environment described by Kadya, there is also no doubt that there is a slight tone of superiority in the words of the jury here. That Diasporic reality was awful; here in Israel, they seem to be suggesting, there is no poverty and filth. As for the "injustice" that Kadya noted, it is doubtful that the capitalism she so railed against was indeed the cause of the misery she described. The inter-war years were (except for a very brief period) uniformly problematic in all of the Western world. The US suffered from a crippling Depression. In Europe, none of the combatants of WWI had properly recovered. And the "Socialist" economy of Communist Russia fared no better than the capitalist systems of the non-Communist states of Europe. The rhetoric of the economic "injustice" of Europe, one that the early settlers of Israel were meant to abolish, had not yet died down in 1971, when the Manger prize was awarded.

The jury then pointed out that despite the terrible conditions of the Jews in Europe, Kadya emphasized the inherent "nobility of her heroes"..." If one only keeps 'all the windows open to the sun', joy streams in even for those whose lives are full of drudgery and grief." Here they quoted the words of the play Kadya wrote to describe what she herself had tried to do in her children's poetry: bring joy even to children whose poverty might otherwise have overwhelmed them.

Lastly, the jury referred to Kadya's cycle of poems about Jerusalem. "In her poems about the land of Israel, the poet does not separate dream from reality. Jerusalem On Earth crosses over to Jerusalem On High."[41]

The last comment of the jury was unquestionably meant as a compliment. And the jury were right on this issue as well. Kadya's cycle of poems about Israel in

Chapter Six: Return to the US: The first Decade 1952-1962

general and Jerusalem in particular were steeped in mysticism. Recall that the title of the small booklet she first put out was "Angels Come In Jerusalem".

And yet, a sense of irony is clearly in place here. The city of Jerusalem that Kadya described is the city of visionaries who live in a world of their imagination, not in a down-to-earth world. The fact was that the actual city of Jerusalem suffered from inter-ethnic disturbances. Then, as now, Arabs and Jews fought over the right to ascend to the Temple Mount. Religious Jews and non-religious kept to themselves, and suspected and often defamed each other. Unlike the "newer" city of Tel Aviv, Jerusalem was not an economically prosperous city. Tourists and the mentally unstable[42] were the ones who usually left Jerusalem singing its praises and describing the angels who had come to live there. Residents and citizens of the country, people who spent prolonged periods of time in the city and knew the nitty-gritty reality, rarely did so.[43]

But writers are allowed, and even encouraged, to live within the world of their imagination. The comments of the jury, then, probably ought to be taken in the spirit in which they were given. For Kadya, Jerusalem and the world of the spirit were inextricably melded together. Her poetry celebrated the epiphany she had experienced there, and all were grateful to her for that.

At the ceremony for the Manger prize, President Shazar reminded Kadya of the three years she had spent in Israel. He pointed out that the journal she had edited while in Israel had been called *Heym*, "Home", and he expressed the hope she would again come to see Israel as her home. [44]

While it was kind, and even sincere, for Shazar to suggest she might return to Israel to live, the reality was that Kadya was not able to make the move once more. At this point, she and Simche were elderly. A move would have been unnecessarily hard on them. Kadya's heart may have been in Israel, but her physical self was irretrievably ensconced in New York.

Kadya's words upon receiving the Manger prize are note-worthy for what they do, as well as what they do not, say. She spoke in that speech about the "baggage" that Jews took with them wherever in the Diaspora they happened to live.

Included in this "hidden",[45] spiritual baggage are: the Hebrew Bible, the Hebrew prayers, Jewish customs, Jewish Holidays, and the sum total of all Jewish creativity throughout the ages. She continued by saying that this Jewish heritage "is spiritually nourished from the declaration [of the Jews] at Mount Sinai: "we will do, then we will listen".[46]

The one Jewish item Kadya did not mention in the above speech is Jewish law, or what is sometimes called Jewish (religious) observance. Interestingly, the declaration she quoted: "we will do, then we will listen", is mentioned in the Bible as the response of the children of Israel to the giving of the laws of Moses.[47] But for all her spirituality, Kadya was not a religiously observant Jew. It is no accident, then, that she refrained from mentioning Jewish law. Her audience, the lovers of Yiddish literature, did not consider Jewish law a part of their spiritual baggage either. For all that this omission is a glaring one, then, Kadya and her secular audience were in agreement. They were cultural, not religious, Jews, and Jewish law/observance was not a concern of theirs.

When she came to Israel to receive the Manger prize, Kadya told an interviewer that her newest book of poems, *Martsepanes*, published only one year earlier, contained new poems that had not – yet – been translated into Hebrew. She promised that if these new poems were translated into Hebrew, she would return to Israel and recite them for an Israeli audience. The newer poems never were translated into Hebrew. But the interviewer was so impressed with her feistiness and her promise, that she sub-titled the interview: "At 78, she's going strong."[48]

When Kadya and Simche returned to New York from Israel, they resumed their joint work: soliciting articles for *Svive*, editing these articles, proof-reading them and finally, printing them. The few letters written by Kadya that have been preserved from the years 1971-1974 all mention previous and coming editions of the journal, and ask outright for the recipient to consider writing for the journal. Kadya had no problems asking for an article in Hebrew. She did the translating herself and then printed the article in Yiddish.

Kadya, Simche and Zionism

The issue of Kadya's Zionism, or strong identification with Israel, is a complex one. In a letter she wrote to Yeshayahu Rabinovitch before she traveled to Israel to receive the Manger prize, Kadya confessed that she "longed to be in Israel". She was amazed, she said, at the courage of the Jewish people in Israel. There is every reason to believe she was sincere when she said that.

But her departure from Israel in 1952, left a tsunami of anger and resentment in its wake. In an essay, written in a literary journal after her death, Avraham Broydes reports that Kadya told him after she left Israel: "I disappointed [my supporters] and I aroused a grievance against myself. One can rightfully consider me one of the emigrants. I am worthy of flogging".[49]

Since the printed page does not easily allow for irony or indicate a change of tone, it is difficult, if not impossible, to know how serious Kadya was when she said she was worthy of flogging. But there is no question that she was well aware of the ill-will she had aroused in Israel. Her (former) friends and supporters there did not look kindly on what they considered desertion.

From a letter that Kadya wrote to Avraham Broydes, we know that Simche had a cataract operation in the beginning of 1974 and that he was in the hospital for 15 days.[50] Clearly that put a crimp in their printing plans. But the next edition of *Svive* went out as planned. In fact, the last edition of *Svive* was that of April 1974. Yet in that very month, Kadya continued to ask Broydes for contributions to *Svive*. If there were no more editions of the journal, that is because Simche was not there to help Kadya. He died later that year.

There is no question that Kadya would not have had the career she did without Simche's help. Rivke Basman Ben-Haim reports that when the two of them were in Israel, and Rivke visited them, Kadya said: "Without Simche,..." and she didn't finish her sentence. Basman Ben-Haim turned to Kadya and said: "Go ahead, finish your sentence." But Kadya answered: "Simche knows and I know." And she said no more.[51]

With Simche's death, there came an end to *Svive*. Kadya did not know how to set type, and there was no one else like Simche, who would do the job free of charge.

Kadya stayed on in their apartment for a while after his death, but neither she nor her work were the same without him. Beila Schechter Gottesman told me that she visited Kadya after Simche had died. They discussed their own poetry and the works of others in what could only be termed a "normal conversation" until Kadya called out "Simche!" expecting her husband to appear. Beila gently told Kadya that Simche was not around. "Then let him come here", Kadya said. Clearly, Kadya's connection to reality had snapped.[52]

Seeing her deterioration, Dora, her devoted and ever-loyal sister, moved her to a "home" in Philadelphia, where the extended family could visit easily. Kadya died there on March 21, 1975.

For all that Kadya had friends among the elite in Israel, and despite the fact that her stories and poems for children were very much admired there, not one major Hebrew-language newspaper reported her death. It was as though she had never existed. This refusal to acknowledge her death publicly has to have been intentional.

Her death met with a wall of silence among the Israeli elite[53] almost certainly because as soon as she emigrated, she became a persona non grata. Anyone who left Israel to live elsewhere was, in those days, guilty of desertion, but Kadya was doubly guilty. She had not only "jumped ship", she had also betrayed the trust and dashed the hopes of her supporters.

They had imagined she would singlehandedly revive the declining interest of Israelis in Yiddish culture. She had not done that during her three-year stay in Israel, true, but they imagined she would somehow have been able to do that had she stayed.

Naturally, her death was reported in the American (secular) Yiddish newspaper of note, the *Forverts*. The front-page article written on March 23, called her "the well-known poet" and added that her death brought on a "great sadness" among writers of Yiddish as well as among her many readers and fans.

The sub-title of that article announced that the funeral would be the following day at one PM, and the last paragraph of that article says:

"The Yiddish PEN club asks all Yiddish writers to come to the funeral to pay their respects to this beloved poet."

Did the editors of the *Forverts* know that the Israeli newspapers had ignored Kadya's death? Is that why they made a point of announcing the hour of her funeral in the sub-title of their report on her death? Is that why they almost begged Yiddish writers to show up at her funeral? One cannot know for sure, but that is certainly a possibility.

Kadya did not have much faith in the continuity of the American Jewish community. She saw the delight of American Jews in their ever-increasing Americanization and assimilation, and she realized that that was the death-knell of Yiddish culture in the US. [54] She did believe that the Jews of Israel would have a vibrant Jewish culture, be it Yiddish-based or Hebrew-based. It is an ironic twist of fate, then, that Kadya's death was noted in the US, where she felt increasingly alien, and ignored in Israel, where she felt she belonged, if only in spirit.

NOTES

[1] Some of the poems here had appeared in *Di Goldene Keyt*, the Yiddish journal put out by Avrohom Sutzkever in Israel.
[2] *Likht Fun Dornboym*, pp. 134-135.
[3] Op. Cit., p. 32.
[4] Op. Cit., pp. 118-119.
[5] Op. Cit., p. 10.
[6] This, in a poem, found in the collection above, entitled "*In Vald*", In the Forest", p. 19.
[7] *Likht Fun Dornboym*, pp. 105-106.
[8] In the prayer said after meals, there is a special addition on Sabbath in which the petitioner asks God to grant him/her a day that is "entirely and endlessly Sabbath". Clearly, such a day could only be granted by God. Chapter 92 of Psalms, a hymn to the Sabbath day, a day that is "entirely and endlessly Sabbath", was said by the rabbis to be a "song for the future/the end of days".
[9] *Likht Fun Dornboym*, the poem entitled "*Mayn Shprakh*", My Speech, p. 107.
[10] Op. Cit., p. 147.
[11] Op. Cit., p. 148.

[12] Op. Cit., pp. 131-132.

[13] Each of these three poems has been translated by Kathryn Hellerstein. For the originals and Hellerstein's translations into English, see Hellerstein, 1999, p. 237, p. 414, and p. 468.

[14] Op. Cit., p. 415.

[15] Op. Cit., p. 147.

[16] Ibid.

[17] The story of Hagar, Abraham's concubine and Sarah's servant, is found in Genesis chapter 21. For Hagar's expulsion from Abraham's house, see verse 14. Admittedly, Hagar is Sarah's servant, not Abraham's. But if Abraham can be so cruel to his wife's servant, how much more so can he be with his own servant.

[18] II Samuel, chapter 13, verse 31.

[19] Jeremiah, chapter 31, verse 14

[20] See Leviticus chapter 10. For Aaron's silence, see verse 3.

[21] There are some Jews who blame the victims' secularizing tendencies for the Holocaust. But this is a minority view.

[22] Recall her poem: "*El Khanun*". See pp. 137-139.

[23] See Chapter five, p.171.

[24] Also found in the YIVO archive.

[25] This, in a letter in the YIVO archive, dated August 15, 1968.

[26] See endnote above. This is found in the YIVO archive.

[27] See Elias Canetti's book <u>Crowds And Power</u>. Originally published in German in 1960, it was translated into English and released in paperback in 1984.

[28] This in a letter from Sarah Dubow, found in the YIVO archive.

[29] I've given Sarah's various addresses to native Chicago residents. I have it on their judgment that the addresses are in increasingly wealthy neighborhoods.

[30] For the details of this episode in Kadya's life see Zelda Kahan Newman's "The Molodowsky-Korn Correspondence" in *Women in Judaism*, pp. 5-7.

[31] I am grateful to Amir Shomroni for pointing this out.

[32] "Inside the Whale", from George Orwell's book: <u>Inside the Whale and Other Essays</u>, p. 32

[33] To be precise, it was not Stalin who did this, but the great Yiddish linguist Aizik Zaretski, who created this new system. Zaretski, author of the finest Yiddish grammar written to date, was eventually tried by Stalin and sentenced to Siberia on trumped-up charges.

[34] This "simplification" held for other consonant pairs as well. Whereas in the Standard Yiddish orthography, there were two symbols, ח and כ, for the velar fricative, written sometimes as "kh", under the "revised", or Communist, spelling, all such sounds were given a כ. In addition, if the vowel [o] was pronounced [oy] in the spoken language, that was reflected in the new orthography. That is why the spelling for the Hebrew-derived word for "month", traditionally written as חודש, now became כוידעש.

[35] One needs to know Hebrew morpho-phonemics to understand why this is so.

[36] This was the Yiddish journal edited by Avrohom Sutzkever. This poem appeared in no. 12 of his journal on p. 91.

[37] In Leviticus 13/49 the colors green and red undergo partial reduplication. In that verse, "green", ordinarily [yarok], appears as: [yerakrak], and "red", ordinarily [adom], appears as: [adamdam]. While the partial reduplication process can be traced to Biblical Hebrew, it is not clear that the semantics of this form in the Bible is identical to the semantics of the form in Modern Hebrew. Classical Jewish exegesis occasionally understands these forms as conveying the meaning of "very strong" [green or red]. In the Song of Songs 1/6, the color "black" appears. Ordinarily [shakhor], the word in this verse undergoes partial reduplication, and becomes: [shekharkhor]. However, since the noun in verse 6 of The Song of Songs is a feminine noun, the feminine agreement particle – et is appended to the partially reduplicated adjective, and the final adjectival form is: [shekharkhoret]. For the suggestion that partial reduplication can be interpreted sometimes as a diminutive and sometimes as a strengthener, see: http://mg.alhatorah.org/Dual/Netziv/Vayikra/13.1#m7e0n6

[38] *Likht fun Dornboym*, p. 158.

[39] Op. Cit., p. 143.

[40] *Dzshike Gas*, Dzshike Street, was the name of Kadya's third book of poetry. She and Simche lived on that street, and in that book, she described the poverty all around her.

[41] All the quotes from the jury's rationale can be found in (the Yiddish language paper) *Di Letste Nayes*, (The Latest News), March 7, 1971, p. 7.

[42] The phenomenon of mentally unstable folks, usually tourists, who "get high" while in Jerusalem, is known in the annals of psychiatry. It is called "the Jerusalem Syndrome".

[43] To be completely fair, religious Jews, even citizens of Israel, have been known to feel the same as Kadya did. An example of a contemporary Jewish author whose feelings mirror Kadya's, is the religious rabbi and writer, Chaim Sabatto.

[44] For his comments, see *Di Letste Nayes* referred to in note xcix. Shazar's comments are on p. 6 of that issue.

[45] Kadya herself uses the word "hidden" baggage. Her comments can also be found in *Di Letste Nayes*, p. 6.

[46] This declaration can be found in Exodus 24/7. It is considered remarkable because it is evidence of the people's commitment to fulfill God's demands, even before they know what God will demand of them.

[47] Kadya seems to have reinterpreted this Biblical phrase. She switched its purport from a commitment to action, to a commitment to belief. This can be seen from a letter she wrote Melekh Ravitch in 1968, in which she praises a common acquaintance of theirs who was a "*bal bitokhn*", (one who has faith in God), who says "We will do, then we will listen". I am indebted to Amir Shomroni for sharing this point with me.

[48] The interviewer was Ala Eilenberg, and the interview can be found in *Ma'ariv*, May 3, 1971, p. 25.

[49] The exact quote in Hebrew is: ‏"אפשר לראות אותי, ובצדק, עם היורדים. מגיע לי מלקות.". This is in *Moznayim*, 1975, volume 41, number 1, p.65.
[50] Once again, I want to thank Amir Shomroni for sharing this with me.
[51] Personal communication.
[52] Personal communication.
[53] There were articles/eulogies about her after death, among them, the article in *Moznayim*, mention above. But there was no real-time report of her death.
[54] This is something she discussed with her friend and colleague Rokhl Korn. It also comes up in her works that deal with American Jewry. This topic is dealt with in Shomroni's doctoral dissertation.

BIBLIOGRAPHY OF KADYA MOLODOWSK'S WORKS

1. A Hoyz oyf Grend Strit (A House on Grand Street), unpublished manuscript YIVO RG 703.
2. A Shtub mit Zibn Fenster (A House with Seven Windows) (Leah Schoolnik, trans.) Syracuse University Press, Syracuse, New York, 2006.
3. Afn Barg (On the Mountain), Cooperative Folk Press of the International Workers' Organization, New York, 1938.
4. Ale Fenster tsu der Zun (All Windows Facing the Sun), Literarishe Bleter, Warsaw, 1938.
5. Baym Toyer (At the Gate), CYCO Press, New York, 1967.
6. Der Melekh Dovid Aleyn iz Geblibn (Only King David Remained), Paper Bridges, New York, 1946.
7. Dzshike Gas (Dzshike Street), Literarishe Bleter, Warsaw, 1933.
8. Freydke (Freydke), Literarishe Bleter, Warsaw, 1935.
9. Fun Lublin biz Nyu York: Der Togbukh fun Rivke Zylberg (From Lublin to New York: the Diary of Rivke Zylberg, Paper Bridges, New York, 1942.
10. In Land fun Mayn Gebeyn (In the Land of My Bones), Stein Publishers, Chicago, 1937.
11. In Yerusholayim Kumen Malokhim (Angels Come in Jerusalem), Paper Bridges, New York, 1952.
12. Kheshvndike Nekht (Late Autumn Nights), Kletzkin Press, Warsaw, 1927.
13. Lider fun Khurbn (Poems of the Holocaust), Y.L. Peretz Press, Tel Aviv, 1962.
14. Likht fun Dornboym (Light of the Thornbush), Kiyum Press, Buenos Aires, 1965.
15. Martsepanes (Marzepans), CYCO Press, New York, 1970.
16. Mayselekh (Short Stories), Jewish School Organization, Warsaw, 1931.

17. Nokhn Got fun Midber (After God of the Desert), Paper Bridges Press, New York, 1949.
18. Oyf di Vegn fun Tsiyon (On the Paths of Zion), National Committee of Jewish Folk Schools, New York, 1957.
19. Oyf Eygene Erd (On Our Own Soil) unpublished manuscript YIVO RG 703.
20. Yidishe Kinder (Jewish Children), Central Committee of Jewish Folk Schools, New York, 1945.
21. Under Pseudonym of Rivke Zylberg: articles prepared for the Forverts, YIVO RG 703.

INDEX OF PEOPLE

Alterman, Nathan, 308
Babel, Isaac, 274
Balfour, Sir Arthur, 27, 30
Barash, Asher, 245
Bashevis. See Singer, I. B.s
Basman Ben-Haim, Rivka, 182, 241, 315
Ben Gurion, David, 203-205, 207, 237
Bercovitch, Mr., 119
Bergelson, Dovid, 29, 31, 34-44, 51, 63, 69, 98, 122, 157-159, 167, 180, 224
Bergstein, Fanya, 316
Blanc, Natan, 228
Blanc, Netta, 235
Broderzon, Moshe, 70
Broydes, Avraham, 314-315
Cohen, Natan, 64, 105
Der Nister, 34, 63
Dobbe, See Molodowsky (Litman), Dora
Dobrushin, Yekhezkel, 34-35
Drost, Hava, 244
Drost, Meir, 239
Dubow, Sarah, 103-104, 115-120, 203, 221, 244, 247, 281, 301, 317
Durkheim, Emile, 144, 180

Fefer, Itzik, 151
Fichman, Ya'akov, 23, 83, 308
Fishman Gonshor, Anna, 50, 64, 70, 75, 76, 83, 84, 97, 83 104, 105, 106
Froebel, Friedrich, 51
Ga'on of Vilna, 7, 268
Goldstein, Bert, 220-221
Gorali, Yakov, 15
Grabski, Wladyslaw, 52, 64
Grade, Chaim, 100
Hadda, Janet, 178, 179
Halperin, Yehiel, 12, 13, 15, 17, 19, 22-24, 27, 36, 40, 176, 234-235, 237
Hellerstein, Kathryn, 65, 70, 104, 154, 193, 243, 249, 292, 325
Hirshbein, Peretz, 84
Hoover, J. Edgar, 232
Idelson, Bebe (Trachtenberg), 32, 33, 188, 205-206, 211, 234-235
Jabotinsky, Ze'ev, 272, 285
Kafri, Sara, 30
Kaplan, Mr., 220
Kazdan, Kh., 92, 95, 97
Khmurner, Y., 97
Kling, Bertha, 107
Koestler, Arthur, 130, 179
Korman, Ezra, 83, 118, 227

Korn, Rokhl, 4, 37-38, 61, 63, 65, 92, 94-95, 121, 125, 176, 180, 190, 194, 207, 223, 226, 229, 234, 236, 277-279, 281-283, 287, 298-299, 300, 317, 318
Kulbak, Moshe, 68
Kvitko, Leib, 34, 36
Lehrer, Lipa, 202, 237, 239
Levinson, Avrrohom, 308
Levita, Rokhl, 45
Lew, Kadya. See Molodowsky, Kadya
Lew (Lev), Simche, 29, 44-63, 66-69, 77-78, 85, 98-99, 102-104, 109, 114, 116, 118-119, 121, 124, 127, 129, 131-132-136, 139, 142, 145-146, 148-150, 153- 154, 166, 170, 178-179, 185, 187-190, 195, 202, 204, 207, 215, 217, 220, 222-224, 226-229, 231, 235-236, 238-239, 241, 242, 244, 248, 278, 279, 280, 282, 285, 286, 287, 290-291, 293, 299-300-303, 305, 313, 315, 318
Leyvik, H., 92-93, 191-192
Leyzer-Ber 5
Litman, Ben, 72, 143, 153
Litman, Bune. See Litman, Ben
Litman, Ben, 143, 153
Litman, Edith, 143, 211, 305
Maimonides, 17, 25, 287

Manger, Itsik, 93
Markish, Peretz, 36, 68, 69
Mayzel, Nachman, 40, 69, 92, 94
Maze, Ida, 52, 56, 62, 107, 109, 110, 12-125, 130, 170, 173-174, 225, 226, 239, 244, 256, 281, 285
McCarthy, Joseph, 232, 287
Mendelsohn, Sh., 97
Mikhoels, Shloyme, 151, 180
Molodowsky, Aizik, 4, 5,7-9, 11, 14-17, 58-59, 63, 136-153, 153, 176, 179, 180, 185, 199, 201, 204, 2010-222, 231, 292, 317
Molodowsky (Litman), Dora, 2, 4-5, 12, 13, 18, 19, 54, 63, 100, 108, 124, 142, 146-148, 150, 151, 152, 153, 171-172, 185, 198-99, 201-204, 206, 207, 210, 212-218, 222, 231-233, 237, 243, 281, 305, 315
Molodowsky, Ilana, 135, 141
Molodowsky, Leibl, 16, 24, 53, 58, 124, 135, 137-139, 141, 150, 171-172, 179, 180
Molodowsky, Lina, 2, 4, 17-19, 63, 100, 108-110, 143, 153, 180, 195, 201, 214,-216, 231, 238, 254
Molodowsky, Lola, 58, 135, 137, 139, 141
Montefiore, Moses, 7
Mordechai Chaim of Slonim, 7, 8

Index

Morowitz, Genia, 242
Novershtern, Avraham, 95, 106
Opatashu, Joseph, 93
Patt, Yankev, 97
Pinski, Dovid, 178, 192
Ravitch, Melekh, 29, 61, 77-79, 83, 92, 103, 118, 125, 174, 193, 206, 230, 225, 277 280, 283, 302
Sabatto, Chaim, 318
Schecter-Gottesman, Beila, 243, 315
Schliefer, Solomon, 151
Shazar, Zalman, 241, 312, 313, 318
Shomroni, Amir, 64, 106, 237, 239, 317, 318
Shumiatcher, Esther, 84, 107

Simkhonit, Yehudit, 30, 209, 210
Singer, Isaac Bashevis, 69, 99, 105, 125-126, 178, 277
Tabachnik, Avraham, 310
Trumpeldor, Joseph, 273, 296
Tsanin, Mordechai, 193
Vagman family, 42
Vilna Ga'on. See Ga'on of Vilna
Weber, Max, 143, 144
Weinreich, Max, 109, 185, 286
Woolf, Virginia, 55
Zaromb, Shmuel, 80
Zeitlin, A(ha)ron., 50, 64, 91-95, 135-136, 248, 251, 283, 285
Zylbeg, Rivke (pseudonym), 265

INDEX OF PLACES

Argentina, 94, 280, 289
Auschwitz-Birkenau, 272
Babylonia, 192
Belarus, 45
Belgium, 59
Berlin, 40, 41, 43, 63, 158, 286
Berze, 10, 12, 15-17, 19, 23, 26, 27, 29, 40, 47, 63, 67, 143, 286
Bialystok, 12-13, 17, 150, 180
Birobidzan, 99
Brest. See Brisk
Brisk, 19, 46, 68-69, 243
Broadway, 245, 265, 280, 286
Bronx, 117, 180, 242-243, 285
Brooklyn, 179, 243, 274
Brownsville, Brooklyn, 173, 184, 249, 281, 292, 313
Buenos Aires, 269, 284, 287, 289
Canada, 54, 62, 64, 102, 104, 107, 124-126, 151, 173, 178, 202, 204, 280, 284
Chicago, 54, 55, 104, 115-116, 124, 145, 238, 244, 301, 317
Cincinnati, 54
Cleveland, 116, 124
Cuba, 135, 136
Detroit, 54, 55, 116, 124, 126, 178
East Village, New York City, 179

Egypt, 192, 298
Europe, 5, 12, 17, 33, 37, 39, 45, 51, 52, 54, 56, 59, 62, 67-68, 84, 90, 94, 100, 104, 111, 113, 115, 119, 121, 127, 129, 131, 133, 135, 143, 144, 145, 150, 152, 161, 164, 165, 171, 172, 173, 179, 180, 182, 184, 188, 196, 226, 229, 234, 236, 243, 251, 253, 254, 260, 263, 264, 268, 272, 273, 274, 275, 276, 282, 283, 286, 303, 305, 306, 308, 311
Florida, 146, 264
France, 57, 58, 85
Great Britain, 27, 151, 184
Hamburg, 102
Iran, 184, 192
Iraq, 184, 189, 192
Israel (See also Palestine), 5, 7, 15, 16, 27, 30, 31, 33, 38, 43, 45, 49, 50, 59, 64, 74, 77, 82, 91, 113, 116, 122, 123, 136, 154, 161, 162, 167, 170, 176-178, 181, 183-198, 200-207, 209-213, 216, 218-223, 225-, 223, 224, 225-229, 230, 231-236, 238, 241- 245, 254, 260-263, 268-275, 277-281, 283-284, 287, 289, 293-296, 298-299, 301-302, 310-318
Italy, 121, 254, 263

Index

Jerusalem, 7, 27, 28, 224, 231, 238, 244, 270, 271, 283, 307, 308, 312, 318

Kartuskaya Beryoze. See Berze

Kiev, 28, 31-63, 67, 69, 80, 159, 200, 207, 279

Lekhevitch, 45-48, 67

Libave, 9

Lithuania, 2, 3, 100, 130

Lodz, 68

London, 267, 284, 286

Los Angeles, 173, 244, 290

Lower East Side, New York City, 179, 243

Manhattan, 180, 244

Mexico City, 284, 310

Minsk, 47, 48, 64, 80

Montreal, 29, 54, 62, 64, 65, 66, 105, 107, 109, 124, 125, 173, 177, 222, 223, 244, 287, 299

Morocco, 184, 192

New York (City), 18, 41, 43, 51, 58, 63, 65, 104, 109, 110, 112, 114, 116, 122, 126, 137, 140, 142, 149, 177, 189, 195, 199, 206, 223, 235-236, 238, 243, 256, 266, 281, 284, 285, 301, 307, 314, 317, 320, 321

Nikolaev, 27

Odessa, 23, 24, 27-29, 84, 166, 274

Onstead, Michigan, 182

Otwock, 68, 69

Palestine (See also Israel), 7, 12, 27, 33, 36, 52, 64, 113, 121, 175, 176, 254, 260-261, 263

Pearl Harbor, 165

Persia, 184

Philadelphia, 18, 56, 65, 100, 109, 120, 137, 139, 14- 144, 149, 152-153, 204, 221-223, 232, 243, 265, 305, 315

Poland, 10, 48, 49, 52, 54, 57-59, 62-63, 68, 85, 96, 99, 102-103, 105, 106, 108, 114, 124-127, 129-130, 133, 135-138, 150, 229 267, 285, 303

Poltava, 24, 25, 28

Rehovot, 275

Romni, 26

Rosh Pina, 275

Russia (See also Soviet Union), 2,-6, 8, 10, 15, 24-25, 27-28, 31, 33, 36, 39, 44, 48, 53, 63, 68, 99, 106, 116, 127, 133-134, 144, 150-152, 172, 180, 182, 188, 213, 229, 232, 239, 278, 299, 311

Safad, 271

Saratov, 26

Sherps, 10-11, 14

Sierpc. See Sherps

Sodom, 168-169, 293

South Africa, 80

Soviet Union (See also Russia), 122, 130, 151, 272

Syria, 192

Tel Aviv, 15, 185, 179, 189-190, 225, 228, 242, 272, 312

Tiberias, 7, 271

Toronto, 54, 124

Vilna, 7, 68, 268

Warsaw, 1, 12-15, 19, 22, 24, 26-28, 41-44, 49 61, 63, 65, 67-104, 105, 109, 118, 125-129, 131-135, 150, 161, 172, 194, 200, 206, 242-244, 265-267, 277, 279, 282-283, 290, 293, 296, 300-303, 305, 310-311

Washington, D.C., 137

Windsor, Canada, 126

Winnipeg, 54

Yemen, 184, 192, 197

INDEX OF WORKS DISCUSSED

A Hoyz oyf Grend Strit, (A House on Grand Street) 245- 265

A Shtub mit Zibn Fenster, (A House with Seven Windows) 272-277

Afn Barg, (On the Mountain) 91, 302-303

Ale Fenster tsu der Zun, (All Windows to the Sun) 134, 303

Baym Toyer, (At the Gate) 295

Der Melekh Dovid Aleyn iz Geblibn, (Only King David Remained) 153-170, 174, 180

A Lid fun Mayn Heym, (A Poem of My Home) 157

A Lid tsu der Papirene Brik, (A Poem to the Paper Bridge) 167

A Lid vegn Zikh, (A Poem about Myself) 165-167

Der Melekh Dovid Aleyn iz Geblibn, 166-168

Echo, 157

El Khanun, (Grace-Granting God) 154-155, 175, 317

Mayne Kinder, (My Children) 164-165

Toyter Shabes, (Dead Sabbath) 161

Dona Grazia Mendes, 169, 269

Dzshike Gas, (Dzshike Street) 43, 84, 93-95, 98, 106, 318.

Chako, 93

Mayn Papirene Brik, (My Paper Bridge) 84

Freydke, 98-102, 106, 132

Dem Tatns Pelts, (My Father's Fur-Coat) 100-102

In Land fun Mayn Gebeyn, (In the Land of My Bones) 29, 87, 105, 127-132, 179

A Mayse She-hoyo, (A True Story), 128

In der Fremd, (In an Alien Place) 131-132

In Likui Khame, (In the Solar Eclipse) 130

Yerushe, (Inheritance) 130-131

In Yerusholayim Kumen Malokhim, (Angels Come in Jerusalem) 223-225, 238, 289, 292

Kheshvndike Nekht, (Late Autumn Nights) 79-86, 90, 98, 104, 105

Froyen Lider, (Women's Poems) 81-82, 265

Goyim, Yidn, Rasn, (Non-Jews, Jews, Races) 84

Kh'bin oyf der Velt Gekumen, (I Came into the World) 83

Lider Fun Khurbn, (Holocaust Poems) 282-285

Likht Fun Dornboym, (Light from the Thorn-bush) 40, 289-295, 307, 317

Oyf di Papirene Brik, (On the Paper Bridge) 293-295

Martsepanes, (Marzipans) 91, 306-308, 313

Di Zun un Der Foygl Tsipilili, (The Sun and the Bird Tsipilili) 306

Blintses, 306-307

Ester Ha-Malke, (Queen Esther) 306

Shalekh Mones, (Purim Gifts) 306

Tomy, Bomy un Semy, (Tommy, Bomy and Sammy) 306

Mayselekh, (Short Stories) 40, 89-91, 98, 105, 302

A Hintl un a Hunt, (A Puppy and a Dog) 82

A Mayse mit a Balye, (The Story of a Wash-basin) 88-89, 225, 303

A Mayse mit a Mantl, (The Story of a Coat) 85

Geyen Shikhelekh Avek Vu di Velt Hot an Ek, (Little Shoes Walk to the End of the World) 83, 89

Kits, Kats, Ketsele, (Kits, Cat, Kitten) 90

Olke mit der Bloye Parasolke, (Olke with the Blue Parasol) 85-88, 105, 303, 308-309

Nokhn Got fun Midber, (After God of the Desert) 269

Oyf di Vegn fun Tsiyon, (On the Roads of Zion) 269-272

Oyf Eygene Erd, (On Our Own Soil) 195-197, 295

Svive, (Milieu) 29, 30, 63-65, 103-105, 125-127, 149, 177-179, 236, 239, 277-281, 285- 286, 301-302, 314-315

Yidishe Kinder, (Jewish Children) 91, 302